The Irish Highwaymen

The Irish Highwaymen

STEPHEN DUNFORD

MERLIN
PUBLISHING

Published in 2000 by
Merlin Publishing
16 Upper Pembroke Street
Dublin 2
Ireland

www.merlin-publishing.com

ISBN 1-903582-02-4

A CIP catalogue record for this book is available from the British Library.

Typeset by Carole Lynch, Dublin.
Printed by Techman Ireland Ltd.

Cover illustration: William Powell Frith (1819–1909), *A Stagecoach Adventure,*
Bagshot Heath (1848: Private Collection/Bridgeman Art Library)

For

Bernie, John and Romy

Acknowledgments

My thanks to everyone who assisted, encouraged and helped me to complete this book, especially...

My father, the late Steve Dunford, who brought me to the crest of
The Comeraghs – we heard the hoofbeats –
and
My mother, the inspirational Bernadette Dunford

Alice Beresford Photography, Dublin; Joe Allen: the best postman in Ireland; Una Phelan, Librarian, and all the staff: Ballyroan Branch Library, Dublin; Patrick Casey, Christine Jones, Nick Roberts: British Library, London; Paschal Bugler; Lynda Unchern, Photographic Dept: Cambridge University Library; Crónán Ó Doibhlin, Librarian: Cardinal Ó Fiach Memorial Library and Archive, Armagh; Maire-Elaine Tierney: Central Library, Derry; Catherine Winters: Cong, Co. Mayo; Kieran Wyse, Niamh Cronin: Cork County Library; Celine Coughlan: County Library, Portlaoise; County Roscommon Historical and Archaeological Society; Michael McShane: Cullyhanna Community Enterprises Ltd; Adam Bentley: Dell Computers; Bernie Campbell: Donegal County Library, Letterkenny; John Donnelly; The Dunford and Mac Nally families; Sheila Doyle, Assistant Librarian: Durham University; Paddy John Feeney, Co. Waterford; Mary Neville: Fermoy Branch Library; Pete Filan, an outstanding history teacher; John Flynn, Co. Waterford; Hugh Collins: Garda Síochána,

Fermoy; John Dunford and all the staff: Hummingbird Records/Publishing; Nicholas Carolan, Joan Mc Dermott, Róisín ní Bhriain, and Treasa Harkin: Irish Traditional Music Archives, Dublin; Kevin McMahon, Editor: Journal of The Creggan Local History Society; David Kiely; the late Cathy Burke, R.I.P.: Kilbrien, Co. Waterford, for all her stories and humanity; Brendan Neary, Past President: Kilkenny Archaeological Society; Jim Fogarty, Declan Mac Auley: Kilkenny County Library; Ann Culhane: Limerick County Library; Maura Connolly and Marie Farrell: Linen Hall Arts Centre, Castlebar; Ivor Hamrock: Mayo County Library, Castlebar; Gerard McCooey; Andy Bennett: Meath County Library, Navan; Kieran Corrigan, Gerry Hargadon, and Gunther Falkenthal: Merlin Films Group; Chenile Keogh, Norman Siderow, Sandra McMahon and all: Merlin Publishing; David Munnelly; Seán and Síle Murphy, authors of *Waterford Heroes, Poets and Villains*; Brian Donnelly, Catriona Crow, The Director, and the staff: the National Archives, Dublin; Colette O Daly, Elizabeth Kirwan, Joanna Finegan, Colette O Flaherty, Teresa Biggins, The Director: National Library, Dublin; Michael Kenny, Sandra McEvoy, Alex Ward: National Museum, Dublin; Northern Irish Tourist Board; John Stokes Powell, author of *Huguenots, Planters, Portarlington*; Gavin Ralston; Mary Smith, Breda Gilligan, Máire Breheny, Denise Staunton: Roscommon County Library; Martin Dunne, Curator: Roscommon County Museum; Fr Gaffney: Rosminian Fathers, Dublin; Lex Hyde, Curator: Rothe House Museum, Kilkenny; Siobháin O Rafferty: Royal Irish Academy; Mary T. McVeigh: Selb Library Service, Armagh; Shannon Development, Tourist Information Office, Limerick; Brian Rankin: Southside Tax Services, Dublin; Steven de Paoire Photography, Dublin; Gary Brown, Brenda Kirwan: The Cock Tavern, Gormanstown, Co. Meath; The Irish Architectural Archive, Dublin; The Royal Irish Academy; Gary Wynne: The Wynne Private Collection, Castlebar, Co. Mayo; the staff, especially Mary Guinan Darmody: Tipperary Library, Thurles; Críostóir MacCárthaigh, Deirdre Hennigan, Folklore Dept: University College Dublin; Lord Waterford; Donal Moore: Waterford City Archives; Geraldine Carey: Waterford City Library; Mary Gorman: Waterford County Council, Dungarvan Branch Library;

and

a very special thanks to a Great Lady and a Wonderful Editor: Selga Medenieks

Introduction

Villains and Heroes

"Rapparee", "highwayman" and "Tory" are names that ring with romance and danger. Place the word "bold" or "Captain" before them and the image of the swashbuckling outlaw-adventurer is complete. He is handsome, dashing, brave, and willingly risks his life to help penniless widows facing eviction at the hands of tyrannical landlords. It's an image that appeals to the popular imagination. Forget Dick Turpin: the Irish highwaymen would have left him standing in the shade, as far as delivering the stuff of legend was concerned. If we must draw a parallel, then it ought to be with Robin Hood, that dispossessed English knight, or Rob Roy Mac Gregor, the Scottish Highland Chieftain and Jacobite outlaw, both of whom made merry hell for the authorities.

Ireland had need of heroes in the seventeenth, eighteenth and nineteenth centuries. Life for the native Irish – as distinct from the "planters" and their descendants – was a miserable, often brutal, existence. We could apply the modern term "ethnic cleansing" to the savage injustices suffered by much of the population. Large areas of Munster, Ulster, and Leinster had been planted; Cromwell had banished whole communities to the inhospitable wilderness of Connacht and Clare in his attempt to transform Ireland into "a second England". Once-proud clan leaders had given up the fight and fled to the Continent.

The introduction of the penal laws had ensured centuries of Catholic mistrust – if not downright hatred – of Protestant neighbours. Catholics were not allowed to own a decent horse: a fleet-footed steed was the forerunner of the fast getaway car.

What little profit Catholics managed to wrest from their few acres of poor land was eroded by rents and tithes to a foreign landlord and his alien priesthood. There was no-one to turn to, until . . .

Into the midst of this misery rode the highwayman. He rode the finest horses – the pick of plundered stables – and was armed with pistol, blunderbuss, sword and dagger. However relentlessly he pursued and robbed wealthy adventurers and land-lords, he observed a code of honourable conduct in relation to the poor. He appro-priated ill-gotten gains at pistol-point and returned them to their rightful owners. His hideouts were inaccessible and the common people ensured an unending succession of safe-houses.

If it sounds a bit fanciful, then consider this: many Irish highwaymen shared a background similar to Robin Hood's or Rob Roy's. They were scions of the Irish aristocracy who, with the coming of the invader and planter, found themselves homeless and landless, outlaws in their native country. In many cases, then, the "work" of the rapparee represented the settling of old scores.

And these gentlemen were very able adversaries. Several had enjoyed the finest military training on the Continent. They had fought for the French, the Spanish, the Dutch, the Flemish – and even for the English. It was not for the first time that an army was to rue the day it recruited future enemies. The Crown had inadvertently provided the Irish highwayman with the skills he needed to pursue his life of insur-gence: horsemanship, marksmanship, swordsmanship, and strategic thought. The common trooper, tasked with safeguarding Ireland's highways, stood little chance against such highly trained and experienced fighters. He was outclassed, outgunned and outridden.

Here, then, depending on your point of view, are some of the worst blackguards who ever stuck a booted foot in a stirrup – or some of Ireland's finest champions. Often betrayed by a friend turned foul informer, most ended life violently, either dangling from a rope or killed by the foe; but they provided Ireland with many colourful pages of history, legend and song.

As we begin to hear the sounds of hoofs galloping down the centuries, we remem-ber the words of author and historian Alice Curtayne:

"The sympathies of the masses of the native Irish were always with the rapparees… their activity is like a thread of light in a long, dark tunnel."

Contents

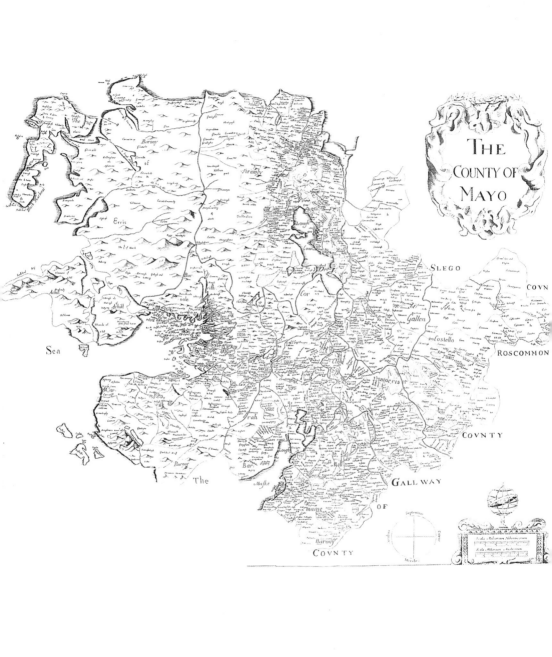

THE
COUNTY OF
MAYO

The
Barony
of

Erris

Sea

Achill
Achill

Sea

Curr

Barony
The

Bar.
Muske

maine

Barony
COVNTY

Arawly

Elough

Cor

Gallen
Costello

ntorris

Clan

rah

Bar

Hill

GALLWAY

OF

COVNTY

SLEGO

COVN

ROSSCOMMON

Septentrio

Meridies

Scala Miliarium Hibernicorum

Dudley Costello

The Scourge of Mayo

It is the spring of 1667 and a carriage approaches the city of Dublin. The man, his wife and three children riding in it have come from the west of Ireland. It is the Sabbath day and, as the travellers draw ever nearer to the city, having forded the river Liffey, they hear the great boebell of Christchurch Cathedral sounding from within the city walls. The man does not know it, but a few short weeks ago in that very neighbourhood a baby boy was born. His parents christened him Jonathan: thirty-two years from now he will be made a prebendary of another cathedral and will enter history as Dean Swift.

But there's still a long way to travel before that time. Charles II sits on the throne of England. He is Protestant, yet has plans to restore Britain to Catholicism; he will attempt this in 1672 and thus precipitate a war with the Dutch King William of Orange. Until that time the Irish will continue to live under one of the most repressive regimes seen in Europe since Roman times. Long gone are the Brehon Laws by which civilised Irish society lived in harmony and prospered. In their place is a foreign system: the island has been carved up into counties, each complete with an English system of governance, judges and juries, sheriffs and bailiffs.

The family draws ever nearer to Dublin; her walls are in sight, beyond Thomas Street and the bustling corn market. The carriage passes through a gate dedicated by medieval pilgrims to Saint Iago, also called Saint James – the patron saint of lepers. The passengers pause here to stare up at something that has been placed on a spike above St James' Gate. It is a human head in an advanced state of putrefaction. The children are frightened by the spectacle – as they were intended to be by the men who had the ghastly object displayed there. A sign affixed to the head reads: "The Scourge of Mayo." This is the head of Dudley Costello, highwayman.

The Dispossessed Irish - a Brief History

Dudley Costello (or Dubhaltach Mac Cosdealbha, as he would have been known in his native tongue) could trace his ancestry back to Norman conquerors of the twelfth and thirteenth centuries. They were the de Angulos, invaders who chose Connacht as the site of their settlement and grew to become one of the mightiest and most well-respected families in that province.

They could have grown to the stature of many such Norman families who settled in Ireland, such as the Butlers, the Ormondes, and the de Burgos. Instead, Dudley Costello's forebears began to intermarry with the prominent Old Irish clans – the like of the MacDermotts, O'Connors, and O'Garas – and within the span of a generation or two had gone native, becoming "more Irish than the Irish themselves".

The de Angulos, having integrated completely into Irish society, became the Nangles and, some generations later, a branch of the Nangles called themselves Costello.[i] The family controlled an area of Mayo stretching from Ballaghaderreen to Ballyhaunis. There were castles and strongholds at Kilcolman and Banada, with the largest built at Castlemore, which gave its name to the present townland.

Ethnicity is a complicated affair. In order to understand Dudley Costello's background, we need to follow the course of the invader from Norman times. At some stage between Dermot Mac Murrough's treachery in 1168 and the Battle of Kinsale in 1601 these families became Hiberno-Norman, a status which differentiated them from the native Irish. Over time, families such as the Costellos' severed ties with the Anglo-Normans and their successors, the English; it was a choice that eventually led to their downfall.

Trouble began for the Costellos during the Composition of Connacht in 1584, when Queen Elizabeth was deciding how best to manage her overseas dominions. Her Lord Deputy in Ireland, Sir John Perrott (who was reputed to be the son of Henry VIII), decreed that every Connacht landowner should pay one penny an acre to Her Majesty; in return, no soldiers would be quartered on the people. The Hiberno-Norman Costellos, who had no allegiance to the English monarchy, refused. This refusal was to cost them dear.

Theobald Dillon, a lawyer, arrived in Connacht in his official capacity as Collector General. Posing as their legal representative and interpreter, he swindled the Irish-speaking natives out of property and land. The Costellos lost Castlemore Castle and most of their barony. The state papers of the time refer to this transaction as a "free gift" to Dillon from Shane Costello, the clan leader; in reality he was the victim of *lucht an róba*, the cunning of the lawyers who acquired many estates from the native chieftains ignorant of the English language and law.

The property was briefly restored, however, in 1595, during the Nine Years War. This was the struggle, spearheaded by Hugh O'Neill, Earl of Tyrone, for the survival of the old Irish aristocracy – and indeed of the national culture itself. The Costellos could not have known that the restoration of their homes and lands was simply the calm before the storm.

The seventeenth century began badly for Jordan Boy Costello, Dudley's father, and his clansmen, who had once ruled their own baronies. Now they were humbled, forced to bend the knee to the invader and accept his ways. Some chose not to. The exodus which came to be known as the "Flight of the Earls" saw chieftains such as O'Neill and O'Donnell take refuge on the Continent rather than submit to ever more humiliating subjection and compromise. Jordan decided to ride out the storm.

But the émigré earls had judged well. In 1604 Sir Arthur Chichester became Lord Deputy and revived the Acts of Supremacy and Uniformity. Their provisions outlawed Catholic clergymen and, under threat of heavy fines, the Old Irish, Anglo-Irish, and Hiberno-Normans were coerced into attending Protestant services and paying tithes. No effort was spared to crush the old ways and beliefs. It was a very short-sighted campaign of suppression on the part of the authorities; the Lord Deputy's actions were to result in public resistance – and the flourishing of the Irish highwayman, the rakehell and rapparee, who was to become the scourge of the invader.

The scribes known as the Four Masters[ii] helped to fuel the fire of nationalistic zeal. Their book, *The Annals*, pleaded Ireland's cause with great scholarship and erudition. The fervour was fanned further by Geoffrey Keating's groundbreaking *History of Ireland* and by the works of other eminent scholars, many of whom had taken refuge in the Irish colleges at Louvain, Rome, Lisbon, Madrid and elsewhere. However, comparatively few Irishmen of the time could actually read books, whether in English or Irish (the language of Keating and the Four Masters). Literacy was, by and large, confined to the great landowners. Many of those who had fled the country had taken service in the armies of mainland Europe, for soldiering was the only honourable occupation open to a high-born emigrant. Many chose to return and put to good use the military skills they had acquired abroad: they would fight for Ireland.

A Boy in the Wars

Official records of the time are scant and the year of Dudley Costello's birth is unknown. Some authorities suggest dates as early as 1600, but we can't be too far off the mark if we accept that Dudley was about twenty-one at the time of the 1641 confederate rebellion. The insurrection was Dudley's first taste of action and the young man acquitted himself with great distinction.

Both Old and Anglo-Irish had had enough of England's high-handed ways. The rising was orchestrated by Owen Roe O'Neill, the Ulster chieftain, and leaders of like stature. They were joined by men such as Rory O'Moore, a returned exile and Armagh landowner whose people had been driven off their lands in County Laois, members of the Maguire, O'Reilly and MacMahon families, and others who had lost their lands to the plantation of Ulster. But the rebellion failed, largely because of a split that arose between the Anglo-Irish – who were in the majority – and the Old Irish. The former, believing that the campaign was going against them, wished to sue for terms with King Charles; the latter were opposed to this course of action. Their Confederate Council "was unable to display the vigour and unity of purpose that the situation demanded".

Even with hindsight it is hard to know which party was the wiser. Charles' reign was in tatters at this time and his days were numbered. In 1640 he had been defeated by the Scots; at the outbreak of the Irish rebellion, his parliament was expressing its grievances against him and the following year it would assume control of the military. All things considered, Charles would probably have given in to all but the most unreasonable of Irish requests. On the other hand, England was so weakened in 1642 that the rebellion could very easily have succeeded, had the rebels not fallen out.

When the split arose Dudley Costello sided with Owen Roe O'Neill, who was at that time possibly the best soldier in Europe and called "the choice champion of His

The seal of the Confederation of Kilkenny.

Holiness, the Pope". Indeed, the Pope sent a special nuncio to Ireland with money and supplies to help the Confederation. The splinter army fought on with some successes, the most celebrated being the rout of Major General Robert Monro. By this time Parliament held the reins of English power and Monro, a Scottish Presbyterian, was one of her ablest commanders. In a bold move to overthrow both the Irish confederates and Charles' royalists alike, he planned to march on Kilkenny with 6,000 men. In 1646 he set out from Carrickfergus, intending to gather reinforcements on the way, but he was surprised by Owen Roe at Benburb, County Tyrone, and his forces scattered. Dudley Costello rode at O'Neill's right hand.

Across the water, King Charles was literally fighting for his life; the royalists were losing ground to the parliamentarians. Oliver Cromwell came to power as Lord Lieutenant at a time when the fortunes of the confederates were at their lowest ebb. He landed in Ireland in 1649 at the head of a formidable army of 20,000 highly disciplined, well-equipped veteran troops. Flushed with his victories in England and Scotland, Cromwell was determined to sort out "the Irish problem". In November of the same year the great O'Neill died in County Cavan. Though his death was a terrible setback to the cause and left the way clear for Cromwell's legions to ravish the country, the confederates fought on.

One by one the Irish leaders succumbed before the fearsome Cromwellian thrust. Philip MacHugh O'Reilly capitulated in Cloughoughter, County Cavan, in April 1653. Rory O'Moore had already fallen back on Inisboffin, off the Mayo coast, the garrison they called "the last spark of freedom", and this surrendered in February. Among its commanders was Dudley Costello.

The Irish commanders on the island, Colonels Cusack (the Governor), Burke and Costello, surrendered on condition that they be free to quit the country and join the Spanish army with 1,000 of their men. The terms on which various Irish armies surrendered permitted them to "transport themselves to any foreign state not in amity with the parliament". Some 40,000 men left for Spain and France, many never to return. Wives, children and widows were prohibited from travelling with their men; shortly afterwards, government agents, with the approval of parliament, had thousands of these dependants transported to slavery in the sugar plantations of the West Indies. Dudley was one of those soldiers who left Ireland for Spain.

Our knowledge of this period of his life is scant. We do know that the future outlaw won his spurs as an officer in the Spanish army. In Flanders he joined the King of England's standard, becoming a captain in the Duke of York's regiment and distinguishing himself at the siege of Betune in French Flanders.

Without an army Ireland was ripe for further plantation. The Act of Settlement was passed, in which the "papists" were classified according to their guilt in the rising of 1641. The country was to pay for its defeat at Cromwell's hands. The lands were to be confiscated by parliament, used to pay its debts and reward its supporters. All Irish Catholics who held property valued at £10 or higher were forced to transport themselves to Clare or Connacht. The common people were to remain on the land as serfs and slaves of the new landlords. The remainder of the land not already in the hands of parliamentary supporters was to be confiscated.

More than eleven million acres of land were taken from the Irish and dispersed amongst the "adventurers" and "servitors", while the government claimed all Church property, towns and some large estates, all of which it planted with new settlers. Meanwhile, Dudley Costello was soldiering abroad, honing his abilities in the cavalry and rising through the ranks of the Spanish army – and awaiting his opportunity to return home.

His patience was rewarded in 1660, when the English monarchy was restored and Charles II crowned king. The Irish Catholics had supported Charles II overseas, and had sided with his father during the confederation; therefore, they assumed that their confiscated lands would be returned to them.

They were mistaken. Charles, mindful of the rashness that had caused his father to lose his head, was reluctant to offend parliament and consequently did nothing to help the Irish. More than that, he announced publicly that there would be no general restoration of lands.

Dudley Costello – now a colonel in the army of Spain – returned to Ireland in 1660 in the hope of recovering at least a portion of his ancestral land, only to discover that most of the estates were now firmly in the grasp of the Dillon family. Dudley was entitled only to a few poor acres of the once-sprawling Castlemore demesne, while Lord Thomas Dillon was in possession of 64,195 acres in Mayo, Roscommon and Westmeath.[iii]

Dudley was sickened by this injustice. He decided that the time had come to avenge his family's honour and to exact vengeance upon the Crown and its lackeys in Ireland. The worst of his ire, of course, was directed at those who had appropriated his land.

One of Ireland's most notorious highwaymen was about to reveal himself.

"The Scourge of Mayo"

Word went forth that Dudley Costello was "enlisting" and it wasn't long before his call was answered. Some recruits were men who had served under him in Spain; others were veterans of the confederate rebellion. He had as his lieutenant a formidable fighting man: Edward "Cornet" Nangle,[iv] a close relative and former comrade-in-arms.

The north-east of Connacht was to be the initial theatre of operations for Dudley and his band. He began to range over the countryside, burning and looting as he went, showing no mercy to the planters but distributing his booty among the unfortunate landless people who served these so-called masters. No road was safe from the highwayman; no traveller could set out upon a journey without fear that from around any bend might appear mounted and heavily armed bandits. From his favourite hideout in Barnalyra Wood, Dudley raided all Mayo and Sligo and soon became "the most talked-of man west of the Shannon", with a price of £20 as reward for his capture, dead or alive.

It was at about this time that a new word entered the Irish vocabulary: "Tory".[v]

In his book, *Irish Tories, Rapparees and Robbers*, John J. Marshall tells us that the first written reference to Tories is found in the *Calendar of Manuscripts* of the Marquis of Ormonde in 1646. From that time onward the term was applied to "men living the life of brigands and preying upon all who had anything to lose". "Tory" derives from the Irish *tóraidhe*, defined as "a robber, a highwayman, a persecuted person".

The authorities of the time would have found that last definition blackly humorous. If anybody was being persecuted, it was Dudley Costello's victims. And they were growing in number. The Tory didn't confine his activities to Mayo and Sligo; when the authorities in those counties stepped up the hunt for him and his band, he ventured into Leitrim. He raided mercilessly, then swept into Cavan and Fermanagh, wreaking his promised vengeance on the planters, robbing and burning their homes, destroying their crops and slaying any who resisted before driving off their cattle and horses.

He went ever deeper into Ulster. In June 1666 Sir Matthew Appleyard, the commanding officer at Charlemont Fort in Tyrone, reported to the Viceroy that both dragoons and troops on foot had pursued "one Dudley Costello and his gang to Dungannon and thence to Fintona". As it was, the outlaws narrowly evaded capture on this occasion. They had stopped for some ale at an inn and been warned by the local people of the impending arrival of the soldiers. By the time Appleyard's men reached Fintona, Dudley and his band had fled in the direction of their hideout in Barnalrya Wood, County Mayo.

They would have travelled cross-country; there was little need to stick to the roads, such as they were. The present-day road system was still in its infancy. Land enclosure was then still comparatively rare in Ireland, although the first hedgerows could be seen in places. A man could gallop the breadth of a county freely, if his mount could take the pace. The countryside still had much of its forest, too, offering almost unlimited concealment and refuge to the highwayman.

Tragedy struck Dudley soon after his escape from Tyrone. He led his men[vi] in a raid on a village that straddled the Mayo-Galway border. Here a community of planters had built houses for their workers, all of whom had been imported from

England. Dudley and his men stormed the village and torched all the English homes, leaving those belonging to the Irish untouched.

The destruction completed, the gang tarried a while to survey their grim handi-work – foolishly, for the smoke from the burning houses had been spotted by a patrol of dragoons. The soldiers descended on the smouldering village, taking the outlaws by surprise, and a fierce battle commenced. Much of it was hand-to-hand combat; no quarter was asked or given.

Edward Nangle, Dudley's right-hand man, was in the thick of the fighting when he was hit by a ball and mortally wounded. Then, in full view of the outlaws, a dragoon cut off the dead man's head with a sword.[vii] It was a foolish act, for it served only to incense Dudley and his Tories further and they fought on with even more determination. The fight ended with the dragoons in full retreat, leaving behind five dead comrades and a dozen captured horses.

The military were seething with outrage. Having Dudley Costello burning and looting the houses of the planters they were charged with protecting – and even mur-dering the occasional foe – was one thing, but killing five dragoons in a single action was quite another. The army was frustrated by its inability to apprehend this brigand who was developing a reputation for humiliating them at every turn.

The authorities in Dublin Castle (dubbed "the Devil's half-acre" by the old Irish) resorted to drastic measures. They issued orders commanding all soldiers, both horse and foot, in Mayo, Sligo, Leitrim, and Roscommon to "tear apart" the country and to run to ground and destroy Dudley Costello and his confederates. All methods, no matter how barbarous, were to be employed in the attempt to capture the outlaws.

Lord Viscount Dillon was a descendant of the rogue lawyer who had appropriated the Costello estate, and incumbent of Castlemore. His brother Theobald had taken an army commission and was now a captain. Both lived in dread that the highwayman would sooner or later come to reclaim his ancestral lands – and might choose to repossess them over the dead bodies of the usurpers.

Exercising his authority in the county of Mayo, Lord Dillon placed his brother at the head of a large force of militia and military. Their primary orders were to hunt down the Tory and bring him to justice. The second order of business was to force the local tenants and peasants, by the use of cruel force, into informing on Dudley Costello. Lord Dillon was fully aware that the outlaw's success in evading capture was due in no small part to the connivance of the local people;[viii] he was, after all, their hero.

The campaign of terror began. Lord Dillon's commands were carried out to the letter, and with horrendous barbarousness. Intimidation and torture became the order of the day for the common people of Mayo and Sligo.

On June 25, 1666 a broadsheet nailed up in every village and town proclaimed Dudley Costello to be a common murderer and traitor with a price on his head.[ix] But

B Y
The Lord Lieutenant and Council
OF
I R E L A N D,
P R O C L A M A T I O N.

[Reward for several rebels.]
Dublin: 25 June 1666.
Whereas Dualtagh Costelo, Edmund Nangle (Cornet Nangle), Christopher Hill, Thomas
Plunket, Cahel alias Charles Mac Cawell, Neil o Neil, and their complices are in the woods
in Meath, Turone, Monaghan, Fermanagh, Longford, Leitrim, Cavan. They are to
surrender
before 17 July on pain of Proclamation as notorious rebels and traitors. £20 reward for
any of them or their head, and a pardon if an accomplice.
Meath, Roscomon, Arran, Anglesey, Dungannon, Henry Tichborne, J. Temple, Paul
Davys,
Robert Forth, Ja. Ware, Rob. Meredith, Theo. Jones.
Dublin: J. Cook : 1666.

Dillon, cunningly, had gone further: the fine print promised that any associate of
Dudley's who brought in the head of a comrade would be rewarded and, moreover,
granted a royal pardon.

News reached Dudley of these terrible bribes, and he was beside himself with
rage. He dispatched a furious letter to Lord Dillon declaring: "from now on all should
take note, for I am going to burn and slay without mercy."

> "I have so much honour yet left me (which my adversaries know very well, though
> they will not own it), that I will not, unawares, seek their destruction as they did
> mine, but do declare by these presents that I will, by burning both corn and
> houses, act my part in their destructive tragedy. Let them prevent it the best way
> they may now that they have timely notice. If they had dealt thus generously by
> me, I would have prevented their design of having me proclaimed a traitor by the
> vindication of my innocence of what was laid to my charge…"

He was as good as his word. Before the end of 1666 the outlaw had set ablaze six big
houses on both sides of the River Moy, the property of planters; he had also torched

the planter villages of Kilmoone and Coyle Cashel, as well as other properties in Connacht. Three hours before dawn on November 26, 1666 Costello and his band of about thirty men burned down Castlemore and the village of Ballyhane. Lord Dillon's plan had backfired spectacularly.

Ireland's western province was in a state of emergency. The Earl poured in more and more troops until Connacht was "crawling with military". This was an extraordinary move, given the circumstances that obtained in those times: Charles II had recourse to a very limited treasury; there was precious little money available to expend on Ireland, much less on a campaign to apprehend a particular Irish villain. Yet hundreds more troops were sent in as reinforcements. Clearly Dudley was regarded as a major threat. The large troop presence in the area made it inevitable that the outlaw gang would eventually be tracked down. In the event, it was barely a matter of months before they were confronted.

In the spring of 1667 Dudley and his comrades carried out a daring raid on a large planted estate at Cruachán Gailing in the parish of Killasser, County Mayo. They set fire to the house and drove off the cattle and horses in the direction of their hideout.

Tumgesh, a ford on the river Moy,[x] was to be the site of Dudley Costello's undoing. Waiting there was Captain Theobald Dillon and a large number of soldiers under his command. The Tories hadn't a prayer: they were hugely outnumbered.

Captain Dillon must have experienced a frisson of joy when the most infamous outlaw of the time came within pistol range. He wasn't only ridding Connacht of the "Scourge of Mayo", but was also striking a blow for the future of his planter friends; he was ensuring that certain parcels of Connacht would remain loyal to the English. Dillon had the hated foe in his sights – and he fired. Dudley toppled from his horse, dead.

The battle was described in a letter to Captain Dillon's brother, the Lord Viscount:

"… Costello fell upon a 'court of guard of Captain Dillon's of about six or seven men,' killed one Walter Jordan and wounded three more men. This gave the alarm to Captain Dillon who arrived with fifteen or sixteen fresh men. The rebels who were as he supposed about forty in number, 'made a stand and prepared themselves to receive their charge, which was so performed by Captain Dillon and his party, that advancing near the enemy and firing on them with the first two ranks, they shot Costello dead on the place with some execution upon others of the party, who were immediately routed, and dispersed themselves to several ways and were pursued for two miles in the dark through the mountains, but without any further account. Three more were found dead on the mountain next day, and one taken who was too severely wounded to fly further. Orders have been given to pick up the stragglers, and to the country to make 'hue and cry' after them, and that without a doubt a good account will be given of these desperate rebels."

Captain Dillon cut off Dudley's head; the outlaw's body was quartered and hung on four gibbets, each displayed in an area of the country over which the outlaw had ranged. Earlier rebellions had accustomed the public to the awful spectacle of a rebel's head spiked on a pole[xi] and mounted high on a public building. The Earl of Ormonde ensured that Ireland's Tories also received this treatment. In the *Calendar of State Papers* of 1667 we read that an assortment of heads was sent to Dublin. A "hanging committee", chaired by Ormonde, decided where each head was to be displayed. That of Dudley Costello was to decorate St James' Gate, "which is upon that part of the town towards Connacht", the province whence it originated. Dudley was survived by his son: he too became an outlaw.[xii]

Lament for Dudley Costello

On the sweet Moy's banks at__ Tum - gesh

Ford, Where__ wild free gar - la-nd__s grow,__

__ A__ lone - ly oak still guards the

spot Where__ they shot brave Cos - tell- o,____

__ As he ap - proached the__ ri - ve - r

wide Framed_in____ the set - ting__ sun,__

__ By a__ ball laid low__ so_ long____ a -

-go___ fr - om Cap - tain_Dill - on's gun.__

No more will Barnalyra Wood
Hear through its dale and glade
The echoes of the Colonel's voice
Nor his feared Toledo Blade.
From Ancient Mask to Regal Erne,
Where with Nangle he ranged wide,
To rob the rich and help the poor
And stem the crimson tide.

So rest in peace bold swordsman,
Though no stone marks your grave,
For on the gibbet you were hung,
Spiked by an Ormond Knave.
But tonight around ruined Castlemore
A Connaught wind will blow
For to praise the name of the one they called
"The Scourge of Old Mayo".

Castle Costello

5

9

12

15
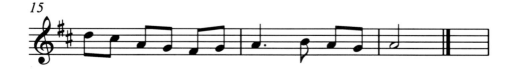

THE
COUNTY OF
KILKENNY

Septentrio

County

Queenes

The

Fassaodining

Catherlagh

Gallmoy

Tip:

:pera:

Oriens

Genran

:ry

Ida

Wexford

Countie

Knock to pher

Countie

Iverk

Waterford

Iberco

County

Meridies

Scala Miliarium Hibernicorum

Scala Miliarium Anglicorum

Patrick, "Tall" James and "Little" James Brennan

The Three Brennans

In 1680, thirteen years after the demise of Dudley Costello, there burst upon County Kilkenny a Tory trio that became one of Ireland's most daring bands of highwaymen. They were cousins: Patrick was born in the townland of Killeshin; "Tall" James and "Little" James hailed from Croghtenclogh.

The Three Brennans could trace their roots to the ancient Sept (clan) of Ossory in pre-Norman times. They were born aristocrats whose family had once held extensive lands in northern Kilkenny. In the wake of the Cromwellian conquest, vast tracts of native-Irish property were given to the Lord Lieutenant's soldiers and adventurers. Some were returned, however, during Charles II's restitution, though no-one was restored all his former lands. The native Irish drew the shortest straws; their ancestral homes and lands were lost to them for ever. Among the dispossessed were the Three Brennans. They took to the roads and the mountain retreats, seeking retribution for the wrongs done to them.

They were extraordinarily successful. This was due in part to the Brennans' courage and determination – and to the rich pickings to be had in Kilkenny and elsewhere, a good proportion of them being the loot of the invader. Between 1680 and 1683 the trio amassed a staggering amount of booty, to the value of £18,000.

It is worth pausing to consider that sum. In 1682 work was completed on the Long Bridge, a structure commissioned by the Belfast city fathers and spanning 2,562 feet; it cost £12,000. Some decades later Oliver Goldsmith's village schoolmaster was "passing rich at forty pounds a year". In today's money, then, the Brennans were multimillionaires.

The Brennans are reputed to have been the founding members of the Kellymount Gang,[xiii] who later operated out of Coolcullen Wood (near the townland of Kellymount) in the parish of Shankill. The notorious Captain Freney in his *Life and Adventures of James Freney* credited the last Brennan member of the Kellymount Gang with having taught him his "trade".[xiv]

By 1683 the Brennans were the scourge of County Kilkenny, orchestrating and participating in numerous raids and robberies, usually on the houses and property of the invaders from the other side of the Irish Sea. It was a time of great foment in the country. In 1681 Oliver Plunkett had been given a staged trial in London and was martyred for treason. There were English fears of "a popish plot" to overthrow the monarchy, which were later realised when James II ascended the throne in 1685. In

James Butler, 1st Duke of Ormonde (1610–1688).

the meantime the Brennans ensured that the English interlopers in County Kilkenny and environs lived almost in a state of siege.

The outlaws' fame and notoriety spread. On February 5, 1683 they were mentioned officially for the first time in a letter from Dr Thomas Otway, Bishop of Ossory. It was addressed to the Earl of Arran, Lord Deputy, to be passed on to his father, the Duke of Ormonde. Otway alludes to "those very Brennans who had done and were still doing so much mischief in that county, and had the morning before, by a wile, lured one of the witnesses against them into a wood, and there with horrid cruelty, cut out his tongue".

A terrible business – if we're to believe it; Otway had a vested interest in blackening the Tories' reputations. On the other hand, such barbarousness was not uncommon in those times. The cruel treatment of informers by a contemporary of theirs, Captain Power, exceeded the Brennans', but these were all desperate men. There was a price on their heads and much to be gained by traitors turning them in to the authorities.

Nor were the authorities above helping to persuade a would-be informer that treachery might be worth his while. In June 1683 a Mr Alexander Marshall, of Lisburn, County Antrim, and two other gentlemen merchants were riding from Ballinakill to Kilcullen on the old Cromwell Road. They were approaching Ballyragget, a village situated a little to the north of Kilkenny city.

As the travellers followed the road through Ballyragget Heath they suddenly became aware of the sound of galloping hoofs behind them. They were startled to find themselves being overtaken by men mounted on fine steeds, who were heavily armed with swords, carbines and pistols. The travellers were in no doubt that they had been waylaid by the Three Brennans.

The outlaws knocked the men from their horses and dragged them into an old fort nearby. Here they robbed the merchants of their possessions and £100, before escaping with the terrified victims' mounts.

Marshall was an influential man, and his colleagues, too, in no less a measure. They went right away to the authorities in Kilkenny city and protested vehemently, giving a full description of their attackers. The regional authorities passed the information on to Dublin. Lord Chief Justice Keatinge wrote to Lord Arran on the subject on July 27:

> "The Brennans commit frequent robberies in these parts, and have of late committed robberies in the County of Limerick. They have in their company a desperate fellow named Munshaglin Byrne, on whose conduct and courage, as they call it, they must depend. I am of the opinion that if I could assure this man his pardon for all acts, murder excepted, he would sell the rest, but this I dare not promise without your Excellency's permission."

Keatinge was correct on one score: the Brennans sometimes worked as a trio, but more often than not rode at the head of an outlaw band, assisted by trusty lieutenants. One such was the aforementioned Munshaglin Byrne, another dispossessed aristocrat. The best-laid plans of the Chief Justice obviously failed because shortly afterwards the Brennans committed one of their most daring – and most lucrative – crimes. It was also to be their undoing.

The cousins probably should have confined their operations to the midlands, where at the best of times troop and militia presence was thin on the ground. The Kilkenny authorities had enlisted reinforcements for the express purpose of running the Brennans to ground; the trio decided to range farther afield until the hunt was called off. And so it was that they found their way to a dwelling that lay some seven miles north of Dublin city. It was the home of a Mr Bolton, a grandson of the Lord Chancellor.

There is no record suggesting that the house was chosen deliberately; in all likelihood the Brennans were attracted by its size and suspected that so big a house must contain ample booty. They surprised the occupants and servants and, with a display of weaponry, made off with all they could carry.

The outlaws must have had some inkling as to the value of the jewellery and silver plate they had looted, together with a substantial amount of cash. It was a fortune. When the Chief Justice arrived on the scene he declared that the take from the Bolton residence exceeded in value that of any robbery he had ever heard of.

So great was the haul, in fact, that it forced the authorities' hand: they launched one of the biggest manhunts the country had ever seen. Extra troops were drafted in and no expense was spared. Eventually, the outlaws were run to earth in their native Kilkenny, captured, brought to trial, convicted, and sentenced to death.

On the day appointed for the execution, however, Munshaglin Byrne appeared with a number of the gang members. In a daring operation the men surrounded the gallows, snatched the Brennans from their guards and spirited them across the border into County Laois, where they had many relatives and friends.

The Tory Hunters

Chief Justice Keatinge was furious. The embarrassment of the Brennans' escape from under the noses of the authorities made him more determined than ever to bring the rogues to justice. It was a matter of honour now: to allow the Brennans to range at will over his jurisdiction would send out the wrong signals to every would-be highwayman and outlaw. It was time to call upon the services of his cousin, the "Tory hunter" Jack Warren.

Tory hunting was as close to sport as many "gentlemen" of the time came. In the absence of sufficient troops, and the offer of large sums of reward money, a sinister group of men were encouraged to join in the hunt for highwaymen. They were bounty hunters who made their living by tracking down Catholic priests and Tories and any other felons with prices on their heads. They showed no mercy towards their victims; one of their favourite methods of execution – especially of the priests – was to drag the unfortunate victim behind a horse until he died.

Jack Warren assembled a group of his Tory-hunting acquaintances and they set out to track down and take the Brennans captive. Warren had contacts throughout the midlands who were only too willing to inform on marked men. The Brennans could trust nobody; safe-houses were no longer so. Wherever the trio ranged, Warren's diligent band was not far behind. Not even the anonymity of Dublin could offer them escape from the net that was closing around them. They decided to leave the country.

Ringsend, on the southern arm of Dublin harbour, was a convenient place at which to hole up while arranging passage to England. Moreover, the Brennans had a distant cousin there, a namesake who ran The King's Head Inn. But Chief Justice Keatinge and Jack Warren had spies everywhere in the capital; no sooner had the Brennans ensconced themselves in the inn but their pursuers were alerted to their whereabouts.

Warren and his party of bloodthirsty Tory hunters saddled up and set out for Dublin with all speed. On their arrival Keatinge dispatched some of his spies to watch the inn while he and Warren waited nearby in concealment.

They had, however, overlooked an important fact: they were dealing with three of the wealthiest men in the country. Eighteen thousand pounds bought much power in 1683, and procured the Brennans a network of spies of their own. No sooner had the agents of the Crown settled into their undercover work at the inn than had the Brennans' own agents passed the word.

The innkeeper had had a secret chamber built into his premises for such clandestine eventualities and he used it to hide the outlaws. It was, as it turned out, an unnecessary precaution. Keatinge and Warren, satisfied by their spies' reports that the highwaymen were secure until morning, retired for the night to Lissen Hall, the Chief Justice's country residence near Swords, north County Dublin.

But their spies quit the inn as well, affording the outlaws the opportunity they needed. The Three Brennans slipped out of the inn under cover of darkness, accompanied by a boy, yet another cousin. They took possession of their horses and cantered off quietly in the direction of the harbour.

The Brennan fortune could buy more than the services of spies; it could also purchase the collusion of an English sea-captain. When the four arrived at the dock they found a dogger boat (a two-masted Dutch fishing vessel) rigged and ready to sail. The highwaymen left their horses in the care of their young cousin, who promised to join them shortly in England.

Nor were the outlaws short of ready cash when they landed. The keeper of The King's Head had arranged for £53 in cobs (a name given in Ireland to the Spanish dollar or "piece of eight") to be drawn on his bank in London. He did not doubt that the debt would be repaid.

The trio chose Chester as their destination and new base of operations, though their reasoning is a mystery. Perhaps they had more cousins there; perhaps they had learned that the area was opportune for their line of work. Chester in the 1680s was a quiet harbour town that had known little upheaval since the civil war, when it lay under siege for two years. Starvation had forced the townspeople to surrender.

In any event, the Brennans passed some carefree months in Chester and its surrounds. They lived comfortably, unhindered by the authorities and Irish Tory hunters. They thought themselves safe – until happenstance intervened that October.

An Unfortunate Coincidence

It was October and Alexander Marshall was a long way from Ballyragget Heath, County Kilkenny, the scene of his waylaying and robbery at the hands of three Irish villains. He had been strolling along the pleasant streets of Chester, having just completed some business, when another group of pedestrians caught his attention.

He could hardly believe his eyes. Here were his assailants, as bold as brass, strutting about the streets as freely as he! The scoundrels looked prosperous, too, and were better dressed than any Irishmen of Marshall's acquaintance. The Antrim merchant hurried to the nearest barracks and roused the troopers.

On seeing the party of soldiers bearing down upon them, the Brennans as one drew their swords. Unfortunately, the odds were too great and the outlaws surrendered, rather than risk being slaughtered on the spot. They were heavily shackled and left to languish in Chester Gaol, awaiting trial.

It has been speculated that the Brennans' motive for settling in Chester was the presence there of relatives. While no record of such persons exists, it is known that at least one member of the scattered Brennan clan lived nearby in Hungerford, Berkshire. It was to this individual – Captain Denis Brennan, an English army officer who resided next door to the Sign of the Coffin public house – that the captured outlaws appealed a few short hours after their arrest. It seems that the English gaolers were as susceptible to bribery as anybody else and not averse to carrying a prisoner's message in return for a sum of money.

In case this cry for help was of no avail, the long arms of the Tory trio reached further. Chief Justice Keatinge had once said that the Brennans would think nothing of giving £3,000 for a pardon or liberty to transport themselves abroad, and having access to such large amounts of money gave them connections in high places. They put one of these connections to the test.

They were quite friendly, it appears, with a Sir Robert Reading. In October 1683, the month of the Brennans' capture, the Earl of Arran received a letter from Reading concerning the outlaws. The knight confessed that he "scarce knew how they could escape hanging" but hoped that His Excellency would "remember the poor devils and let them quit the Kingdom, if they had no hand in blood". Reading went on to say that he believed his word would have weight, confessing that it had been he who had convinced the outlaws to quit Ireland "when Captain Bishop and all the country could not catch them".

Yet it was to neither military nor society connections that the Brennans would owe their liberty, but to their own resourcefulness. Two days after their capture they simply overpowered their keeper, took his keys, and freed themselves.

Escape from Chester Gaol

Richard Wright, keeper of the gaol at the North Gate at Chester, had received three prisoners into his custody on October 19 "charged with the highway robbery of Mr Alexander Marshall on Ballyragget Heath in Ireland".

Wright went on record to say that, so conscious was he of the importance of the three, he kept them in irons all day and when they went to bed at night took away their clothes. He went on to relate that on October 21 he and his wife had been eating supper in the lower room called the Hall. The Brennans were well "ironed" and being watched over by Thomas Greene, a prisoner gaoled for debt who had found employment as Wright's assistant.

Midway through the meal, Tall James Brennan said something in Irish to his companions. In a flash Little James drew a knife, immediately charged at Wright and struck at his throat, wounding the man in the arm as he tried to protect himself. The outlaw then grabbed the keeper and thrust his head under a bed. He pummelled the man with his knees, only stopping when Wright promised to be quiet and stop yelling.

Meanwhile, Tall James had caught hold of Thomas Greene and was threatening to cut his throat. He eventually clapped the assistant in irons. Patrick Brennan tied up the terrified Mrs Wright. He went upstairs to her husband's closet, where he found a sword and the keys to the fetters securing himself and his companions. Once free of the irons, Patrick searched Wright and discovered the keys to the outer gate in one of his pockets.

Wright claimed that, as the outlaws made their escape, he ran to one of the upper windows to raise the alarm, but was spotted by the Brennans. They headed back in his direction and threatened to kill him. He was certain they meant it.

There had been yet another witness to the desperate escape. Mary Swethenham, a maid in the North Gate gaol, chanced into the room when Patrick was securing Mrs Wright. On seeing her mistress in distress, the girl instinctively rushed to her aid, jumped on Patrick's back and tried to beat him off. Despite her best efforts she failed and, fearing for her own safety, fled to the cellar and locked herself in.

One of the outlaws – probably Patrick – followed her. He had taken possession of all the keys to the gaol, including that to the cellar. Before making good his escape, Patrick went and unlocked the door. The frightened girl was cowering with a lighted candle.

"Sweetheart," the outlaw said in an endearing voice, "it may be that you and I may meet again."

"In another country, then!" was Mary's response.

Patrick then blew out the girl's candle and joined his fleeing comrades at the main gate of the prison. They locked it behind them.

The Three Brennans had escaped from gaol again, once more making fools of the English authorities. A number of men in high places were incensed by their boldness. Among them was the Earl of Arran, who was convinced that the escapees couldn't have worked alone. It was his opinion that the Brennans had bribed the gaol keeper, his wife, and assistant, and he said so in a letter to Ormonde dated November 6. "The Brennans have broke gaol at Chester," he wrote, "or rather bought themselves out of it."

His suspicion was never proven true, and it may very well be that Arran refused to countenance the fact that three Irishman were more than a match for the country's legal custodians. The Three Brennans had so far outsmarted everybody.

A tremendous hue and cry was raised, with all available troops and constables joining in the manhunt on both sides of the Irish Sea but, despite the outlaws' known associates being questioned and all their haunts searched, no trace of them was found. The Three Brennans had disappeared without trace.

Time passed. For almost two years nothing was heard of the trio. They lay low, living off their huge fortune, probably reasoning that it was better to allow the outcry over their daring escape to blow over. They cleverly reckoned that the tumultuous affairs of state of the time would soon take priority over the recapture of three outlaws.

Where the cousins passed the time is not known, but they were next heard of on their old stamping-ground of Kilkenny. This time, however, they were engaged in a burglary that, for sheer daring and foolhardiness, exceeded anything they had ever before attempted. The Brennans must have had a mischievous sense of humour, for the residence they chose to rob was none other than that of the man who had called upon every authority in the land to hunt them down. It was Kilkenny Castle, home of the Duke of Ormonde, the most powerful man in Ireland.

On September 17, 1685, evading the Duke's sentries, the highwaymen entered the fortress and made off with a large quantity of His Grace's plate, to the value of £1,000, and a small chest containing plate belonging to Captain George Mathew, the Duke's half-brother and agent. It was a stunning achievement that struck a blow at the very heart of the establishment.

Not unnaturally, Ormonde's blood was up. He vowed that this time every method and measure would be deployed in apprehending the outlaws. However, political events of great magnitude had overtaken the players.

A Surprising Twist of Fate

Charles II had died in that year and been succeeded by his brother, James II. The new king was a devout Catholic, who swiftly set about repealing the penal measures against his co-religionists throughout the realm. He sent his brother-in-law, the Earl of Clarendon, to Ireland as the new Lord Lieutenant and appointed Richard Talbot (later the Earl of Tyrconnell) in charge of the army. The latter began promoting Catholics to positions in the Irish army, to the detriment of Protestant officers. Ireland was once more in political, religious and military turmoil. The country was awash with talk and rumour of invasions and victories. The Brennans might have perpetrated an audacious and spectacular theft, but against this backdrop it was merely, according to Lord Chief Justice Keatinge, "a nine days talk throughout the Kingdom".

In the end it was not "all the king's horses and all the king's men" who brought the rogues to justice. Ormonde's agent, Captain Mathew, had been severely disadvantaged by the burglary and was intent on retrieving his stolen plate. Taking advantage of the chaos in the country, he made contact with the Brennans and offered them terms. The outlaws would enjoy a form of immunity and be allowed to keep their horses and firearms, on condition that they returned the stolen plate. The Brennans accepted this unexpected offer and in due course handed back the valuable haul, pretending that they had discovered it themselves in some caves in the vicinity of Kilkenny.[xv]

If ever there were outlaws who disproved the notion that "crime does not pay", then it was the Three Brennans. In 1687 they were as rich as ever and enjoying the comforts and privileges that their extensive hoard of booty bought them. In that year

Kilkenny Castle and City in 1695.

James II recalled Clarendon and appointed Tyrconnell as Lord Lieutenant in his stead. The Catholic monarch by this stage was employing the Declaration of Indulgence, an Act which Charles II had attempted to pass in 1672, which granted complete freedom of religion in both Ireland and England. With each passing day it was making him more unpopular with English Protestants.

Tyrconnell heard the rumblings and, believing that a conflict was looming, began the process of raising an army; he set his goal at 50,000 men. Above all, he needed fighters with weapons skills and combat experience. He was later accused by William of Orange's followers of recruiting Tories, rapparees, highwaymen and other outlaws into the ranks of the Jacobite Army and of showing them great leniency in relation to their crimes in return for their participation in the war.

The Williamites had grounds for complaint. Tyrconnell did indeed issue instructions to this effect. At the Kilkenny assizes of March 1687 the grand jury of the county decided that there was no better way of suppressing robberies and felonies in the region than "to take the Brennans into protection for a term of years". In other words, the cousins could fight for the king or go to prison.

The outlaws, having obtained full pardons, duly joined the army and fought under the Jacobite banner. That they acquitted themselves well on the field of battle need not be in dispute; perhaps James might have won the day at the river Boyne had he commissioned more like them.

One of the last references to the Three Brennans is to be found in King's *State of the Protestants of Ireland*, 1682. "The Famous Tories, the Brennans," we learn, "who had been guilty not only of Burglary and Robbery, but of murder also, who were under sentence of death and escaped by breaking Gaol, were made among the rest, Officers."

A drawing of a late seventeenth century playing card.

The Felons of Our Land

Fill up once more, we'll drink a toast to com-rades far a-way;_ No na-tion up-on earth_ can boast of bra - ver hearts than they.   And though they sleep in dun - geons deep, or flee, out - lawed and banned,   We love them yet,_____We can't for - get, the fel - ons of our land._____   In

boy - hood's bloom and man - hood's pride fore

- doomed by al - ien laws,_____ Some

on the scaf - fold proud - ly died for

ho - ly Ire - land's cause. And,

bro - thers say, shall we to - day un -

- moved like cow - ards stand, While

trai- tors shame and— foes de - fame the fe - lons of our land.

Some in the convict's dreary cell
Have found a living tomb;
And some unseen, unfriended fell,
Within the dungeon's gloom.
Yet, what care we, although it be trod by a ruffian band –
God bless the clay where rest today the felons of our land.

Let coward mock and tyrant frown,
Ah, little do we care!
An outlaw's cap is the noblest crown
An Irish head can wear.
And every Gael in Innishfail who scorns the serf's vile brand
From the Lee to the Boyne would gladly join the felons of our land.

The Brennans' Jig

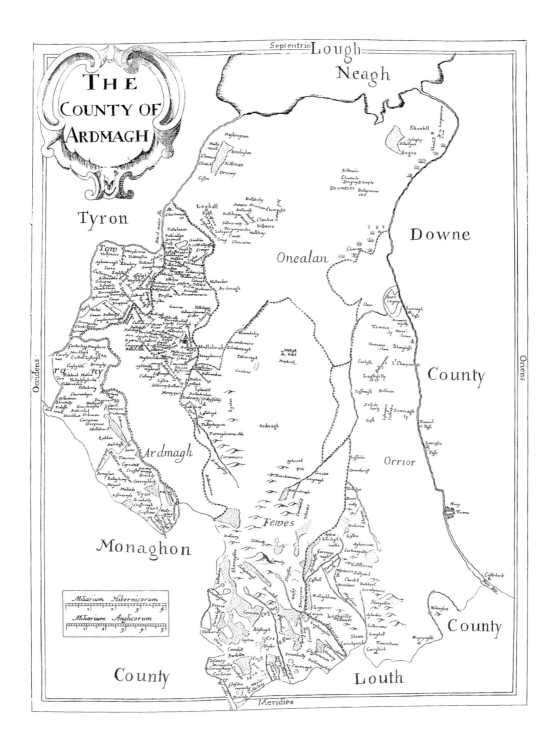

THE
COUNTY OF
ARDMAGH

Septentrio Lough Neagh

Tyron

Downe

Onealan

County

Ardmagh

Orrior

Monaghon

Fewes

County

Louth

County

Miliarium Hibernicorum
Miliarium Anglicorum

Occidens

Oriens

Meridies

Count Redmond O'Hanlon

The Irish Scanderbeg[xvi]

There's a part of Northern Ireland known (affectionately by nationalist locals) as Bandit Country. It acquired this nickname some thirty years ago because of the huge number of republican paramilitaries whose home territory it was. Bandit Country extends, roughly, over an area of south Armagh bounded by Newry in the east and Middletown in the west. It is no coincidence that halfway between these extremities is a geographical feature known as Deadman's Hill. It is also no surprise that in the 1660s it was the stamping-ground of one of Ulster's most celebrated bandits, the highwayman known as Count Redmond O'Hanlon.

The title was no affectation. Up until the plantation of 1609 the O'Hanlon clan – the Lords of Orior – ruled large tracts of land in what are present-day Armagh and parts of north Louth. The surname appears in *The Annals of The Four Masters*, where it is recorded that Flaithbeartach O'Hanlon, Lord of Uí Niallan, was murdered by the clan O'Bruascal in 938AD. Another ancestor, however, seems to have fought on the "wrong" side, for the record states that one Oghie O'Hanlon was knighted by Elizabeth I for the part he played in her struggle against Hugh O'Neill, Earl of Tyrone.

Redmond's date of birth was given as 1640 by the author of an anonymous pamphlet published in 1682,[xvii] but the evidence indicates that 1620 is more likely; the pamphleteer gives the place of birth as Poyntzpass, County Armagh, midway between Newry and Portadown. Tradition has it that Redmond O'Hanlon was born with an unusual birthmark which caused great speculation.

"His first appearance in the world did administer great cause of wonder and chatt to the assisting Gossips who were surprised to see him sprawling with the Brand of a *Roman* T in his brest, which the Neighbours did in Flatery interpret to portend some great fortune to the Babe; and that the Mark representing a headless Cross he should at least be a Martyr for Christian Religion; but success hath shewn, that it barely denoted a *Thief*, or was a Character to Prognosticate an Eminent Tory."

Redmond was said to have inherited from his mother an interest in the supernatural, which he retained all his life, and he was rumoured to have sought out fortune tellers. An early prediction, credited with encouraging Redmond to begin his life of crime, was extraordinarily prescient:

"he diligently inquired out the renown'd man of Art, who had foretold something of him before; and with a good fee obliged him to cast the Scheme of his Nativity, and resolve him, what would be his Progress, and end: the Learned Southsayer putting on his Conjuring Face, and drawing many Lines and Circles, dappled with Figures and signs of the Planets, at last presented him with this ambiguous Prediction:
'Thou Son of Fortune, and Darling of Fame, thy enterprises shall be great, and thy Successs Unparalled; thy Hazards numerous; and thy Escapes miraculous, thy Army shall be small, but thy command great, thy Territory not vast, but thy Revenue unlimitted, thou shalt live without a House, and yet dye in a Bed, the hand of Justice shall not reach thee, neither shalt thou be a Victim to the Law, thou shalt ly in State after thou art dead; and be Bury'd in two several places in one day; thou shalt dy among thy friends, and thy Enemyes shall not see thy Head.'
The Rover was so tickled with this Encouraging presage (which he Literally believed, and altogether interpreted in his own Favour) especially his Impunity, and Protection from the Gallows; that he resolved immediately to be in Action, and began to furnish himself with good Armes, nimble Companions, and exquisite Spyes."

When he came into the world, Redmond's parents were reduced to living on a meagre portion of the lands once ruled by his ancestors. Nevertheless, they found sufficient funds to send the boy to England at an early age to be educated. There he became fluent in French and, more importantly, in English, a language not generally spoken by the native Irish. His knowledge of both languages was to serve him well.

On his return to Armagh Redmond was employed as a footman by Sir George Acheson of Markethill, and it is during this period of his life that he is said to have learned "the rudiments of highway robbery". From whom he learned these skills we do not know, nor are we acquainted with the circumstances of his training. We have only a sketchy but amusing anecdote relating Redmond's dismissal from Acheson's service for attempting to sell a stolen horse. The young man had stuck a false tail on the animal in order to disguise it. As a result of this misdemeanour he was forced to leave the area.[xviii]

When he judged the time safe to return, Redmond made his way back to County Armagh. He found work as a collector of poll taxes, an occupation that was not as innocuous as it sounds today: taxes sometimes had to be collected at gunpoint.

Then, in a move that surprised everyone who knew him, Redmond joined a newly formed religious organisation, one of many that had sprung up during the 1630s. There is no doubt that his zeal was genuine, for we learn that Redmond went on to become a minister of God. At about this time the young man also met a rich and respectable lady whom he married, though shortly afterwards he lost both his wife and her fortune: the one to illness, the other to the gaming tables.

Penniless and disillusioned, Redmond gave way to the lure of adventure. The year was 1641 and Irish chieftains in Ulster, Connacht and Leinster were rising up in an effort to recover their planted lands and to re-establish their authority and standing.

Redmond joined the forces of the Confederation and fought under the command of Owen Roe O'Neill, most notably at the Battle of Benburb on June 5, 1646. When the great chieftain died in November 1649, O'Hanlon continued the campaign and fought with the army of the Old Irish against Cromwell and his forces. It is known that he was active until 1653, the year in which the last Irish garrison on Inishboffin surrendered. In the ensuing exodus, Redmond left for the Continent in the company of thousands of other soldiers.

He joined the French Army and so distinguished himself that he was awarded the title Count of the French Empire, one of the highest honours that could be bestowed at that time, a title equal in its authority and regard to that of a British earl. Yet, in 1653, while Redmond was winning accolades in European wars, the remainder of the O'Hanlon lands was being confiscated by Cromwell and settled by his parliamentarians, as a result of the family's open support for the Confederation.

No evidence exists of the date that this successful and dashing swordsman[xix] returned to Ireland, but it is possible that it was around 1660, when Charles II became King. The Irish landowners who had been stripped of their lands by Cromwell assumed that these would be restored, but most were to be sadly disappointed.

Count Redmond O'Hanlon falls neatly into the mould of the seventeenth-century Irish highwayman. He was typical of the high-born scion whose purpose in returning home was to seek redress for the wrongs done to his family. He is likely to have seen himself as one of the chieftains of the clan and therefore honour-bound to exact justice. On his homecoming Redmond discovered, as did many others, that there was no general restitution of confiscated lands. He was left with no alternative but to take to the hills and highways in order to right the wrong.

At first Redmond operated around Slieve Gullion and the hills of South Armagh near Forkhill, Mullaghbawn and Lislea, and by most accounts he seems to have been working alone at this stage, directing his operations against the local planters and their kind, burning and robbing "their" properties.

He also operated a protection racket[xx] that would have delighted the Chicago gangsters of the 1920s – or even the eleventh-century Vikings who levied the in-famous Danegeld (land tax) on Ethelred the Unready. Redmond demanded of the settlers that they each pay him a half-crown per annum and "for this small sum his contributors lived in perfect security, requiring neither bolt nor bar". Word of Count O'Hanlon's audacity soon spread beyond Armagh.[xxi]

When the final disaster of the Cromwellian War overtook the Catholic land-owners, several of their most active young men had remained in the vicinity of their ancestral estates, rather than go into exile abroad or transplant to Connacht. In many counties these desperate men formed themselves into groups under the leadership of a former local chieftain and waged guerrilla war on those who had dispossessed them. All available resources of law and government were employed to hunt down these Tories. Many of the renegades flocked to Redmond's side, seeking direction.

Scourge of the Military

Redmond was a born commander. He formed the men into military-style companies, each reporting to a hand-picked captain, and widened his theatre of "violence and terrorism" to include the English and Scottish settlers in Counties Down, Monaghan and Tyrone. Local folklore suggests that every Tory who roamed the hills of Ulster at this time operated directly or indirectly under the command of the outlaw Count and could be mobilised at short notice to appear at one of his various hideouts if the need arose. Without doubt Redmond had the respect and devotion of his men; he was also truly loved by the common people, who invariably benefited from his sorties, and who on occasion risked their own lives to save his.

It is said that "when, instead of fearing or hating an outlaw, the people fear for him, the outlaw sees with many eyes and hears with many ears". This was certainly true in Redmond's case. As his fame and notoriety spread throughout the land and beyond, tales of his exploits and daring deeds appeared in a French gazette; he became a romantic figure and favourite of the people, known as The Count Hanlon.

One old story tells of a grand country gentleman of English origin – a planter – who one day rode into the city of Armagh and, having dined at the best inn, went to the garrison and sought out the commanding officer. The gentleman wanted to transact some business; a large sum of money would have to be transported back to his estate in Mullaghbawn. Fearing the outlaw O'Hanlon, he requested that the commanding officer provide an escort of mounted troops. The officer, for a consideration, granted the request and later that same day the gentleman, escorted by a squad of heavily armed troops, rode out through the gates of Armagh and in the direction of Dundalk.

As they continued on their journey it became evident that this well-armed contingent was in no real danger of attack. The day was a warm one and soon the gentleman, lulled by the sun and his escort into a feeling of security, suggested they halt for a drink. The officer readily agreed and the riders dismounted at the Four-Mile-House, a roadside inn. The gentleman allowed the soldiers to avail freely of his bulging purse and many drinks were consumed.

The party was in a merry mood on quitting the inn. Some time later the gentleman informed the officer that they were within a short distance of his home. It was highly unlikely that the outlaw was about, he said; therefore, the services of the soldiers could now be dispensed with. The gentleman presented each trooper with a silver coin and, by way of celebration, the inebriated men fired a volley into the air.[xxii]

But as the sound of the shots died away, and while hands were being shaken, a band of highwaymen led by Redmond O'Hanlon came galloping out from a nearby wood and surrounded the startled escort. The outlaws disarmed the troopers, stripped them of their uniforms and boots, commandeered their mounts, and sent them back to Armagh in disgrace. The gentleman forfeited his fat purse and his horse, but was allowed to keep his clothes.

It is probable that O'Hanlon initiated this attack in order to acquire horses and weapons for a new batch of recruits who had recently joined his ranks. The full purse was a bonus.

It is said that history repeats itself, and Bandit Country can ably attest to this. The present-day British army barracks and bases that mar much of south Armagh's beautiful scenery are eerie echoes of the military outposts erected in Redmond's time. There were more than a dozen of them, thrown up at remote sites throughout the county. From these, daily patrols went out to scour the countryside in search of the outlaw, but to little avail.

The highwayman thumbed his nose at the authorities. On one occasion troops stationed in one of the outposts between the borders of Armagh and Monaghan chanced upon their enemy by accident as he was watering his horse. Redmond dismissed the animal with a slap on the rump, ran into a big field covered with furze bushes, plunged headlong into the thorns and vanished from sight. The soldiers set about a thorough search of the furze with sabre and long bayonet, but eventually gave up and left, cursing and calling down the wrath of God on the outlaw and his family. The oath-takers were unaware that the outlaw had been watching and listening in the concealing branches and foliage of a nearby tree.

Some hours later, after the troops had returned to barracks, Redmond retrieved his horse and left the area, only to return that very night with a band of his most trusted men.[xxiii] They stole into the fortification and, without making a sound, bound and gagged the sentries, and made off with eighteen military horses. They headed in the direction of County Monaghan and the fair in Ballybay.

As dawn broke, the small band of outlaws and their stolen steeds were surprised by a patrol of cavalry and called upon to halt. O'Hanlon, with the confidence of an experienced commander, ordered his men to form a semi-circle, level their murderous guns and prepare to fight to the end: there would be no surrender. The cavalry suddenly found themselves in a vulnerable position, outgunned by a well-disciplined gang of steely fighters.

The officer in charge, a brave young man, approached Redmond under the safety of a white flag and informed him that no hostilities would take place if the horses were returned there and then. Redmond agreed, provided he was given a guinea per animal. Coolly, he added that if this proposition was not agreeable to the officer, he would shoot dead every single member of his patrol.

The young officer had no choice. The money was handed over — all eighteen guineas — along with his promise as an officer and gentleman to allow the outlaw and his men to retire a thousand yards without fear of reprisal. Once again Count O'Hanlon escaped.

The planter landowners of Ulster had had a bellyful of the outlaw. They were tormented and frustrated by the campaign of terror being waged by Redmond and by the complete failure of the authorities to even curtail, much less apprehend, his activities. In an effort to solve the problem themselves, the landlords employed a group of thirty hand-picked mercenaries[xxiv] and agreed to pay each of them nine pence per day for a period of three months, in the hope that they would rid the county of the O'Hanlon gang.

Throughout the summer of 1675 the hirelings scoured the countryside in search of the outlaws. They felled all the trees in Glen Woods, which was reputed to be one of Redmond's hideouts. They caught sight of him on one noteworthy occasion and succeeded in wounding him, but with the help of local people the outlaw managed to flee to Ram's Island, where he remained until his injuries healed. By summer's end the mercenaries' "tour of duty" was over and they left without their prize, prompting four of the wealthiest local businessmen to convene at Hillsborough and hatch another plan.[xxv]

They decided to establish and fund a local volunteer force to defend the region against the highwaymen and offer reward money – £30 for O'Hanlon and £20 each for certain other outlaws – but their efforts were futile. The volunteer force failed to trace their target and Count O'Hanlon continued to roam and range at will, never failing to assist the poor and put-upon.

Worse, perhaps, for the authorities was the fact that Redmond had his "intelligencers", or spies, in the army. To add insult to injury, he also counted members of the Armagh and Down gentry among his allies. In an anonymous letter – possibly written by the Reverend Lawrence Power of Tandragee – to the Duke of Ormonde, the writer implores the Viceroy to root out some well-respected local citizens whom he claimed aided and abetted the outlaw O'Hanlon in an escape.[xxvi] Among these were justice of the peace Sir Toby Poyntz and his son, Captain Charles Poyntz, who was in charge of the local garrison.[xxvii]

Ormonde was outraged to discover that the Tory Count was now being "coshered" (protected) by members of the aristocracy. He saw to it that in 1676 a proclamation was issued offering £100 for O'Hanlon's head and £50 each for those of his men. A Captain Trevor Lloyd was ordered by the Viceroy to take command of a crack force assembled from the local commands, and to strengthen the County Armagh garrisons of Tandragee and Loughbrickland with reinforcements from Lisburn. He was to employ every means at his disposal, whether fair or foul, to rid society of the menace that was Count Redmond O'Hanlon.

Captain Lloyd was only marginally successful: the huge number of troops under his command managed to down only a handful of O'Hanlon's men. Indeed, these successes served only to exacerbate the Count's terror tactics. The Viceroy issued yet another proclamation, threatening that four men in the locality would be transported to the plantations in America should "the outlaws guilty of outrages" not be apprehended within twenty-eight days.

But the threat had little or no effect on the people who held Redmond and his men in high regard and were prepared to help him – by hindering the authorities – at every turn. Nevertheless, a massive military operation was now in place in Ulster. Clever and elusive though O'Hanlon might be, it was proving ever more difficult for him to remain one step ahead of the law.

He was nothing if not resourceful. Legend has it that when the need arose Redmond was known to reverse his horse's shoes to confuse his pursuers. There are also accounts of him and his gang using reversible jackets – possibly made from the uniforms taken from the gentleman's escort near Dundalk. When turned inside out they became the red coats of the army, and were used on many occasions to outwit the authorities and unsuspecting travellers.

The legend grew. So many tales of Redmond abounded that today it is difficult, if not impossible, to separate fact from fiction. The search for the truth is further hampered by the absence of a reliable contemporary account of him. The best description is contained in a pamphlet produced in 1681:[xxviii]

"He was a well timber'd man, tho not of the best Proportion; of Stature indifferently tall; his Body rather nimble, than strong; more subtil, then Valient; naturally bold but not cruel, shedding no man's Blood out of wantonness, or delight, but in his own defence, or by the Chance of a shot; he was rapacious, but not covetous; he gather'd much money to save himself, and to inrich others; like a Bird of Prey, he was greedy to devour, but all went thro him as fast as he swallowed; had his inclinations been virtuous, as his parts were quick, he might have proved a good Subject to his King, and servicable to his Country; Necessity first prompted him to evil courses and success hardened him in them, he did not rob to mantein his own prodigality, but to gratify his spyes, and pensioners: Temperance, Liberality and Reservedness were the three qualityes that preserved him; none but they of the House where he was, knew till the next morning where he lay all night; he allowed his followers to stuff themselves with meat and good Liquor, but confined himself to milk and water; he thought it better thrift to disperse his money among his Receivers and Intelligencers, than to carry it in a purse, or hide it in a hole; he prolonged his life by a general distrust…"

Luck, too, appears to have helped him prolong his life. A tale from the Donegal region recounts an incident that occurred when Redmond became separated from his followers. He was exhausted, and lay down in some bushes to sleep.

He was awakened two or three times by a lizard running over his face, and at first was irritated by this little creature that repeatedly interrupted his slumber. Brushing the reptile from his face, the outlaw was about to get up and find another "bed" where he might sleep soundly when he spotted a wild boar just about to attack him. The little lizard had warned him.

Taking this to be an omen, Redmond dashed into the nearby wood and ran in a direction opposite to that he had planned on taking – with the boar in pursuit. He evaded the beast by climbing up a tall tree, one which afforded a clear view of the surrounding countryside. It also gave him a clear view of a party of military, lying in wait for him in a ditch by the road he had intended to travel.

Though he seemed invincible to the authorities, it should be noted that there is at least one record of O'Hanlon being beaten at his own game.

A Dundalk merchant was owed £100 by a business acquaintance in Newry, but was afraid to travel to County Down in case he was set upon and robbed by the "good

Count". One of his employees, a clever and ambitious young man, offered to make the journey and collect the money. In the event of failure, he was prepared to accept any punishment the merchant thought appropriate. After much deliberation the employer agreed to the proposal. The young man put a guinea's worth of coppers into his purse and, saddling one of his master's ponies, set out for Newry.

Near Jonesborough he was met on the highway by a friendly traveller mounted on a fine black stallion – O'Hanlon himself. The two struck up a conversation and journeyed on together. The young man had recognised the outlaw from the many descriptions and proclamations, but kept this to himself. He told the stranger where he was bound and of the errand he was running for his master. After a mile or so the stranger turned off the highway and onto a boreen. He paused long enough to caution the young man about the dangers of disclosing too much information to strangers. Then, with a wave of his hat, he galloped away.

Redmond O'Hanlon gave the young man what he deemed sufficient time for the transaction in Newry, then returned to the highway to lie in wait. In due course he saw his victim approaching. Spurring his stallion, he charged out onto the road, levelled his blunderbuss and gave the order to "stand and deliver".

"I have no money," confessed the seemingly frightened victim.

With that Redmond whipped off his mask.

"Do you remember me?" he laughed.

The young man looked indignant. He pulled out his purse but, instead of handing it to the highwayman, flung it as far as he could into a nearby bog.

"If you desire it," he said, "then you can follow it!"

The highwayman, bemused, dismounted and leaped the ditch into the bog, landing up to his ankles in mud. His victim then set off back to Dundalk at a gallop – taking Redmond's magnificent black stallion with him.

The loss of his fine mount was a bitter blow to the outlaw – but the contents of the purse would compensate. He made his way with difficulty to where the purse lay and retrieved it. When he undid the thongs, however, he found that it contained but a guinea in copper coin. The shrewd young man arrived safely in Dundalk and handed over the £100 to his employer. He was well rewarded and allowed to keep the black stallion to dispose of as he saw fit.

So incredulous was Redmond at the young man's brazenness that he himself was fond of recounting the story. He was not without a wicked sense of humour. He once described himself during a mail-coach robbery as "Lord Examiner of all passengers", and on another occasion as "Surveyor-General of all the high-roads in Ireland".

It must not be thought, though, that Count Redmond O'Hanlon was simply some sort of likeable rogue, for he could be vicious and merciless when he chose. The planter owner of the castle and manor of Ballymore was to discover this to his cost.

Henry St John was a very prominent "new citizen" and grandnephew of Sir Oliver St John, Lord Deputy of Ireland from 1615 to 1620. The family had confiscated and planted ancient O'Hanlon land and had thus become sworn enemies of the outlaw Count.

The enmity was reciprocated: Henry St John had declared open war on Redmond O'Hanlon. When pursuing the outlaw, his nineteen-year-old son had caught a chill and died. This had spurred St John to double his efforts, dealing ruthlessly and cruelly with anyone even suspected of assisting the gang.

On September 9, 1679 St John was out riding on his estate with the Reverend Lawrence Power of Tandragee and a manservant. Without warning, St John was seized by outlaws, members of the O'Hanlon gang. Evidently the plan was to hold the planter to ransom. Their leader warned Reverend Power that if a rescue was attempted, then the hostage would be shot.

No sooner had the threat been made than several of St John's men appeared and engaged the outlaws. Henry St John received two bullets in the forehead. Though Redmond himself may not have been present at the murder, a Rubicon had been crossed.

At St John's funeral Reverend Power delivered a powerful sermon which is credited with directly influencing and hardening the government's attitude towards outlaws. He castigated the Tories for the murder and chastised those who supported them. He thundered:

> "I must make some reflection upon this country too, concerning these skulking scoundrels that are the distributors of the best planted country in the Kingdom; no part of Ireland having so many inhabitants, yet no place so pestered with the vermin. And you know, gentlemen, the obloquy you lie under, as if some of you did shelter and protect them. I confess I abhor the thought of it, that English people and Protestants should harbour such pernicious vipers in their bosom. Yet it is certain some of you do, and that of the better sort too, or else some half-a-score of ruffians could never lurk so long among you, which is such a prodigious shame that you can never wipe out the infamy of it... Pardon me, sirs, if I express my just resentment against such dealing. I reflect upon no individual person, but this I can boldly say in front of you all, that I have heard many of you accuse one another for harbouring these infamous rebels and that they help to furnish your kitchens and tables."

The Viceroy, equally aghast at Henry St John's murder, had his own brand of revenge planned. He issued a proclamation stating that the crimes of the Tories would be visited on their families, on the "wives, fathers, mothers, brothers, and sisters of such of them as shall be out upon their keeping, that is not amenable to law and committing them to close prison, until such outlaws shall be either killed or taken".

Tradition has it that the outlaw's father, mother and siblings were forced to leave the Armagh of their ancestors and flee to County Donegal. They purchased a house and business premises in the town of Letterkenny.[xxix] That the family found refuge there was owing to the protection of Sir Cahir O'Doherty and Sir John Conyngham. O'Doherty was an old family friend while Conyngham's brother, David, had married Isabel O'Hanlon, the outlaw's sister.

In the summer of 1680 Count Redmond made a secret journey, alone, to visit his family in their adopted home. He stayed in Letterkenny Castle and tradition has it that he had a dalliance with John Conyngham's daughter. At the close of his visit the outlaw was escorted safely back to Armagh by a troop of Sir John's men.

On his return to his home county Redmond resumed his career with renewed gusto. Thomas Harte, in *A History of the Life of James, Duke of Ormonde*, notes that "Redmond O'Hanlon and his gang kept the whole province of Ulster, with a considerable portion of Leinster, in such a state of alarm as was almost incredible".

Incredible, too, was the fact that the outlaw Redmond, when not "out upon his keeping", spent a considerable amount of time in the company of some of Ulster's most prominent figures, the like of Sir Toby Poyntz of Poyntzpass and the Annesleys of Castlewellan.

Deborah Annesley was the daughter of Harry Jones, Bishop of Meath, and very sympathetic to the outlaw's predicament. Acting on her advice, and through the good offices of her father the bishop, Redmond made an approach to the Viceroy, seeking a pardon. The approach was treated with contempt. Ormonde was now using all the means at his disposal to destroy the O'Hanlon gang and pardoning the outlaw was not an action he was willing to contemplate. A saga was nearing its end – and the end was to be bloody.

The Viceroy's Plot

It was in the spring of 1681 that the Viceroy hatched the plot which was to be Redmond O'Hanlon's downfall. He selected one of his Dublin spies and ordered him to find "an army man in the Armagh area with the credentials to carry out a dangerous undercover task".

The chosen man was one Lieutenant William Lucas of Dromantine, near Newry, a young officer of bad reputation (bad, that is, among the native Irish), from a good

COUNT HANLAN'S

DOWNFALL,

OR

A True and Exact Account of the KILLING
that Arch Traytor and Tory

REDMON ó HANLAN:

BY

ART ó HANLAN,

One of his own Party, on the 25. day of *April*, 1681. near the *Eight Mile Bridge*, in the County of *Down*.

Being the Copy of a LETTER writ by a Country Gentleman (now in *Dublin*) to a Person of Quality (his Friend) in the Country.

DUBLIN;

Printed for *William Winter*, Bookseller at the *Wandring Jew* in *Castle-street*. 1681.

[7]

On *Monday* the 25th. Instant, the said *Art O Hanlan* and *William O Sheel*, in company with *Redmond O Hanlan*, were near the *Eight Mile Bridge*, in the County of *Down*, waiting for Prize, on the score of a Fair that was held there, at which place, while they were watching for their Prey, *Redmond* took some occasion to quarel with *Art*, as they were smoaking their Pipes, and in the close bid him provide for himself, for he should not be any longer a Tory in any of the three Counties, (viz. *Monaghan, Down,* or *Ardmagh*) whereupon *Art* rose up and said, I am very glad of it, and will go pist now; and then taking up his Arms (having his Authority and Protection about him) imediately he shot *Redmond* in the left Breast, with his Carbine, and forthwith ran to the *Eight Mile Bridge* for a Guard, but *Art* returned with a Guard, and Mr. *Lucas*, who soon had notice at the *Newry* where he was waiting *Redmonds* motions, for the same Ends, found *Redmonds* Body, but the Head was taken off by *O Sheel*, who fled with it. the Body they removed to the *Newry*, where it lies under a Guard till Orders be sent how it should be disposed of; and since that Mr. *Lucas* has sent out a Protection and Assurance to *O Sheel*, to bring in the Head of that Arch Traytor and Tory *Redmond O Hanlan*.

This Evening *Art O Hanlan* gave in a Relation of this Adventure, to the Lord Lieutenant and Council, who ordered him to have a Sum of Mony paid forthwith, for the good Service he has done. And to Mr. *Lucas* His Grace has promised the Honour of a Command in the Army. These I mention to shew the extraordinary Care, Vigilance and Honour of our Government. If this Relation of mine may prove any way diverting to you, 'twill be a sufficient Reward for this trouble of Letter writing, which is in self irksom to

Your Obliged Humble
Servant.

Dublin April 27 1681

A pamphlet published in 1681 containing Art O'Hanlon's account of Redmond O'Hanlon's death.

planter family "who never spared the back of a peasant". Ormonde issued him with personal instructions and official orders, granting him full powers to act effectively against O'Hanlon.

Redmond had two personal bodyguards, William O'Shiel and Art O'Hanlon: the latter was the outlaw's foster-brother and confidante. Lucas sought out Art and "enlisted" him. The outlaw did not sell his loyalty cheaply: in return for his co-operation he received a written assurance of immunity and the promise of a generous £200 reward. As Lucas and the traitor plotted, Redmond continued his activities, never suspecting that his life-long comrade was to betray him.

At the beginning of April Lieutenant Lucas received Ormonde's instructions that the plan was to proceed. The outlaw O'Hanlon was to be captured or killed without delay; failure on this occasion would not be countenanced. It took three more weeks, however, before the plotters saw their opportunity to obey the Viceroy's orders. On April 25 Redmond O'Hanlon, accompanied by Art and William Shiel, set out for Hilltown, in the Mourne Mountains. The purpose of their journey was to ambush the local landowners and gentry as they returned home from the fair in Banbridge, laden with money and purchases, and escorting their prize animals.

Upon their arrival early in the afternoon, the outlaws decided to "lay up" and snatch a few hours of sleep. Their prey would not be along before dusk. They chose the shell of an abandoned cottage by the roadside and secured their mounts out of sight at the rear. Art and Redmond would sleep first; William was to guard the front from a place of concealment, taking the first watch.

Art's moment came at two o'clock, when Redmond had drifted off to sleep, wrapped in his cloak, on the earthen floor of the cottage. The traitor shot him dead.[xxx]

Hearing the shot, William O'Shiel rushed inside. Art had been expecting him and knocked him unconscious with a single blow. Lieutenant Lucas appeared with a body of men. They had been lying in hiding nearby, awaiting the sound of the gunshot that would signal the Tory's end.

Lucas drew his sabre. Ormonde had requested the outlaw, dead or alive. The officer had no need of the body; the head alone would be sufficient proof that the Viceroy's orders had been carried out.

Art, despite his treachery, must have had some humanity left in him, for he buried his foster-brother's headless corpse in the little Catholic graveyard in Ballynabeck, on the road from Tandragee to Scarva. Lucas took the head to Downpatrick and had it spiked on the gates of the gaol. The traitor Art O'Hanlon duly collected his £200 in Judas money and a pardon for his part in the murder; Lucas was rewarded with a promotion.

Tradition has it that, when news of the killing reached him, Sir John Conyngham dispatched an escort of troops and swordsmen from Letterkenny. They accompanied the O'Hanlon family as far as Ballynabeck, where the body of the slain outlaw was exhumed and brought back to Donegal. After a decent Christian burial it was re-interred in the Church of Ireland graveyard in Letterkenny, the Conwall parish church.

Tradition also states that Redmond's mother made a pilgrimage to Downpatrick Gaol. The grief-stricken woman, on seeing the bleached head of her son spiked like that of a common criminal, composed this *caoineadh*:

> Dear head of my darling,
> How gory and pale;
> These aged eyes see thee,
> High spiked on their jail.
> That cheek in the summer,
> No more shall grow warm;
> Nor that eye e'er catch light,
> But the flash of the storm.

In the 1930s a worn and weather-beaten tombstone was discovered at Conwall parish church bearing the O'Hanlon coat of arms. The inscription, in so far as it is legible, states that there lie:

"The five sons of Redmond Hanlen, Mercht. in Letterkenny: John, the firstborn, Alexander, Francis, John and Redmond. Also here lieth the body of William, the son of the aforesaid Redmond Hanlen who departed this life the 27th… 1708, aged… 3 years… months and 14 days.

Also the remains of David Conyngham, Gent., and Cath[?], his wife, daughter to Redmond Hanlen. They were esteemed more for goodness of heart than for affluence of fortune. Died lamented here on… December, 1752, 72 years old. She: 21st August, 1775, aged 80."

Could this be the final resting place of the outlaw, Count Redmond O'Hanlon, who "banked his Treasure in the hearts of the people" and whose ghost is still seen riding the highways of Armagh?

Redmond O'Hanlon

A shep-herd that lives on Slieve Gul-lion Came
down to the Coun-ty Ty - rone, And
told us how Red - mond O' Han - lon Won't
let the rich Sax-ons a - lone! He rides o-ver moor-land and
moun-tain, By night, 'till a stran-ger is
found, Saying "Take your own choice to be
lod-ging Right o - ver, or un-der the ground!"

If you whistle out Whoo! like a native,
  He leaves you the way to go clear;
    If you squeeze out a Hew!
      like a Scotchman,
    You'll pay him a guinea a year.
  But if you cry Haw! like a Saxon,
Och, then, 'tis your life or your gold!
By stages Count Redmond O'Hanlon
Gets back what they pilfered of old!

Old Coote of Cootehill is heart-broken;
  And Johnston beyond in the Fews
Has wasted eight barrels of powder
    Upon him, but all to no use!
  Although there's four hundred
      pounds sterling
If Redmond you'd put out of sight;
Mind, if the heart's dark in your body,
  'Tis Redmond will let in the light!

The great Duke of Ormond is frantic—
  His soldiers got up with the lark
    To catch this bold Redmond
      by daylight;
But Redmond caught them in the dark.
  Says he, when he stripped them and
      bound them—
"Take back my best thanks to his Grace
  For all the fine pistols and powder
    He sent to this desolate place!"

    Then here's to you,
      Redmond O'Hanlon!
Long may your excellency reign,
High ranger of woods and of rivers!
Surveyor of mountains and plain!
  Examiner-chief of all traitors!
  Protector of all that are true—
Henceforward, King Charlie of England
  May take what he gets, after you!

The Ballad of Douglas Bridge

On Doug-las Bridge I met a man Who

lived ad - ja - cent to Stra - bane, Be -

fore the Eng - lish hanged him high for

ri - ding with O' Han-lon. The eyes of him were just as fresh as

when they burned with - in the flesh___ A - nd

his boot - legs were wide a - part from

ri - ding with O' Han- lon.

"God save you, Sir," I said with fear,
  "You seem to be a stranger here."
    "Not I," said he, "nor any man,
    Who rides with Count O'Hanlon.

"I know each glen from North Tyrone,
To Monaghan, and I've been known,
    By every clan and parish, since
    I rode with Count O'Hanlon."

"Before that time," said he to me,
"My fathers owned the land you see;
But they are now among the moors
    A-riding with O'Hanlon."

"Before that time," said he with pride,
"My fathers rode where they now ride
    As rapparees, before the time
    Of trouble and O'Hanlon."

"Good night to you, and God be with
    The tellers of the tale and myth,
    For they are of the spirit stuff
    That rides with Count O'Hanlon."

"Good night to you," said I, "and God
    Be with the chargers, fairy-shod,
    That bear the Ulster heroes forth
    To ride with Count O'Hanlon."

On Douglas Bridge we parted, but
The Gap o'Dreams is never shut
To one whose saddled soul tonight
Rides out with Count O'Hanlon.

THE
COUNTY
OF CORKE

PART

OF KERRY

COUNTY.

Limrick

Tippera
ry

Water

Counte

County of

Coun

Richard Power

Captain Power, A Genteel Robber

Night was falling over a remote corner of Leinster as a lone horseman picked his way through the hills. He stopped every so often and cocked his head to listen, satisfying himself that his pursuers had lost sight and sound of him.

He was a stranger to these parts and there was no-one he could turn to for shelter, warmth and concealment. All at once he caught sight of a light flickering in the distance. As he drew nearer he saw that it came from the window of a little cabin; smoke issued from its chimney. The sight caused the fugitive to think of his own home, so many miles behind him. His thoughts turned again to hot food and a place to sleep. He dismounted at the door.

As is the way of the Irish, the stranger was welcomed into the humble home. The couple occupying the house pulled a stool to the hearth for their visitor. Some time later, seated beside the fire with food inside him and a gill (¼ pint cup) of poteen in his hand, the stranger couldn't help noticing that his hosts seemed sad and uneasy. He enquired of them the cause but they evaded his questions; he persisted and learned the truth. The occupants of the cabin faced eviction.

The tenant farmer had fallen behind with the rent. In doing so he had played into the hands of the landlord, who wanted nothing better than to see his lands "cleared" and the tiny holding amalgamated to ensure a better yield. An eviction notice had already been served and on the appointed day the family were to be thrown out onto the road. Their few possessions would be thrown out with them — that is, what little remained after the landlord had confiscated all he could in part-payment for the arrears.

It was a cruel fate that awaited the stranger's hosts and the callousness of this particular landlord went further: he had decreed that any neighbours or friends who were found giving help or shelter to the couple were to be fined, evicted, or even imprisoned. The couple were despondent and feared for the lives of their little ones, who at that moment were sleeping peacefully in the loft above the stranger's head, oblivious to the dreadful fate that awaited them.

The farmer and his wife must have thought it odd that the stranger should show such curiosity concerning their troubles. They were, after all, not the only poor tenants who were being treated thus in the 1680s. James II had not yet acceded to the throne of England; the Irish were still being treated as vermin in their own land. Yet the kindly stranger persisted with his questions. When was the eviction due to take place? Was there nobody the farmer could turn to for help?

There was not. According to the landlord, the arrears amounted to £50 and no friend of the farmer's had anything like that sum of money.

"Supposing a friend were to give you the money to clear your debt," the stranger said. "Would you repay it if you could?"

"I would," replied the farmer at once. "I would repay every penny, or die trying."

Impressed by the honesty and integrity of the man, the stranger reached into his purse and counted out £50 in gold, which he placed in the weather-beaten hand of his disbelieving host. He then wrote a promissory note and had the farmer sign it with his mark.

"Do not," he instructed, "pay over the gold until the house is about to be knocked down around you. Then spin the landlord a yarn to anger him."

The astonished farmer agreed, another drop of poteen was had, and early the following morning the grateful couple waved goodbye to their benefactor.

The day of the eviction arrived and the landlord, accompanied by the sheriff and his hired thugs, plus a detachment of the military in case of trouble, approached the little cottage in the hills.

There was consternation; women and children were crying and neighbours stood in surly, rebellious groups, forbidden by the harsh decree to lend assistance or offer shelter to the unfortunate family. With blows accompanied by oaths and threats, the soldiers and officials cleared a path through the throng until the landlord, mounted on his fine horse, could confront his "hapless" tenant.

"Well, have you my rent?" he demanded.

The farmer delayed as long as possible before replying, much to the landlord's annoyance. Then, just as the sheriff's men were about to begin throwing out whatever meagre possessions were in the cottage, he handed a bag to the landlord.

"There are your fifty pounds," he said. "They were given to me by a friend for safe-keeping. Now I must use them to save my family from eviction and becoming beggars."

The landlord was flabbergasted. This was the last thing he had expected, but he could not refuse the money with the sheriff and the throng of people gathered around him. Ungraciously he accepted the gold and, grudgingly, wrote a note declaring that all the farmer's arrears were now fully cleared and no further moneys were owing. He then proceeded to berate his tenant for dragging him and all his company up into the hills for no reason. He was still muttering darkly when he wheeled his hunter around, dismissed his men with a gesture, and galloped off alone back in the direction of his fine residence.

His departure had not gone unseen, however, by a rider who had remained in concealment at a safe distance. As the furious landlord made his way homeward he had to pass a lonely thicket on a remote stretch of the road. Out from among the trees thundered a horseman, blocking the landlord's path. He was masked and was brandishing an evil-looking horse pistol.

"Stand and deliver!" cried the masked man.

The victim was relieved of the £50 in gold, whatever cash he had on his person, his watch and fob, and sundry other valuables. Before the masked man galloped away he cautioned the landlord about his treatment of his tenants.

Word spread quickly about the robbery and in no time at all there was a hue and cry in the area. Extensive parties of military, accompanied by the sheriff and local landlords, scoured the countryside for the mysterious highwayman. They had not much of a description to go on: all the shocked landlord could tell them was that the stranger had been wearing "dark clothes and a mask".

Within days of the robbery the farmer once again received a nocturnal visitor. The stranger had returned. He was made doubly welcome and passed another night in the company of the couple, who regaled him with an account of how their landlord was robbed of the gold by an unknown masked highwayman.

As they were finishing breakfast the following morning, the farmer assured the stranger that he would begin immediately the task of raising the £50 he owed. He thanked him yet again for his generosity and promised to work hard to have as much as he could of the money by the year's end. The stranger nodded and went to saddle his horse.

Outside the cottage, mounted and ready to take his leave of the family, the stranger smiled, reached into a coat pocket and removed a piece of paper. It was the promissory note. Smiling down on the poor but honest family he tore the note into a dozen pieces and scattered them to the winds.

Captain Richard Power then galloped off into the morning, having added yet another chapter to his story.

The Ubiquitous Captain Power

"Your Grace must consider that Power is an absolute ubiquitous, and tarries in no place long enough to be discovered and taken. He is sometimes in the County of Waterford, and sometimes in Kilkenny, and immediately after we hear of his pranks in the County of Limerick, and in Kerry and in Cork; so that it is an impossible thing to pursue him from place to place."

Primate Boyle in a letter to the Duke of Ormonde, October 17, 1685

They sought him here, they sought him there: Ireland's very own Scarlet Pimpernel, the "ubiquitous" highwayman and outlaw Richard Power, was a native of Kilbolane, County Cork. He was the second son of an Irish Catholic gentleman who owned a small freehold estate in the area. As the younger of two brothers, Richard had no claim to the family property and it seems that it was a disagreement with his brother over this very matter which caused him to leave home and take to the roads as an outlaw.

The title of "Captain" was bestowed on him by the ordinary people, as it was on many highwaymen, because of his success and pre-eminence as a Tory. By that stage he had established quite a reputation for himself. Richard is mentioned in public records in 1683, the year he was first proclaimed an outlaw. The price placed on his head was £20, but in another proclamation two years later the value placed on Captain Power's apprehension had increased five-fold: on July 17, 1685 the authorities promised £100 to any man who could bring the Tory to them, dead or alive. In a letter dated September 17, 1685 the Duke of Ormonde revealed the reasoning behind this reward:

"the Government have taken care to set a considerable price upon Power, the Tory's [head]; if that be seconded by placing [some] parties of the Army in apt stations both will either apprehend him or drive him where he is not so well acquainted."

The bane of the high-placed was a friend to the poor and downtrodden. It appears that he derived great pleasure in telling his wealthy victims, while in the process of robbing them, that the contents of their fat wallets and purses would be distributed among the less well-off.

Captain Power was no saint, however. In exchange for his looking after the poor, this gentleman outlaw demanded loyalty and respect and was ruthless in dealing with any person who double-crossed him. On one occasion he tracked down an individual whom he knew to be an informer and cut out the traitor's tongue before lopping off both his ears. Like so many others before and after him who were for whatever reason "out upon their keeping", Power depended upon the loyalty of ordinary people just as much as they depended on him for the money, valuables and food which he brought to them. The rewards offered for information leading to the capture or killing of known Tories and outlaws were enormous and would have in many instances enabled a peasant family to live well for years, but the common people detested the informer, believing that he got whatever was coming to him if caught. They preferred to live with dignity, in dire poverty, if need be. Richard Power and other outlaws and rapparees were looked upon as being patriots of a kind, unwilling to bow beneath the yoke of oppression, but willing to fight for their rights.[xxxi]

Richard Power came to prominence at a propitious time for one bent on following the "trade" of the highwayman. Troops were thin on the ground in Munster, owing to the dispersal of many soldiers in Ulster as a result of the Scottish rebellion. With the counties of Cork, Limerick and Tipperary loosely guarded, Tories like Power could range virtually at will and unmolested. By the time the second proclamation was published, he was known to be responsible for numerous highway robberies and burglaries across many counties and had become increasingly daring in his raids.

No crime, it seemed, was too audacious for him. He even attempted on one occasion to rob Sir John Meade, the Chief Justice of The Royalties and Liberty of Tipperary, but chance intervened and Power missed his quarry by minutes on the highway. Meade's brother-in-law happened along on the same day, though, and the outlaw had the privilege of rendering his purse £80 lighter. It was this outrageous act which led to the proclamation in 1685 of Power as an outlaw for the second time.

But for bare-faced cheek it was hard to beat Captain Power's most infamous deed, which he perpetrated in the town of Newcastle, County Limerick. The outlaw was given information that the daughter of a well-known and wealthy merchant was about to be married. At about ten o'clock on the morning of the wedding, Richard rode boldly up the avenue leading to the merchant's house and dismounted at the front door.[xxxii]

The outlaw always dressed well and, coupled with the fact that he was well-spoken and educated, his appearance raised no eyebrows among the servants and workmen completing the preparations for the wedding feast. Handing a footman the reins to his fine steed and looking for all the world the proper gentleman, Richard informed the servant that he wished to speak to the bride's parents. He had, he added, brought a present for the young lady.

The footman dutifully announced the arrival of the gentleman stranger "bearing gifts" and the Captain was ushered into a reception room where the master and mistress were seated. He introduced himself, using a fictitious name, and proceeded to engage the couple in polite conversation. After some time he apologised for his lack of manners in not presenting them with the gift he had brought and reached inside his waistcoat. But instead of the promised wedding present, Richard drew out one of his terrifying pistols and cocked the weapon. He ordered the frightened couple to hand over whatever cash they had on the premises. This amounted to over £60, which the outlaw pocketed before marching the distraught couple at pistol-point to the front door. Richard then called for his horse and mounted it, all the while holding the bride's parents at pistol-point. Those present who were tempted to tackle the outlaw were dissuaded from doing so by the sight of a large, fearsome blunderbuss at his saddle.

Enjoying the sport, Captain Power called for wine to be brought out. He then drank a toast to the bride's health, before dashing the glass to the ground and galloping away from the town without hindrance.

With £100 on his head – a small fortune – Captain Power made a handsome prey for Tory hunters. There were also other adventurous spirits who were willing to "try their hand" at his apprehension. One such an attempt was made while Power was enjoying a quiet drink at an inn outside Kilworth, a village close to Fermoy.

Someone present recognised Power and word of his whereabouts reached a young English Ensign[xxxiii] stationed in Cork city. The Ensign was aware of the £100 reward; the promotion he was certain to receive for the capture of the outlaw must also have crossed his mind… and Power was all alone. Mustering a small group of men, the Ensign set out from barracks without informing his superiors.

The soldiers arrived at the inn at dusk and entered the taproom, where they found the innkeeper alone. The Ensign demanded to know the whereabouts of the notorious outlaw whom he believed to be on the premises. Not wishing to have a bloodbath on his hands, the innkeeper directed the callow officer to a small parlour at the rear. A stranger was having a quiet drink there.

The Ensign left his men supping free ale in the taproom and made his way nonchalantly to the back room. Sure enough, a well-dressed man was sitting at a table by the fire, a bottle of fine liquor in front of him. The gentleman invited the soldier to join him, which he did. Each drank a dram or two to the other's health. Presently, however, as the gentleman leaned across the table to pour yet another glass for his guest, the Ensign spied the butt of a pistol under his coat. This was sufficient "proof" for him; he challenged his host.

But he had foolishly neglected to draw his weapon first – and now the outlaw produced his. Before the Ensign could raise the alarm, Richard Power had cocked his pistol and levelled it at the officer's head. He next drew the soldier's sword and held the tip against the young man's throat. He forced him to hand over his valuables and pistol, before gagging him and tying him to a little couch that stood in a corner of the parlour.

The outlaw then bade his helpless foe a good night, scooped up his liquor bottle and slipped out through the window. Some time later the Ensign's companions came in search of their officer, to discover him lying disarmed and shamefaced, still bound to the couch. It was an embarrassed and pitiful troop that returned to Cork city that night.

Captain Power and Count Redmond O'Hanlon

One of the most colourful stories told about Captain Power concerns a journey he made to Ulster. His intention was to meet Count Redmond O'Hanlon, whose fame had spread throughout Ireland. On arriving in Armagh the Captain found lodgings at an inn where, while eating his evening meal, he spotted at a nearby table a gentleman counting out a large sum of money. Never being one to look a gift horse in the mouth, and not wishing to pass up such a fine opportunity for acquiring booty, Richard summoned one of the servants.

"There's money in it," he told the man, "if you can find out for me which road that wealthy fellow will be taking on the morrow." The servant complied and early the following morning the highwayman took the road the servant had indicated. He found a secluded and remote spot, ideal for his purpose, and lay in wait. After a short time the unsuspecting gentleman appeared. Power sprang into the roadway and accosted him, demanding at pistol-point that he stand and deliver.

"And it's no use trying to deny you have not any money," the Captain added. "Did I not see you counting it last night?"

The traveller admitted that he was indeed carrying a substantial amount of money, but was not prepared to hand it over without a struggle. He promptly drew his own pistol.

Both men discharged their weapons without either party suffering a hit. They next drew their swords and set to on horseback, slashing and thrusting, and the sound of steel clashing against steel was heard a good way off. The two fought for some time, neither being able to draw blood, and were eventually forced to concede that there would be no victor. Mollified, they agreed a truce. Laying their weapons aside, the two went and sat together in the shade of a tree, where they shared a bottle, rested and conversed amiably.

The story goes that the chief robber of Munster asked his adversary's name. To his surprise, the other introduced himself as Redmond O'Hanlon. Power exclaimed that he had ridden many miles solely to see him – and to satisfy his curiosity about the type of man Redmond was.

"You have satisfied your curiosity," the Ulsterman said, "for I am the man. And I must confess you are the heartiest lad I ever met. I never was worsted before."

The outcome of the meeting was that Captain Richard Power and Count Redmond O'Hanlon became staunch friends and partners in crime. It is said that Power remained with O'Hanlon for eighteen months, became a member of his gang, and rode side by side with him, before returning to his own hunting grounds in Munster.

Before departing from Armagh, the Captain made a pact with the Count that if either was captured and imprisoned, then word should be sent to the other, and he who was at liberty would do all in his power to rescue the detainee. This pact turned out to be a fortuitous one for Richard Power. Shortly after his return to Munster, he was arrested and charged with the robbery and slaying of a merchant on the road near Ballyneety, County Limerick – the site of Galloping Hogan and Patrick Sarsfield's later triumph – and thrown into Clonmel Gaol.

Power dispatched news of his plight without delay to Armagh. On receiving the letter O'Hanlon convened an emergency meeting of some of his lieutenants.[xxxiv] Time was of the essence: a proclaimed Tory was not always granted the courtesy of a trial and Power could be executed at any time. O'Hanlon instructed his men to take care of any outstanding "business" and to join him in Munster. He then set off southward.

Fortunately, the Count reached Clonmel on the eve of his friend's execution. In typical O'Hanlon fashion, he managed to get word to Power immediately upon his arrival. It is possible that he disguised himself in order to gain access to the gaol – but it is equally likely that he went to no such trouble, as few in those parts knew him by sight. In any event he informed Captain Power that he was going to set the town ablaze that very night. His plan was to start a series of fires in different locations and spirit away the prisoner under cover of the general confusion and panic which would surely ensue.

But Power dissuaded him. To attempt such a thing would be foolish, he said, and result only in O'Hanlon's death; one of his people had informed him of a huge military presence in Clonmel. The Captain, it transpired, had a better plan. He was to be transported to Kilnagowna, near Ballyneety, the next day, for execution at the exact place where the merchant he was accused of killing had died. A small troop of infantry, led by the local sheriff, would escort him. The journey was relatively long and Power shrewdly reckoned that the party would have to make a comfort stop at a certain halfway house of his acquaintance…

The following morning the manacled and sullen prisoner was taken from the gaol. The troopers set off with their charge, with the sheriff leading the way. As Power had predicted, midway into the journey the escort party stopped at an inn. The outlaw was led into a small room and left with four troopers standing guard over him. The sheriff and the remainder of the escort retired to the taproom, a large area at the opposite end of the house, where they commenced drinking, easy in the knowledge that their prisoner was secure. By all accounts the landlord was a party to the whole plan; it is said that he refused to give any assistance to Redmond O'Hanlon unless the outlaw administered to him a small wound, enough to allay any suspicion of his complicity.

And so it came to pass that Redmond entered the inn, dressed in the fine clothes of a gentleman. On seeing the soldiers he affected surprise and enquired as to their presence. The sheriff informed him that they were escorting "the former highway-man" Captain Power to his place of execution and assured him that the outlaw was well secured and under armed guard.

After praising their bravery, the stranger with the northern accent called for a round of ale for the soldiers, and added a few bottles of liquor for good measure. Having drunk a glass or two, the gentleman asked the sheriff if it would be possible to see the once-notorious outlaw. Nothing, the sheriff said, would please him better, and he led the stranger to the little room at the rear. The Ulsterman, on seeing the prisoner chained and cowed, once again praised the valour and sterling conduct of the troopers. The pair returned to the taproom, where the stranger called for "liquor of the best" to be sent to the four guards.

By now the drink was flowing freely and the whole company was in splendid spirits. Under the pretext of going outside "to make my water", O'Hanlon left the room and went to the back of the inn, satisfying himself that there were no other sentries posted. He gave a prearranged signal – and from the nearby hills eight heavily armed riders descended on the inn to rendezvous with their commander.

O'Hanlon acquainted his men with the exact location of the prisoner and his guards and then went to rejoin the sheriff and the rest of the party. While one of the gang took care of the horses, the other seven stole into the inn and hurried to the place where Power was being held. They burst in and quickly overpowered the four drinking guards, who were not given any time to cry for help.

O'Hanlon's plan had been simply to put the men out of commission, but one of his ruthless lieutenants, Brian Kelly, a man who took no chances, disobeyed orders and killed the guards instead. With the help of a strong dagger and the stock of a blunderbuss, two of the gang released Power from his manacles. They then exited as stealthily as they had entered, with the Captain in tow, and made for the mountains.

O'Hanlon was still drinking with the sheriff and the soldiers. The story goes that, on the pretext of bringing more liquor to the four guards, he "discovered" them dead and the prisoner missing. The alarm was raised. Without hesitation O'Hanlon mounted his horse and set off with the sheriff and the troopers in pursuit of Power and his rescuers.

The posse was hampered by the darkness and the amount of alcohol consumed. Redmond O'Hanlon had no difficulty in slipping away unnoticed, and joining his comrades at a prearranged meeting place on the Bog Of Allen. Captain Power's daring escape was toasted long into the night.

The Accursed Informer

The year 1685 saw great turmoil in Ireland and her neighbouring island. The Catholic James Stuart became monarch and the threat of insurgence and war was almost palpable. Throughout this period Captain Power continued to harry and rob the wealthy planter landowners and merchants, who were already nervous and feeling vulnerable in a country awash with political and military difficulties. Yet, despite the social and political upheavals, it was Power's exploits that caused the greatest embarrassment to the local authorities.

An incensed Earl of Granard, the Lord Justice, acting on the earlier theory and remarks of Duke Ormonde, ordered Captain Aungier, an extremely competent and loyal soldier, to move his troops from Cork city to Charleville. This was due entirely to Richard Power's "depredations" in that area: Aungier was charged with apprehending the outlaw by whatever means necessary. When the officer arrived in the region he discovered that the local gentry, though appalled by Power and his misdeeds, were afraid to help the authorities because of the ruthless and deadly way in which the outlaw dealt with informers.

There was, however, a gentleman who was willing to help. He was Reverend Vowell, the local Protestant clergyman, whom Power had threatened to hang if he ever caught him, on account of the churchman's collusion with the authorities.

The Reverend informed Captain Aungier that he had a spy in his employ who would, for a small consideration, give them notice next time Power appeared in the neighbourhood.[xxxv] The officer assured the clergyman that in those circumstances he would dispatch immediately a party of his troopers to take the outlaw, dead or alive.

On October 20, 1685, at around five p.m., Reverend Vowell rode red-faced and excited into town and sought out Captain Aungier. His spy, he confided, had told him that Richard Power was in the vicinity. The Tory had been observed at three o'clock going into the house of John Power – probably a relative – who lived about a mile and a half from Kilbolane, a village lying about five miles from Charleville. According to the spy, the outlaw used this particular house frequently and often stayed the night while the owner was absent.

Aungier ordered his quartermaster to choose a dozen of his best men and arm them well. They were to prepare their weapons and saddle up as quietly as possible so as not to attract any unwanted attention from the "hostile natives". Reverend Vowell offered the services of his spy, which were eagerly and appreciatively accepted.

At one a.m. the party slipped out of Charleville unnoticed and by half past two they were within three hundred yards of John Power's house. The quartermaster gave the order to dismount. He detailed three of the men to look after the horses; three more were to guard the back door, which faced a bog some three hundred yards distant; the remainder of his troops were positioned at the front door. From inside the house came faint sounds of a voice raised in song.

Satisfied with his deployment, the quartermaster summoned the spy, who was familiar with the layout of the house. The pair proceeded to reconnoitre the building. They saw that the light of several candles was showing at a window; keeping close to the outside wall, they made their way to it. There was still no sign that the occupants had got wind of anything amiss. The sound of singing had grown louder; the officer and the spy peered in through the window.

There were three men and three women in the room, seated at the fire and surrounded by bottles of wine and liquor, many empty. One of the men had a woman upon his knee and it was he who was doing the singing.

"That's Power," the spy said. "I wish you the best of luck!" Quickly she turned and ran away into the night.

The quartermaster padded silently back to the men he had deployed at the front door. They tried the latch. To their surprise, the door was unsecured. They entered the house which, apart from the room where the party was in progress, was in darkness. The quartermaster cursed the cowardice of the spy; no-one else was familiar with the layout of the interior. He and his men made enough noise finding their bearings that they awakened a man who was asleep in a room off the entrance. The fellow leaped from his bed and saw the soldiers. He had just enough time to sound the alarm before being felled by a blow to the head with a musket stock.

Captain Power had heard his henchman's cry. The outlaw grabbed his carbine.[xxxvi] He rushed to the door of the room, opened it a fraction, and poked the barrel out just as the quartermaster came into sight. The soldier spotted the gun in the nick of time. He dodged, caught hold of the barrel and pushed it aside as Power discharged a ball.

The pair struggled fiercely as they fought for possession of the carbine. Power managed to slam the door shut, catching the soldier's wrist between the door and the post, forcing him to let go of the weapon. The outlaw quickly bolted the door.

Power reloaded and snatched up one of his pistols. He fired both weapons through the timber of the door but failed to hit any of the soldiers. The attackers returned fire, three of the troopers firing simultaneously. The women screamed. Three lead balls splintered the wood and two struck the outlaw: one lodged in his belly, the other in his groin.

"Surrender, man!" the quartermaster called from the hall.

Richard refused in the most colourful of language. He was bleeding from his wounds, yet was confident that he and his companions could escape. Unseen by the soldiers, one of the women had slipped out through a side window and was on her way to summon five more of Power's band of outlaws, who were stationed in a hut on the nearby bog.

Richard and the others had by now extinguished all the candles in the room and the whole house was in darkness, lit only sporadically by flashes of gunpowder. It was a dangerous situation, with ball and shot flying about. During a lull in the shooting the quartermaster again called out to Power to surrender. This time there came no reply from the darkened room. The soldier was so angered by this that he threatened to set fire to the house.

Captain Power was in a quandary. His wounds, though they were not as serious as they might have been, were troubling him. The hoped-for reinforcements had not arrived and he did not know why. Perhaps his comrades had come when summoned, considered the odds too great and fled. Perhaps the message had never reached them. Further speculation was soon rendered academic, however, because the quartermaster's patience ran out. He set deed to word and the house was put to the torch.

The dampness of the thatched roof resulted in smoke billowing into the interior. Within a quarter of an hour the roof was completely engulfed in flames. Blazing beams and rafters began to collapse onto the trapped outlaws and their women. Resigned by now to the fact that his comrades, for whatever reason, had abandoned him, the wounded and bleeding Captain Power surrendered, if only to save the others from a gruesome death.

The vanquished came out one at a time, coughing and spluttering. As the outlaws handed over their weapons to the soldiers, the quartermaster learned for the first time that Power was wounded. He decided to make a pact with the outlaw: he would bring Power to a surgeon once they had reached Charleville; in return, Power must give his word as a gentleman that he would not attempt to escape.

The bargain was made and the Captain's comrades, escorted by the soldiers, bore him on a litter to Kilbolane. The following morning the quartermaster conveyed Power to Charleville and delivered him into Captain Aungier's custody. Aungier was delighted. Having been apprised of the bargain Power had struck, he gave the outlaw the use of his own quarters so that the wounded man might receive medical attention.

Captain Power recovered speedily and was back on his feet within three weeks – just in time for his execution. When he was judged well enough to travel he was taken from Captain Aungier's agreeable quarters and brought to the cold confines of Clonmel Gaol. There, on Tuesday, November 10, 1685, he was hanged by the neck until dead.

One of the Lords Justices, the Earl of Boyle, wrote at the time:

"Power the Tory was executed upon Tuesday last (Nov. 1685) at Clonmel, and, as my informer tells me, he died very magnanimously by the help of three bottles of sack [sherry], which he took that morning for his morning's draught."

As he waited for the hangman to loop the noose around his neck, Power gave a caution to all young men, desiring them to shun the company of lewd women – perhaps thinking of the one who became the clergyman's spy, or the girl who reportedly dissuaded him from accepting a conditional offer of pardon.

"By women," said he, "was I enticed to continue in sin, and by a woman was I at last betrayed, though she pretended to be my friend."

The speech, it is said, reduced the spectators to tears.

Bold Captain Power

Come gath - er 'round me peo - ple and we'll

sup____ the man - tl - ing bliss, And

drink to the bo - ld Cap - tain and cur - se the trait - or's

kiss; With pis - tol and with fal - chion his

ti - tle__ wa-s well won, No car - pe-t

knight,_ he'd sta - nd and fight,__ a

true____ Kil - bo - lane son.

From Dunanore to Seskinore, all out upon the land,
His fealty to the poor well known, he robbed the recreant.
Let his name be placed in the Realms of Gold and never a jag let lie,
While he lays his head in his earthen bed, he will not doubly die.

So here's a gramercy to him who put the lightning in our blood,
And, just like Bonnivard of old, against the foe he stood;
Woe-worth to Ormonde and to Boyle and their orders from the Pale,
Hung this rapparee from the gallows tree by a clew in Clonmel Gaol.

There's Whiskey in the Jar

did - dle, O____   There's whis - key   in   the

jar.

He counted out his money and it made a pretty penny;
I put it in my pocket and I gave it to my Jenny.
She sighed and she swore that she never would betray me
But the devil take the women, for they never can be easy.

Chorus

I went into my chamber all for to take a slumber
I dreamt of gold and jewels and for sure it was no wonder,
But Jenny drew my charges and she filled them up with water
An' she sent for Captain Farrell, to be ready for the slaughter.

Chorus

And 'twas early in the morning before I rose to travel
Up comes a band of footmen and likewise Captain Farrell;
I then produced my pistol, for she stole away my rapier
But I couldn't shoot the water so a prisoner I was taken.

Chorus

And if any one can aid me, 'tis my brother in the army.
If I could learn his station, in Cork or in Killarney,
And if he'd come and join me, we'd go roving in Kilkenny.
I'll engage he'd treat me fairer than my darling sporting Jenny.

Chorus

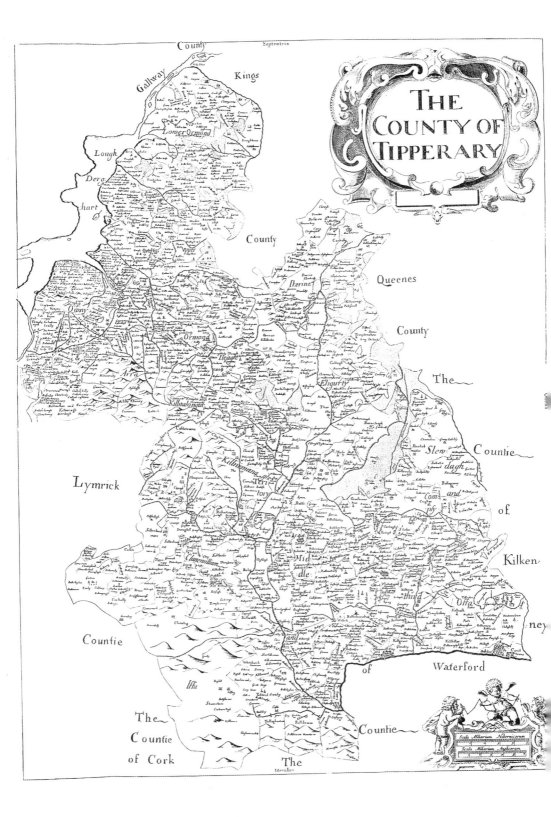

THE
COUNTY OF
TIPPERARY

Daniel Hogan

Galloping Hogan

Ireland was in chaos. The Great O'Neill lay dead and Oliver Cromwell was raising hell. Drogheda lay in ashes, its defenders and townspeople butchered most brutally. Wexford shared a similar fate. The puritan General was systematically quelling a rebellion set in train by the royalist adherents of Charles of England. Now his Ironsides, the cavalry, roamed the countryside in search of surviving rebels and those who had succoured them.

The blacksmith John Hogan[xxxvii] must have been expecting trouble when a troop of Cromwell's cavalry clattered into the village of Goldenbridge, County Tipperary, and halted at his little forge. They had come for a purpose: local blacksmiths were known to have made weapons for the insurgents. The troopers' faces were hard beneath their close-fitting skull helmets and they all looked alike dressed in drab, brown leather jerkins.

John Hogan was being assisted by his young son, Daniel. Man and boy stood sullenly by as the roundheads ransacked the forge. They found nothing: far from convincing them of John's innocence, their lack of success only infuriated them.

They rounded on the father and beat him unconscious. Next they turned their attention to the boy. A trooper produced a length of rope, made a noose in it, and flung the rope over a bough, swearing an oath to hang Daniel as a punishment for his father's insurgence. Just as they were about to string up the boy, the commanding officer noticed that his charger had lost a shoe. He postponed the lynching and ordered Daniel to replace it.

The boy, having learned the farrier's trade from his father, set to work and soon the shoe was ready. Sweating and shaking with fright, for he knew that once the horse was shod he would lose his life, Daniel grasped the horse's foot – but the animal must have sensed his fear because it lashed out, sending the boy sprawling.

The officer agreed to hold the horse's reins while Daniel nailed on the shoe, all the while berating him for incompetence. When the last nail was in place, Daniel suddenly straightened up, hammer in hand. He struck the trooper a fierce blow to the head, grabbed the charger's reins, leaped into the saddle and raced away, leaving the astonished troops dumbstruck. When they regained their composure, they set off in pursuit. They failed to catch the boy: the roundhead officer's charger was swift and Daniel had an intimate knowledge of the countryside.

It is fitting that a horse was involved and that the lad made his escape at the gallop. The soldiers and their masters would, in time, have much cause to regret that the boy's neck had not been stretched when the opportunity arose, for Daniel Hogan went on to become Galloping Hogan, one of the most celebrated of Ireland's outlaw rapparees.

The Emergence of the Kern

The Hogans were descended from the Dalcassians, whose territories extended over parts of Clare, Tipperary and Limerick.[xxxviii] Daniel's forebears occupied lands around the stronghold of Ardcrony, near Nenagh, and his ancestry can be traced back to Ogan, an eleventh-century warrior prince. Along with many other old Irish families, the Hogans were driven from their lands to make way for the plantations and settlements of Henry VIII and forced to live in the heavily wooded hills and mountains of Munster and west Leinster. Some of the O'Hogan clan managed to hold on to their lands at Ardcroney up until the Cromwellian plantation of 1652–53, when most of the territory was given to Nicholas Toler,[xxxix] a quartermaster in the Puritan army.

The invader did not know that he was sowing the wind to reap the whirlwind. The dispossessed organised themselves into irregular bands of foot and horse raiders, capable of swooping down and attacking the numerically superior English forces before melting back into the hills.

Such companies of determined "kerns" gradually developed into larger and more lethal forces. Their commanders and instructors were experienced Irish soldiers, lately returned from the battlefields of Europe. These "swordsmen" had an ancient model:

the Chinese guerrilla fighters who had operated with deadly efficiency for centuries and whose methods were widely used by military strategists on the Continent.[xl]

Thus began a system of warfare in Ireland that would endure almost to the present day. The armies of the interloper were relatively safe when ensconced behind the stout walls of their keeps, but once out in the open they were vulnerable to the hit-and-run strategy of the Irish. The guerrillas knew the terrain and were more mobile; they could wreak havoc on army convoys and supply lines.

Some of these raiders operated alone, while others struck in bands, but all employed the same tactics of speed and agility. They also had the people on their side – an enviable advantage.

Over time, the daring guerrilla bands matured into formidable cavalry units and (to a lesser extent) infantry, who assisted the Irish armies in the wars with England. Though they never became "regular" soldiers, the generals nevertheless welcomed them with open arms, and prized their martial skills highly.

Horsemen and Guerrillas

One man stood out among the rest of the rapparees,[xli] as they became known in the 1680s. He was Daniel Hogan, one of the finest soldiers and horsemen Ireland ever produced. To be given the sobriquet "Galloping" in Hogan's era, when most people handled horses as easily as we drive cars today, a man had to be an exceptional rider and "be one" with his horse.

The rapparees had a secret riding trick which they used in emergencies: they were able to summon their horses by means of a whistle or some other signal. As the animal galloped towards him, the rapparee would grab hold of the left ear of the careering animal. Using the horse's momentum, its owner would then swing neatly into the saddle – and race to safety. No doubt Hogan was capable of this feat. Legend has it that he acquired the nickname "Galloping" because of the great skill with which he rode and handled his huge mare. In all likelihood it was a Cashel, one of the great old breeds of Irish horse originating in that County Tipperary town. This was one of the biggest, strongest and noblest breeds in Europe, renowned also for its speed. Hogan's mare was eventually captured in Kilkenny by the Williamite forces.

Equestrian skills, though important in themselves, were not enough to win a would-be guerrilla a place among the rapparees. Daniel Hogan probably began his training as a runner or a lookout before being allowed into the ranks of the fighters. His training proper would have followed the pattern laid down by men such as the Munsterman known as the White Sergeant.

Tradition has it that this individual had served in the Irish army at one time but had been drummed out for roguery. He had taken to the highways and was "out upon his keeping" as an outlaw. He rose to become the leader of a band of rapparees and was known as the White Sergeant because of the white feather he wore in his hat. No-one, not even those who served with him, was privy to his real name; he likewise insisted on his men never using their own names, lest they be discovered and arrested by the authorities. By all accounts he was a ruthless and vicious man, but a brave one who never shirked his duty and would not ask a comrade to perform a deed he himself would not carry out.

The White Sergeant is reputed to have devised a terrible test for recruits wishing to join the irregulars. The young man would be taken from the camp at night, accompanied by four seasoned veterans, and brought to a local bog. The destination was a certain bog-hole that had been "treated". The recruit was placed in a waxed hessian sack with a rope about his body, secured beneath the armpits. Sack and occupant were then lowered into the hole and allowed to sink, until the man's feet were touching a ledge purposely hewn out for the test. The other end of the rope was then attached to some saplings arranged above the hole. All was then concealed by freshly cut bog weeds and heather. The rapparees would have left the top of the sack open so that the captive was able to peer out. He was left thus in his watery "grave" for three hours or more. If the cadet survived this frightening experience, he was then invited into the ranks. Galloping Hogan would have been subjected to such an ordeal when earning his spurs.

If this terrifying rite of passage seems unnecessarily cruel, and even senseless, then it should be considered in light of a method favoured by the rapparees to spy on the enemy troop encampments. Submerged in a bog-hole and concealed by vegetation, a scout was able to observe troop movements and eavesdrop on the conversations of the soldiers. There was method in the White Sergeant's madness.

Reverend George Story, writing in *A True and Impartial History of the Most Material Occurrences in the Kingdom of Ireland During the Last Two Years*, revealed:

"When the rapparees have no mind to show themselves upon the bogs they commonly sink down between two or three little hills, grown over with long grass, so that you may as soon find a hare as one of them. They conceal their arms thus, they take off the lock, and put it in their pocket or hide it in some dry place; they stop the muzzle close with a cork, and the touch-hole with a small quill, and then throw the piece itself into a running water or pond; you may search till you are weary before you find one gun: but yet when they have a mind to do mischief, they can all be ready in an hour's warning, for every one knows where to go and fetch his own arms, though you do not."

Clearly Hogan's rise through the ranks of the rapparees was meteoric, because he went on to command a large and successful band of his own. Shortly before the siege of Limerick, Galloping Hogan and some of his scouts happened to be reconnoitring near the Slieve Bloom mountains. They caught sight of the fluttering banners of the vanguard column of the Williamite army as it emerged from a wooded area at the edge of a bog. Hogan immediately recognised them as detachments of Dutch dragoons and Danish infantry and, after ordering his scouts to take cover, he galloped forward alone through the treacherous bog, taking a route known only to rapparees of the area. He reined in his Cashel directly opposite the leading flank of the column, where he coolly began to count the number of troops and the cannon which they hauled.

R.D. Joyce, in *Legends of the Wars in Ireland*, wrote:

"It seemed to tickle their fancy mightily that a single man should thus put himself in such dangerous proximity to them with a broad marsh behind him; for in a few moments, with a shout of laughter, an officer and about a dozen men dashed out from the regiment of blue dragoons, and came at a thundering pace across the moor towards Hogan. But they knew little of the man they had to deal with."

The wily rapparee, like a fox mesmerising rabbits by chasing his tail, slowly began to canter around the bog, leaping from one safe spot to another, lulling the soldiers into a false sense of security. The pursuing dragoons – all except their captain – spurred their mounts across the bog after the insolent rebel, only to find themselves floundering up to their saddle-girths in the thick, cloying mud.

The captain, a fine horseman, eventually reached the solid dry spot of land where Hogan sat smiling astride his horse. As they were now within range of each other, the Dutch officer whipped out his long menacing pistols and pointed them at Hogan, calling on him to surrender. The rapparee retorted that he would never surrender and began advancing toward his adversary, the smile never leaving his face. The dragoon, unnerved by Hogan's ice-cold bravery, panicked and fired off his weapons. The balls whistled by the rapparee's head, narrowly missing him, yet on the man came, unperturbed. When he was within a few feet of the officer, Hogan drew his sword and bade the Dutchman do the same. As soon as the soldier had his sword unsheathed, he spurred his mount and charged towards Hogan in an attempt to unhorse him. The rapparee anticipated the charge and, reining his dextrous Cashel to one side, he allowed the officer to gallop by. As he passed, Hogan swung his mighty blade and struck the officer a sickening blow between the shoulders, almost knocking him from his charger. The Dutchman recovered admirably and came about for a second attack.

With his left hand Hogan pulled his horse pistol from its saddle holster and levelled it at the approaching soldier, thinking that he would finish the contest off in one
flash – but he could not bring himself to pull the trigger because he deemed it unfair
to his brave adversary, so he holstered the gun and once more advanced with his
naked blade. The riders engaged and the countryside rang with the sound of steel
clashing upon steel, as each blow was matched by an equal blow, the two being
expert fighters. At length the superior swordsmanship of the rapparee shone through
and, with a lightning strike, he drove his razor sharp blade into the side of the brave
Dutch officer. The captain dropped his weapon, let go of the reins and fell from his
charger, landing on the grassy knoll where he lay, dead, in a pool of blood.

The commander of the column, who was watching the encounter from a safe distance, saw his captain fall and immediately ordered that one of the cannons be fired
at Hogan. The ball missed the rapparee but struck instead the poor dragoon's horse,
killing it instantly. It fell beside its dead rider. The story goes that Galloping Hogan
then stood tall in his stirrups and, with a wicked grin, shook his bloodied blade in
the direction of the despondent enemy commander, shouting out that this was what
he should expect from then on – this was a taste of things to come! Then the outlaw
flitted once more across the bog as a succession of Dutch cannon balls flew through
the sky, only to land harmlessly in the bog-holes around him.

King John's Castle, Limerick, c. 1840.

Exploding the Limerick Siege Train

It is more than likely that Hogan fought in Sarsfield's cavalry at the Battle of the Boyne in July 1690 and he almost certainly participated in the Battle of Aughrim the following year. From the Boyne, the defeated Irish retreated into Connacht, in an attempt to hold the strongholds of the Shannon at Athlone and Limerick. William next secured all the garrisons of Leinster and most of Munster with the help of John Churchill, later the Duke of Marlborough, and marched on Limerick with his huge army and massive siege train.[xlii] He camped at Cashel in Tipperary and decided to let the train follow at its own pace while he pressed onward with the troops and a much less cumbersome train of light artillery.

William arrived at Caherconlish, eight miles south of Limerick, on August 7, 1690 and within the week had begun the bombardment of the city with the light artillery pieces. Many of his great officers, including the Dutch aristocrat and future commander Lieutenant-General Ginkel, watched the show from the nearby hills. They were confident that this initial attack would result in the Jacobites' capitulation before the arrival of the train. The army, even without the big guns, was formidable: 20,000 foot and 3,500 mounted soldiers.

The rapparees had harried and sniped at William's troops during their march on Limerick, only to fall back eventually behind its walls in search of protection. But no comfort was to be had in the besieged city. Its garrison was commanded jointly by Richard Talbot, Earl of Tyrconnell – or "Lying Dick" Talbot, as this swaggering philanderer was called in the English court – and by Count de Lauzun. The French general had arrived the previous year with 7,000 troops, but he had no stomach for a siege. Nor had he much confidence in Limerick's fortifications: he declared openly that her walls could be battered down with roasted apples. Under a flag of truce de Lauzun marched his troops out of the city, fell back on Clare and Galway, and proceeded to France.

This left Tyrconnell in absolute command. Patrick Sarsfield, a proud grandson of Rory O'Moore,[xliii] held neither Tyrconnell nor de Lauzun in high regard. At the Battle of the Boyne he had been scathing about Lying Dick's efforts and there was no love lost between the two. Before Tyrconnell, too, abandoned the city, he appointed Major General Boisseleau as governor with the Duke of Berwick[xliv] as his second-in-command. Major Generals Sarsfield and Dorrington, and Brigadiers Henry Luttrell, Wauchope and Maxwell were his highest-ranking officers.

Boisseleau and Berwick were on good terms with Sarsfield; they respected and valued his skills as a soldier and leader of men. The Duke of Berwick, in particular, seems to have greatly admired Sarsfield. In conversation and correspondence he often referred to him by his sobriquet "Notorious".

This, then, was the company in which Daniel Hogan found himself. One notorious soldier was about to ride out with another – and inflict on William an extremely bitter blow.

Sarsfield was in overall command of the Jacobite cavalry. Heavily augmented by rapparees, they numbered 3,500 in total and were stationed close to Limerick. As the bombardment by William's light artillery continued without much success, the besieged army learned of the approach of the massive siege train. It was making slow but steady progress towards Limerick, escorted by a body of musketeers and two troops of Colonel Villiers' horsemen under the command of Captain Poultney. As more sightings and descriptions of the huge artillery were reported, the commanders of the city realised that they stood no chance against such formidable weaponry; the city would be pulverised and its 15,000 soldiers and civilians annihilated.

The Limerick defenders held a council of war and a decision was made, one which is attributed to Sarsfield. The train had to be intercepted and destroyed before its guns came within range of the city walls. The governor and the other officers agreed that Sarsfield would be in command of the attempt to blow up the siege train. The choice of men and weapons was at his discretion. Sarsfield went immediately to recruit the man most suited to be his lieutenant: Galloping Hogan. Together they set about mustering six hundred more volunteers: the finest and most seasoned horsemen available. At nine o'clock in the evening of August 10, 1690, the warriors, led by Sarsfield and guided by Hogan, set off in the utmost secrecy through the north gate of the city – and rode into immortality.

Secrecy was essential: William's scouts were everywhere. There was also the possibility that the council of war had been infiltrated by informers and traitors. Whatever the case, Sarsfield and Hogan were to outwit the enemy. The siege train was approaching from the east, from the direction of Cashel; Hogan led the horsemen northward. He led them through Harold's Cross, near Blackwater, bypassing O'Brien's Bridge; past Bridgetown, and on to Ballycorney. Here, at the bridge, they came across and arrested a young Protestant (known only as Cecil), working on the assumption that all Irish Protestants supported William, with a view to getting information from him about the Williamite army posts in Killaloe.

Killaloe lies some twelve miles to the north-east of Limerick city. Had a Williamite scout followed Sarsfield and Hogan, he would never have suspected that their destination was the siege train, now far to the south.

At Killaloe the riders found the bridge to be heavily guarded by enemy troops. The ever-vigilant Hogan led the riders to a ford on the Shannon, about a mile upstream, between Pier Head and Ballyvalley. There they crossed the mighty river and rode into Tipperary, unseen and unheard. It was an extraordinary feat, considering that there were six hundred men and horses involved.

Hogan knew this territory well and made for Labbadiha Bridge – or Hogan's Glen, as it is now called – where the contingent was met by a band of his rapparees. The newcomers guided them due east, to Bushfield and the ford of Aughbee, onto the old Cromwell Road, thence to Crishanny, and down to Keeper Hill. At Ballyhourigan Wood, near Killoscully, they called a halt at around 3 a.m. They rested for the first time that night, having journeyed approximately thirty-five miles. Members of the O'Ryan clan, the family of the highwayman Ned of the Hill, fed and watered the men's horses.

However, the intrepid foray did not go entirely unnoticed. A certain Manus O'Brien, a country gentleman, got wind of the departure from Limerick of a large group of riders. A Williamite sympathiser, O'Brien immediately passed on this information, but the soldiers took his account lightly. Only when word reached William himself was action taken. The King had O'Brien brought before him; after questioning the gentleman closely, William ordered five hundred horsemen to be sent out to defend and bolster the escort of the siege train and bring it safely to his headquarters at Cahernarry.

William was aware that the train was not too far off; if it was indeed the target of the body of Jacobite horsemen, then the enemy's good head-start meant that they might arrive at their destination at any moment. The King's orders were not acted upon immediately – Sir John Lanier, the officer ordered to command the troop, delayed his start for four hours. He was subsequently suspected of treachery, a charge he strenuously denied.

In Tipperary, meanwhile, Hogan and Sarsfield set out southward with their riders, heading for Toor, through Capparoe and onto Glengar (near Losset). From here Sarsfield sent out scouts. They picked up the trail of the train and followed it as far as the village of Cullen. Having crossed a stream east of the village, they came upon the wife of a Williamite soldier who had remained behind when the train had journeyed on. She was bathing her tired feet in the cool, soothing waters.

This innocent encounter was to prove extremely fortuitous for the Irish. Taking pity on a woman alone in a war-torn land, the rapparees escorted her to the public house in Cullen. Here she drank some whiskey and beer – and became dangerously loose of tongue. To the scouts' surprise, she carelessly and unhesitatingly revealed the password for entry into the siege-train camp. It was "Sarsfield".

Armed with this crucial piece of information, the scouts resumed their tracking of the train and followed it as far as the ruins of the old castle at Ballyneety, a little way inside the Limerick border, where it had made camp for the night. This, as it turned out, was a major military blunder.

The Jacobite plan was proceeding more successfully than anyone had hoped: there were whoops of joy when the scouts returned with both the whereabouts of the enemy camp and the password. The diversionary ruse had also been a success. The rapparees had covered some ninety miles since the previous night – about five times the length of the direct route from Limerick to Ballyneety. Nobody could have guessed their true purpose.

At midnight Sarsfield and Hogan broke camp and set out for Cullen, a village close to the Tipperary-Limerick border; they were taking the same route the Williamite train had followed. As the rapparee band approached Ballyneety, they were challenged by the outlying guards, who demanded the password. It was duly given and the horsemen were allowed to pass at an easy trot.

Let us pause here for a moment and consider the situation. An English sentry is posted to guard his comrades' camp. He is approached by a huge body of Irish horse-men – the sworn enemy – and allows them to proceed, simply because they know the password.

Would that matters had been so clear-cut. The truth is that when William of Orange went to war against his father-in-law, James II, he did so with an army that consisted of Dutch, English, Germans, Danes – and Irish. The forces fighting under the Jacobite banner were Irish, French, German and Walloon. These were confusing times: so much so, in fact, that at the Battle of the Boyne the Enniskilling cavalry had been engaging the Huguenot horse for some time before their commander realised that they were supposed to be fighting on the same side.

And so it was that the rapparees could forge deep into the enemy camp without arousing suspicion. They now approached the second, inner, ring of sentinels and, having increased their pace, were challenged again. A rider came out of the shadows.

"Password!" he bellowed.

"'Sarsfield' is the word," replied Patrick Sarsfield himself. "And Sarsfield is the man!"

The alarm was raised – but too late. Sarsfield and Hogan charged into the camp at the head of their well-trained and well-armed horsemen shouting the Jacobite war cry: "Now or never! Now and forever!"

With pistols firing and sabres slashing, they quickly overpowered the sleeping escort, who were taken completely by surprise. The battle lasted but a few minutes: some sixty Williamite troopers and one officer perished.[xlv]

Sarsfield and Hogan then set about the real work. The enemy horses were rounded up and stampeded away in the direction of Limerick. Sarsfield next ordered the siege-guns to be formed into a circle. Their barrels were filled with powder, pointed into the ground, and a powder trail laid down to where the men were stand-ing. Sarsfield gave Hogan the honour of lighting the fuse.

"Now give it the match, Hogan," he said, "and we'll have an earthquake all our own."

Daniel Hogan laid the match to the powder. There was a tremendous explosion as the guns blew to pieces, and powder and ammunition ignited.

Sir John Lanier and his five hundred troops, having set out four hours too late, had just arrived in Caherconlish when they saw an enormous flash and heard a thunderous roar. Lanier knew that he was too late to save the train, but hoped to be able to head off the attackers as they fled the camp. However, unfamiliar with the area, he turned his forces in the direction of the Shannon – and went the wrong way.

Sarsfield and Hogan did not return the way they had come; instead, they led their men in a north-easterly direction, from Ballyneety to Borrisoleigh and on to Banagher. They forded the Shannon there and blew up part of the bridge, effectively cutting off the approach of any pursuers, before turning south and heading back to Limerick.

Their return journey was not without incident. There was a troop of dragoons camped in the Banagher area under the command of Sir Albert Cunningham. On hearing the rapparees pass by, the dragoons quickly mounted up and engaged the rearguard, killing sixteen and wounding some others. Astonishingly, these were the only casualties sustained by the rapparees in the course of the entire action.[xlvi] The victorious horsemen made their getaway from Banagher via Portumna, arriving in Limerick on August 15 to a huge and rousing reception from the besieged citizens. Hogan and Sarsfield had saved the day.

News of the daring raid quickly spread across Europe, causing an international sensation. The *Gazette de France* gave a good, if slightly inflated, account of the attack. The *London Gazette* of August 25, 1690, however, played down the whole affair, reporting the losses as minimal and of no great account.

"This incident will only lose us three or four days, for in that time our cannon (being 24-pounders) will arrive from Waterford; in the meantime our batteries are preparing and all things are put in posture for a vigorous attack on the town."

Although the assault on Limerick failed as a result of the Ballyneety action, the matter did not end there. Shortly afterward, William withdrew his army and returned to Dublin. He crossed to England, leaving his Dutch general Ginkel in command.

In May 1691 the hapless fugitive King James, aided by Louis XIV, dispatched the Marquis de St Ruth to take overall command of his forces in Ireland. St Ruth, a capable and sincere soldier, quickly mustered an army of some 15,000 men and marched to Athlone, which was under attack from Ginkel. Inspiring deeds of heroism were performed by the Irish at Athlone; nevertheless, Ginkel crossed over the undefended ford there on June 30, forcing St Ruth to retreat westwards.

The decisive battle of the war was fought on July 22, 1691 at Aughrim, near Ballinasloe.[xlvii] As St Ruth stood in his stirrups to order the final charge, he was struck by a cannon ball and killed. The army fell into confusion and was routed. After the

The Treaty Stone, Limerick.

battle, Galway capitulated and Ginkel marched on Limerick, again laying siege to the city. The second siege lasted barely a month; yet again the Irish were hopelessly out-numbered. However, with winter rapidly approaching, Ginkel was prepared to offer favourable terms. Sarsfield accepted.

The Treaty of Limerick was signed on October 3, 1691: the signatories were Ginkel and his Chief Justices on one hand, and Sarsfield and his commanders on the other. Ironically, within a few days of the siege ending, a French fleet sailed up the Shannon, with an army and plentiful supplies of weapons and rations on board. Tradition has it that, on seeing the ships, Sarsfield said: "Too late, too late! The Treaty is signed and Ireland's honour is pledged."

He left for France, taking the Irish army with him.

The Rapparee's Demise

Daniel Hogan, however, remained on his native soil. It would be cynical to say that he was swayed in his decision by the lure of easy booty, yet it is also true that he saw no reason to resist its allure. It is believed that he was in command of a band of more than one hundred rapparees, mounted and on foot. By targeting the Williamite convoys, the outlaws amassed a huge store of plunder, weapons and booty.

On June 1, 1691 Hogan and Captain Grace, another rapparee, at the head of eighty men, attacked and took Castle Camgart near Birr, County Offaly, which had been garrisoned during the winter by a party of military. A battle then ensued to retake the castle. The Williamites were unsuccessful and a certain Ensign Story, brother of the Reverend George, was killed in the battle. The Reverend, writing about the event in his *True and Impartial History*, describes the chivalry of Hogan and his men.

"The Irish proffered to bury him [Ensign Story] honourably which they did, allowing his own drum to beat the dead march and themselves fired three volleys at his grave, acknowledging at his death certain former civilities from him which is very rare with that sort of people."

There are conflicting accounts of the manner in which the rapparee known as Galloping Hogan continued his career.

In September of that year Hogan attacked a lightly escorted party of "carrs" (wagons or carts) heading for camp, relieving them of seventy-one horses but doing no harm or injury to the escort or drivers. The same month he attacked, by some accounts single-handedly, a party of dragoons near Roscrea, killing seven, with the eighth man barely escaping with his life. ·

George Story states that Hogan and most of his men surrendered at Roscrea, taking advantage of the Proclamation of Pardon issued for the second time on October 14, 1691. It promised "pardon and protection to all robbers, thieves and rapparees who before the 5th of November, following, should surrender their arms to any Justice of the Peace and take the Oath of Fidelity to their Majesties described in the Articles of Limerick".

But not all the Irish were agreeable to the treaty and there are those who maintain that Daniel Hogan was among those renegades. He was rumoured to have continued as a rapparee, attacking the supply trains as before and gathering supplies and arms for the continuation of the struggle, while others used the same methods for personal gain. Whether or not Hogan was among them, these bands of outlaws were an immense problem for the Williamites. There is even an outlandish story that Ginkel, in a masterly stroke, recruited Hogan and placed him at the head of twenty-four of his most loyal men, all heavily armed with the best weapons and horses, with orders to suppress the rapparees. We may believe what we will.

If speculation surrounds the rest of Daniel Hogan's life, then as much conjecture is attached to the manner of his passing. Some say he was murdered in Roscrea by others of his kind, prior to October 19, 1691;[xlviii] others would have us believe that he was hanged in Portroe, County Tipperary. Whatever the truth, one thing is not in dispute: the man known as Galloping Hogan deserves his place in the pantheon of Irish folk heroes.

In 1838 on a farm near Labbadiha Bridge, Tipperary, Michael Andrews, a farmer, was digging a field with his brothers when they came upon some old timber-works. On digging further they unearthed an underground chamber formed from black oak. Inside were about twenty pairs of wooden shoes and a large quantity of ashes.

It was an intriguing discovery. Judging from their age, and if the old Orange toast to King William ("who saved us from brass money and wooden shoes") is anything to go by, then it is entirely possible that the shoes were among supplies sent by the French to aid King James. However, local folklore has it that this was a hideout of the famous rapparee Galloping Hogan.[xlix] The chamber was filled in and remains thus to this day. It is now known as Hogan's Glen.

Galloping Hogan Jig

Galloping Hogan

Old Lime-rick is in dan-ger and

Ire - land is not free; So

Sars - field sends_ a message_ to a

fear - less rap - par - ee: "Com - e

ride ac - ross the___ Shann - on At the

soun-ding of the drum and we'll blow the en-em-y siege_ train

To the land of King - dom come."___

Gall - op - ing Hog-an, Gall - op - ing Hog - an,

Gall - op - ing all a - long, In___ his

sad - dle is a___ sa - bre, on his lips there is a song; He's_

off a - cross the Shan - non To_ des

-troy the enemy___ cannon; And_ he goes gallop-ing,

he goes galloping,_ Galloping, galloping_ on.

The Rapparee is bearded,
There's a twinkle in his eye;
As he rides into the city,
The Limerick ladies cry:
"Mr Outlaw, Mr Outlaw,
Will you tarry here with me?"
"Ah, I'm off to Ballyneety,
To blow up a battery!"

Chorus

So tonight along the Shannon,
By the pale light of the moon,
There flows an eerie brightness,
As of an Indian noon;
Then clippody-clop resounding
Through the lattice of the shade,
The ghost of Galloping Hogan
Goes a-riding down the glade.

Chorus

THE
COUNTY OF
TIPPERARY

County
Gallway   Kings

Lower Ormond

Lough
Derg
hart

County

Iherine

Queenes

County

Onny

The

Ormond

Teagh

Elhurity

Arra

Killnalongan

Counties

Slem
dagh

and

Lymrick

Killnomana
Terri
tory

Com
psy

of

Clanwilliam

Mid
dle

Kilken

thind

Offa

ney

Countie

Iffa

and

of

Waterford

The
Countie
of Cork

The

Countie

Edmund O'Ryan

Ned of the Hill (Éamonn an Chnuic)

Edmund O'Ryan might have been a saint or a scholar, had it not been for the tears of a woman. As a boy he had been sent to France and Spain for a formal education. It appears that he intended initially to join the priesthood – instead, Edmund became a highwayman.

It was not a deliberate decision. Edmund was at home, enjoying a break from his studies on the Continent. One day, while out riding, he heard wailing and crying coming from within a small cottage nearby. The obvious distress in the woman's voice caused him to stop and investigate.

The occupant of the cottage was a poor, elderly widow Edmund had known since childhood. She told him that she was unable to pay her taxes, and was being visited that same day by the bailiff and his deputies. The bailiff had threatened to seize the woman's only cow, her sole means of support, in lieu of the taxes.

The honourable Edmund did not stand idly by. He waited in the cottage until the tax collectors arrived – and challenged them. Tempers flared and a fierce fight ensued. Pistols were drawn and, whether by accident or design, Edmund shot the bailiff dead. Realising the enormity of his crime, Edmund leapt into the saddle and galloped away into the hills, pursued by the bailiff's shocked deputies.

As a result of this unfortunate incident Edmund O'Ryan was proclaimed an outlaw and a large reward offered for his arrest, dead or alive. With one short, sharp action the scholar-postulant had become the friend of the oppressed and the foe of the oppressor.

On the Battlefield

Edmund was born in Atshanbohy in the parish of Templebeg, in the upper half-barony of Kilnamanagh, County Tipperary, in the latter part of the seventeenth century. The boy was of good fighting stock: his mother was descended from the ancient O'Dwyers, Lords of Kilnamanagh, while his paternal ancestors were the great warrior O'Ryans of Kilnalongurty.[1] There is some dispute over how Edmund acquired his nickname, Ned of the Hill (Éamonn an Chnuic). It may have been because, as an outlaw, he frequented the hills, but it is more likely that he was so called in his youth because the O'Ryan home was built on a hill, known locally as Knockmehil, and the title distinguished him from other O'Ryan sons called Edmund. Indeed, his sister was known as Sally of the Hill (Sadhbh an Chnuic).

Ned ranged over his native parish in the aftermath of the shooting. Hunted night and day, he embarked upon a one-man crusade against the foreign landlords and authorities. He robbed, he plundered, and he disrupted the peace of the area.

Political events had overtaken the country – the great struggle between James II and William embroiled Irishmen of every persuasion. Ned joined the Jacobite army. The move afforded him both the opportunity of fighting for his beliefs and temporary respite from the forces of law. These forces were, by and large, engaged in the Williamite cause.

Ned fought at the battles of the Boyne and Aughrim, under James' banner, and also played a vital role in the action that resulted in the destruction of William's great siege-train at Ballyneety. He was, according to the nineteenth century author and poet R.D. Joyce, "one of the noblest gentlemen and bravest rapparee captains that ever drew sword or shook bridle free in the cause of worthless, war-minded King James the Second".

Ned formed a band of guerrillas who harried and sniped at William's convoys on their way to besiege Limerick – and it was on one of these raids that his cousin Hugh O'Ryan lost his life. Hugh, not only a first cousin but a great friend of Ned's, was slain at the time of the first siege of Limerick, during an ambush of Williamite troops at the Bridge of Tern. Joyce records a romantic description of Edmund at his cousin's funeral:

"There, erect as a spear-shaft, stood a young man, slightly above middle height, with eyes black and piercing, like those of an eagle, and a sun-embrowned face, eminently beautiful in its contour and proportions. A bright helmet, in the crown spike of which was stuck a spray of heather with its purple flowers all in bloom, defended his proud head; and from beneath it flowed down a mass of raven-black and shining hair upon a glittering steel corslet, under which in its turn, the skirts of a light green coat fell in graceful folds over the manly leg of its wearer. Over the corslet was flung a broad green leathern belt, from which depended a heavy cavalry sabre and a long skean or dagger, with the hilt of which latter the hand of its owner was playing nervously…"

The death of "Hugh of Glenurra" had a profound effect on Ned; later, accompanied by Hugh's father (Ned's uncle Owen O'Ryan) and Galloping Hogan, he would avenge his cousin.

It was also during the time of the siege of Limerick that another personal tragedy befell the outlaw. One of Sarsfield's scouts, a friend of Ned's, was returning to his column and passing through O'Ryan country. He noticed that there were many Williamite troops in the area. Knowing that Ned's mother lived nearby and thinking it likely that Ned would call and see her, he knocked on her door and urged her to warn her son.

As the scout left the house he was observed by several Williamite soldiers, who set out in pursuit. He fled into the hills and found refuge in a remote cabin belonging to a mutual friend of his and Ned's. He waited there for a few hours until convinced that the troops had left the area and that it was safe to return to quarters. Believing the coast to be clear, the scout mounted his horse and had a final word with his host. It then occurred to him that he had no means of lighting his pipe, and asked for an ember from the hearth.

No sooner had the friend returned with a glowing sod than a volley of shots rang out. The friend fell dead with two balls lodged in his body – the glow had alerted the troops, still keenly searching the area. The scout, unhurt by the musket-fire, gave his horse the rowels and fled in the direction of Inch, a village close to Kilcommon, in the foothills of the Galtee Mountains.

As chance would have it, Ned had chosen that very evening to visit his mother. He had heeded her warning concerning the enemy soldiers and was returning to his column by a circuitous route, one that led him through the hills. Suddenly he heard shots and guessed that a brother-in-arms was in danger. He galloped in the direction of the gunfire.

There was a small hill nearby. Ned knew that its brow would give him a vantage point. On reaching the summit he saw that one of the Williamite dragoons had forged ahead of the others and was gaining on his friend, the scout, after a chase of six miles. Ned drew his brace of pistols and urged his steed down the incline – straight into the path of the enemy. He fired both guns and the dragoon toppled from his saddle, mortally wounded.[li] Ned and his comrade made their escape back to Sarsfield's band.

After the signing of the Limerick Treaty in October 1691, many rapparees and swordsmen joined Sarsfield when he left for France, to seek glory on the battlefields of mainland Europe. Some remained in Ireland, to continue the fight as highwaymen or rapparees. One such was Ned of the Hill. The Williamite war had interrupted his lucrative – and vengeful – career and he now sought to make up for lost time. Once more he took to the Kilnamanagh Hills. However, stories that circulated at the time attest to the qualities which set him apart from other outlaws.

The Gallant Highwayman

Ned was nothing if not gallant. One morning he held up a coach on the main highway to Dublin and disarmed the driver. He then ordered the sole passenger, a married woman, to "stand and deliver".

Terrified, she handed over her purse, which contained £100. She informed Ned that her husband had given her the money for living expenses. He was, she explained, in England on business, and would be there for quite some time. The money was to last her for the duration of her husband's sojourn.

Ned opened the purse and extracted a half-crown.

"I'll keep but a half-crown to support life 'till I reach home," he said, and returned the purse to the astounded woman. Gallantry was the last thing she had expected from a highwayman.

She thanked him profusely for his kindness and ventured to ask his name. He bowed.

"It is Ned of the Hill that has robbed you, madam," he told her, "and not some common criminal. Be sure to say that when you recount this incident."

The lady readily agreed. So taken was she by the outlaw's conduct that she assured him that she would use her husband's good offices, influence and connections to secure a pardon for him. Ned thanked her, bade her Godspeed and rode off into the distance.

He had not gone too far, however, when he himself was surprised and ambushed by another highwayman, and obliged at pistol-point to hand over all his money. Ned proffered the recently-acquired half-crown. But, as the stranger reached over to take the coin, Ned whipped out his pistol and levelled it at a point between the other's eyes. He retook possession of his half-crown, grinning, and proceeded to part the other highwayman from his purse and weapons. Disarmed, penniless and at

Ned's mercy, the stranger begged to know the name of the person who had out-smarted him.

"Éamonn an Chnuic," Ned replied in the language the highwaymen shared.

The stranger laughed loudly on hearing this, as if in disbelief. He then began to goad Ned and jeer, saying that he had often heard the name but believed the real Éamonn an Chnuic to be an outstanding athlete, fearless in deed, especially in unarmed combat.

"Very well," said Ned, rising to the challenge. "I'll prove to you that I am he."

He cast aside his weapons, dismounted, and the two highwaymen proceeded to settle the issue toe to toe. The bout was short, but fierce, and Ned emerged the victor. He left his opponent in no doubt as to his identity.

Chastened, the stranger shook Ned's hand and the two parted in friendship and respect, each promising to help aid the other in the future – they had, after all, a common enemy.

Legend has it that the man Ned fought that day was none other than Count Redmond O'Hanlon.

O'Ryan's gallantry went hand in glove with his kindness toward the poor and downtrodden. Not long after his encounter with the Ulster outlaw O'Hanlon, Ned happened to call at the home of a poor family in Gurtnahalla, near Borrisoleigh, County Tipperary.

On entering the cottage he was both appalled and touched by the abject poverty of the occupants – appalled by the penury of their circumstances and touched by their dignity. He quickly devised a plan that would improve their situation. He advised the man of the house to go to the garrison in Borrisoleigh and inform the officer in charge that Ned of the Hill was in the vicinity. In return for this information, the outlaw assured the tenant, he would be given a £5 reward – the standard informer's "fee". Five pounds was a sum that could keep a man and his family well fed and sheltered for a year. At first the poor man refused, protesting that he would not be an informer for any money, but was soon convinced by Ned's assurances that no harm would befall him.

The man did as Ned suggested, received his reward, and duly led troops to the area. The soldiers spotted the brazen outlaw riding in the direction of some nearby woods and gave chase. Ned plunged ever deeper into woods unfamiliar to his pur-suers, and had great and deadly sport with them. He resorted to his guerrilla tactics of old, sniping at the troopers' flanks before vanishing back into the trees, only to emerge again, guns blazing.

That day Ned single-handedly killed seven troopers. The rest of the squadron limped back to quarters with the bodies of their dead comrades. The information they had bought had cost them dear – but the incident was to prove costly to Ned as well.

As a result of the shootings, a large military force was drafted into the area with instructions to apprehend the outlaw: the authorities were determined to show that the slaughter of seven of His Majesty's men would not go unpunished.

The hunt was on and the outlaw was kept continually on the move. He rarely spent two nights under the same roof, going from safe house to safe house, the common people keeping him out of the clutches of the authorities. Those good men and women worshipped him. At one time he even slipped back into the heavily garrisoned region around the Castle of Borrisoleigh, where allies hid him underneath the noses of the troops. Security should have been at its tightest here but the army simply assumed that the outlaw would not be daring enough to enter the area – they were to learn not to underestimate Ned's boldness.

An officer from the castle garrison was dispatched to Nenagh to collect the troopers' pay. He journeyed well-armed, but alone. One of the local people got wind of his departure and alerted Ned. Thus it came about that the officer, on his return journey, was joined on the highway by a finely dressed and well-spoken gentleman. Ned's upbringing and foreign education served him impeccably. The officer was glad of the company; they rode on together for a few miles. Abruptly, as they were nearing a remote stretch of the road, the soldier quickened his pace and urged Ned to do likewise.

"For what reason?" Ned enquired.

"There is every likelihood that we shall be waylaid by the infamous, murdering highwayman, Ned of the Hill."

Ned suppressed a grin.

Onward the pair journeyed together, through Ballyruan, heading for the castle at Borrisoleigh, the officer blissfully unaware of the true identity of his gentleman companion. As they drew close to an inn, Ned could not restrain himself any longer. He reined in his mount and informed the officer that he had been travelling all the while in the company of the "ruthless murderer" Ned of the Hill. He then invited the thunderstruck officer to share a jug of ale.

Having spent most of the day with the outlaw and coming to no harm, and not a little chagrined at having earlier displayed his fear of the highwayman, the soldier gave his word as an officer and a gentleman that he would not attempt an arrest. He agreed to stop for an ale and the pair entered the inn.

The officer was, alas, no gentleman in the chivalrous sense of the word. History does not record his method, but somehow he managed to get word to his barracks that he was in the company of one of Tipperary's most wanted men. A message was delivered to the commander of the troops – one Garcy Boate – that reinforcements should be sent at the double. Soon the inn was surrounded by uniformed men and Boate lost no time in calling on Ned to lay down his arms and surrender.

Ned's drinking companion was both relieved and delighted. Ned was appalled.

He prided himself on his good judgment of character and had regarded this officer's word as his bond. Seeing no immediate way of escape, Ned surrendered, and graciously made the commanding officer an offer of drinks for his soldiers. The commander saw a way of ingratiating himself with his men at no cost to himself – and, after all, the outlaw was quite outnumbered – so he allowed the troopers into the inn. He ought to have suspected trickery, for Ned faced the gallows for his crimes.

Ned requested that a barrel of ale be placed in the middle of the floor and its lid struck off. He then urged all present to dip their cans into it and drink a toast, before they placed him in irons and led him away. The officers and men needed little encouragement.

Ned waited until the troopers' cans had emptied the barrel somewhat. Then he rose to his considerable height, lifted the barrel, and flung its contents into the soldiers' faces. In the moment they stood startled, Ned dashed through the doorway, mounted a horse and made his escape.

The story has an epilogue. That evening the outlaw infiltrated the grounds of Borrisoleigh Castle and shot dead the officer who had betrayed him. Ned of the Hill strongly disapproved of men who went back on their word.

The Most Wanted Outlaw

Without a doubt Ned of the Hill was one of the most dangerous Tories who ever lived; the soldiers provoked him at their peril.

One Sunday a sports meeting was taking place on the hill of Liss, near Borrisoleigh. It was here that Ned met a Mr Edward Shanahan,[lii] who observed that the outlaw was openly bearing arms. Shanahan requested that Ned put away his weapons: not only did the organisers of the meeting wish to avoid trouble on the Sabbath, but there was a group of soldiers from the castle present and doubtless they would regard a gentleman so heavily armed as suspect. The outlaw accordingly obliged, concealed his weapons in a ditch, and joined in the sport and merriment, much to the delight of the ordinary folk, who had recognised their champion.

On observing Ned's gentlemanly demeanour and the good cut of his cloth, the officer in charge of the contingent approached him and engaged him in conversation. Unlike the local people, he was unaware of the outlaw's identity. The talk eventually turned to the topic of the time – Ned of the Hill. The soldier's language became heated and, drawing his sabre, he sliced the head off a thistle.

"There!" he cried. "I would gladly pay a large sum of money for the privilege of doing the same to this Ned fellow – a cowardly criminal who skulks behind ditches and shoots men in the back!"

Ned said nothing; outlaw and army officer parted company. Some time later the sports meeting came to an end. Ned returned to the group mounted, with pistols, sabre and blunderbuss in plain view.

"Where is the braggart?" he called out. "Tell him that the 'cowardly criminal' is here!"

The officer appeared – and Ned shot him dead without preamble. Next he began firing at the confused and bewildered troopers, who fled the area. The outlaw pursued them to the outskirts of Borrisoleigh and killed fourteen soldiers. By this time the alarm had been raised and the entire garrison – cavalry and infantry – had been mobilised. Ned turned tail and galloped off in the direction of Rathmoy. The mounted soldiers set off in pursuit.

Ned lay in wait at a narrow stretch in the road. He ambushed the pursuing riders, discharging his blunderbuss into the tightly packed group, injuring and panicking both soldiers and mounts. Before the troopers could recover and ascertain if the outlaw was alone, Ned was gone again. They chased him for five miles across open country, eventually losing his trail in the woods near Shanballyduff.

Ned was now the most wanted man in two provinces. There was a correspondingly high price on his head, payable whether his captors killed him or brought him in alive. The bounty was increasing with each successive outrage. The Tory hunters began to gather like vultures.

One such individual was a man named Reuben Lee, a resident of Gurtnaskehy. Lee was of planter stock, reputed to have either been a Cromwellian soldier or the son of one who had settled in the area and joined one of the many outlaw bands. By all accounts he was one of the most dauntless and ruthless highwaymen in the locality. He was also one of the most despised; he always kept for himself that which he robbed, even when riding in the company of others. This flew in the face of the unwritten tradition of Tory conduct, which was that spoils were always divided equally.

Local folklore has it that Lee had robbed more than enough to enable him to live comfortably for the rest of his days; he only wanted the freedom to do so. He approached the authorities and offered to deliver Ned of the Hill to them in exchange for a pardon for his crimes: a sprat to catch a salmon, as it were. Not unnaturally, considering the tally of soldiers Ned had killed, the authorities agreed.

Lee arranged to have Ned come to his home in Gurtnaskehy on a certain day; the house was to be surrounded and the outlaw captured once and for all. However, the plan was complicated by the unexpected arrival of another outlaw visitor. He was one of the Ryans of Templederry, a respected family of loyal Irishmen.

Ryan had his suspicions about Lee and voiced them to Ned. He spoke to him in their native Irish, a language Lee did not understand. Both men noticed that Lee was stealing furtive glances out of the window, but Ned said nothing. Instead, he moved casually to the window and looked out. A large force of troopers was approaching the house, some taking cover in the ditch by the lane leading to the yard.

Without a word, Ned picked up Lee's gun, which was lying on the table. He looked the Cromwellian straight in the eye – and shot him dead.[liii]

The two outlaws escaped through the back door and raced to freedom. As they rode away, Ned confided to his comrade that Lee had a sizeable hoard of money hidden near the house. If they made good their escape, then Ryan was to return and retrieve it for himself.

"You earned it with this day's work," said the outlaw in gratitude.

They escaped successfully and local tradition has it that Ryan did indeed return to find the traitor's treasure exactly where Ned had said it would be: wrapped in a foal skin and buried at the rear of the house.

In the wake of this dramatic escape Ned must have felt that the net was closing and that it was only a matter of time before he was run to earth. He headed deeper into the Keeper Mountains and, in the early 1700s, resumed his trade from a base near Hollyford. For a number of years little was heard of him outside that immediate area; when his name came to public attention again, it was through no fault of his own.

A Mr Maude was robbed of eighty pounds by a highwayman claiming to be Ned of the Hill. When news of the impersonation reached the real Ned, he was incensed. He swore he would track down the impostor and have the money returned to the victim in less than three weeks. He was as good as his word: before the three weeks were up Mr Maude's purse was filled again and the impostor in custody.

The man was so impressed by this show of integrity that he vowed to do all in his power to obtain a pardon for Ned. In fact, the two men became great friends. They passed many evenings together talking and smoking a good pipe, while Ned stayed at the home of an old acquaintance, Thomas Bawn Dwyer ("White Tom" Dwyer), also known as Dwyer Broc ("The Badger" Dwyer).[liv]

Ned had chosen his safe-house poorly, however. There was still an enormous price on the outlaw's head: £300, a sum that in those times would have tempted an angel. One evening in 1724 Ned arrived at Badger Dwyer's house, tired and bedraggled, having been pursued for two days and nights by the military. Exhausted, he lay down to sleep while Dwyer kept watch.

The Badger seized his opportunity. Taking an axe, he crept silently to Ned's bunk. With one mighty blow he struck off the outlaw's head. Ned of the Hill, folk-hero of Tipperary and nemesis of England's soldiery, had not even had time to cry out.

Dwyer put the head in a sack and hurried off to the authorities, wild with excitement at the thought of the fortune he was about to collect. A bitter disappointment

awaited him:[lv] only two days before, Ned had obtained his pardon. Mr Maude's
overtures on the outlaw's behalf had been successful.

Nevertheless, the authorities confiscated the severed head of Ned of the Hill and
set it on a spike above the entrance to Cashel Gaol. Not long after, it was removed by
some local men and presented to Ned's sister, Sally of the Hill; she gave them a guinea
for this service.

Sally buried her brother with dignity.[lvi] His remains lie interred in the townland of
Curraheen, near Foilachluig in the parish of Toem, in the barony of Kilnamanagh.[lvii]
The people of Curraheen may not have buried a saint or a scholar, but they buried a
true gentleman outlaw – and a hero and champion that Tipperary and Ireland will
never forget.

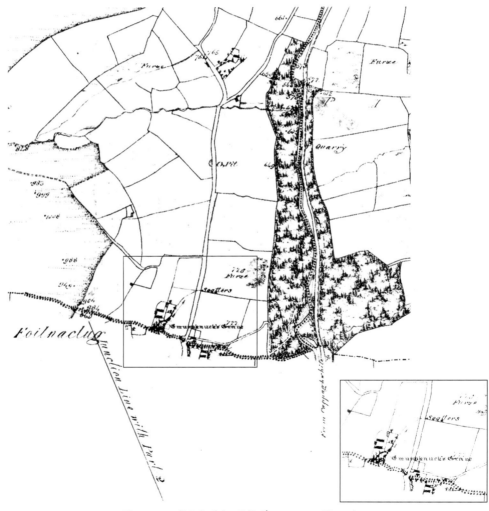

The grave of Ned of the Hill (Éamonn an Chnuic)

Ned of the Hill

16
walk - ing. O my dear love and true What

20
could I do for you But_ un - der my man - t - le

24
dr - a - w you? For_ the bul - lets like hail fa-ll

28
thick on your trail And to - geth - er we both may be

slaugh - tered.

Long lonely I go;
Under frost, under snow,
Hunted through hill and through hollow.
No comrade I know,
No furrow I sow:
My team stands unyoked in the fallow.

No friend will give ear
Or harbour me here –
'Tis that makes the weight of my sorrow!
So my journey must be
To the East o'er the sea
Where no kindred will find me or follow!

Éamonn An Chnuic

"Cia súd amuigh a' réabadh na nguirt,
Nó ag éisteacht mo dhorus dúnta?"
"'Mise Éamonn a' Chnuic, nó a' leigfeá
mé 'steach,
Ag éileamh mo chuid fearainn dúithche?"
"A rún agus a chuid, god é
dhéanfad-sa annsin
Mara dtóigfead-sa suas mo thúirne?
Buin díot do chuid éadaigh is luigh
in do léine,
Agus fuireocha mé féin 'mo dhúsacht!"

"Who is that without, that is trampling
the fields,
And listening at my bolted door?"
"I am Eamonn an Chnuic,
will you not let me in,
Who am seeking my own rightful lands?"
"Dear love, what shall I do then
But take up my spinning-wheel?
Take off your clothing and lie
in your shirt,
And I will stay awake."

"A bhláth breagh na finne, a ghrádh gach
uile dhuine,
Nó'n ngluaisfeá-sa seal don Muighe liom,
Mar bhfuighmist ól fada is imirt is
ceolta dá sinim,
Agus mórán do na h-úbhlaibh úra:
Mar bhíonn sméara is biolar is caora
a' chuilinn,
'S a' cuaichín i mbarr an úirigh?
Is go bráth ní thiocfadh an bás i
n-ár gcuinne
Faoi bhruach na coille cúmhartha."

"Fair blossom of whiteness, beloved by all,
Will you come for a space to Moy
with me?
There we shall have long drinking and
gaming and music,
And ripe apples in abundance;
There are blackberries and cress
and holly bushes,
And the little cuckoo in the top
of the greenwood;
And never shall death come nigh us
On the fringe of the fragrant wood."

"Is cruaidhe thú ná'n stíl nó leacracha
an aoil,
'S is carraic do chroidhe, a dheigh-bhean,
Ná dtigeann ins an oidhche 'gus síneadh
liom-sa síos,
Agus páirt do mo phian a réidhteach!"
"B'fhearr liom-sa bheith 'mo luighe
ráithe agus mí
Ar leabaidh chruaidh chaoil gan éin-fhear
Nó do leanbh ar mo chích nó um asgall
ins an oidhche,
Agus tusa ag do mhian gá bréagadh!"

"You are harder than steel
or limestone
And your heart is a rock fair lady;
You never come at night to lie down
by my side
And relieve me of part of my pain!"
"I would rather be lying for a quarter
and a month
On a hard, narrow bed, husbandless,
Than to have your babe at my breast
or on my arm at night,
With you away courting your fancy!"

Bean Dubh An Ghleanna

Tá bó agam ar an slíabh agus táim le seal ina diaidh
ó chailleas mo chiall le nuachar,
á seoladh soir is siar ins an áit a dtéann an ghrian
ó mhaidin go dtí an tráthnóna.
Nuair a fhéachaim féin anonn ins an áit a mbíonn mo rún
ritheann óm shúil sruth deora
is, a Rí ghil na gcumhacht, go bhfóirir ar mo chúis
mar is í bean dubh an Ghleanna do bhreoigh mé.

Bean dubh an Ghleanna an bhean dubh a b'fhearra,
bean dubh ba deise gáire,
a bhfuil a grua mar an sneachta is a píb mar an eala
is a com seang singil álainn.
Níl óganach cailce ó Bhaile Átha Cliath go Gaillimh
nó as siúd go Tuaim Uí Mheára
nach bhfuil ag triall is ag tarraingt ar eacha donna deasa
is iad ag tnúth leis an mbean dubh álainn.

Geobhainnse bean sa Mhumhain, triúr bean i Laighean,
bean ó Rí geal Seoirse,
bean na lúba buí a d'fháiscfeadh mé lena croí,
bean agus dhá mhíle bó léi.
Iníon óg an Iarla atá go tinn dubhach diacrach
ag iarraidh mise a fháil le pósadh,
ach dá bhfaighinnse féin mo rogha de mhná deasa an domhain
is í an bhean dubh ón nGleann a thoghfainn.

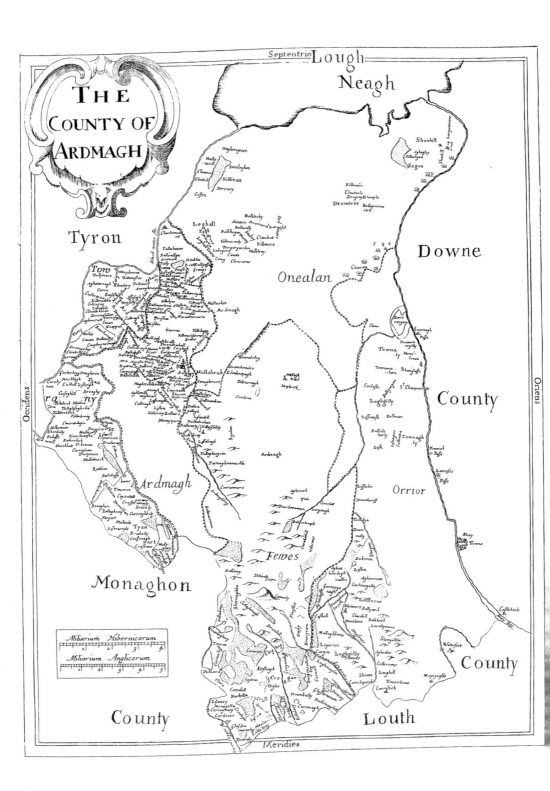

THE COUNTY OF ARDMAGH

Septentrio

Lough Neagh

Tyron

Downe

Onealan

Occidens

Oriens

Ardmagh

Orrior

Monaghon

Fewes

County

County

Louth

County

Meridies

Miliarium Hibernicorum

Miliarium Anglicorum

Charles Carragher

Big Charlie Carragher

At the same time as the infamous Count Redmond O'Hanlon was nearing the close of his career as a highwayman, a son born to another south Armagh family was growing into the man who would become the outlaw dubbed Big Charlie Carragher, or Cathal Mór.[lviii]

By all accounts Charles was a ruthless man who was not above the shedding of innocent blood. By the time of his death he had acquired a reputation so terrible that more than 250 years would pass before a Carragher family in south Armagh named a son Charles, nor even the Irish equivalent, Cathal.

But he was not born an outlaw: like so many others, his violent life as a highwayman stemmed from the circumstances of his birth and ancestry.

Tradition informs us that Charles was the son of a dispossessed Irish gentleman who lost his lands to the planters. Though in straitened circumstances, the family never lost their gentility. Charles would give to anybody who listened a full account of his family history and he burned with a belief in his ancestral rights. As he grew into manhood, he developed an air of grandeur; he was known as something of a dandy and was rarely seen abroad without fine clothes, his wig and tricorn hat – and a brace of expensive pistols. In short, there was nothing about Charles Carragher in his early twenties that would have led anyone to believe that his life would be anything other than respectable.

The young Charles was sent to live and work on the premises of a Mr Blykes, an innkeeper of Dorsey in the area known as The Fews, County Armagh.[lix] He worked well and without incident for a number of years, until he secured the job of "sheriff's bailiff" (or "keeper") of the Dorsey cattle pound. It appears that he was recommended by Mr Blykes. This was fortunate for Charles, for positions of authority were not readily given to Catholics. A good measure of responsibility came along with the position but the job put temptation in the young man's path and directed his thoughts to crime.

Soon after Charles began work as sheriff's bailiff, his employers noticed that cattle were disappearing in mysterious circumstances. Naturally enough, suspicion fell on their keeper. One of Charles' duties was to look after livestock confiscated by the authorities in lieu of unpaid rents. The tenants who had lost their animals in this way would have been Charles' "own" people – the dispossessed native Irish. It would not be unfair to say that Charles was working for the enemy, but at the same time he might have chosen to accept the privileged position for the reason that he might turn it to the good. Whatever his motive, a watch was set on Charles and, sure enough, he was caught red-handed in the act of illicitly slaughtering a cow. Instant dismissal followed.

It is intriguing that no further action was taken. Charles' crime amounted to cattle stealing or rustling. A man could be hanged for less – and men frequently were. Charles' light punishment was in all probability due to his having influential connections. However, the incident would have put paid to the possibility of any other respectable employment. Charles believed that he had only one road left open to him: the highway.

Out Upon His Keeping

Charles quickly became quite proficient in his new "trade" and a force to be reckoned with. It was as though the ghost of Redmond O'Hanlon stalked the roads of south Armagh. He was a very successful horse and cattle rustler who also regularly robbed the mail coaches and transports on a stretch of the old road between Dundalk and Armagh. John J. Marshall, in *Irish Tories, Rapparees and Robbers*, recounts how Charles made the transition from minor cattle thief to dangerous outlaw. He "progressed in his career from one atrocity to another, until he became a relentless, cruel, and it is said, dastardly and treacherous assassin and murderer".

Charles gathered around him a formidable band of outlaws with himself as leader. No-one was admitted into the group who had not already proved himself by some serious unlawful act and, it was rumoured, at least one capital crime. This last was relatively easy to commit. In keeping with most European countries, Irish law made the death penalty mandatory for all state crimes and for varying degrees of felonies, including murder, rape, arson, counterfeiting, the embezzlement of state funds and theft. There was a practical reason behind this readiness with the rope: it was cheaper than putting the miscreants behind bars.

Corporal punishment, such as flogging or being placed in the stocks, was also in favour in the early eighteenth century, as was transportation to the British colonies. Many Irish men, women and children were sent to America as either indentured servants or slaves. The historian Peter Kolchin relates how colonial newspapers of the time were

> "filled with advertisements for fugitives, both white and black; a typical notice from the *Pennsylvania Journal* of September 26, 1751, advertised for return of 'an Irish Servant Man, Named Christopher Cooney, of Short Stature, pale Complexion, short brown Hair'; the listing noted that he 'has a Scarr on his left Cheek, near his Nose, has lost one of his under fore Teeth, has had his Right Leg broke, and walks with his Toes turning outwards.'"[lx]

Unsurprisingly, criminals would go to desperate lengths to avoid this fate and keep the authorities confused. In the company of his outlaw confederates, Charles Carragher terrorised – largely unhindered – the wealthier inhabitants of Armagh and neighbouring counties, while showing kindness to the poor. However, he was no Robin Hood: a series of cold-blooded murders accompanied his many acts of robbery and plunder.

So great a reign of terror did he unleash that the authorities were forced to take unusual measures to curb his activities. Big Charlie, as he had then become known, was originally "presented" as an outlaw and Tory on January 11, 1714 at a general quarters session by the County Louth grand jury. On February 8 of the same year, a government proclamation gave him until March 21 to surrender: if he failed to do so, he would be deemed guilty of high treason. A reward of £20 was placed on his head.[lxi]

Needless to say, Big Charlie did not surrender. On December 24, 1717 he was again proclaimed "a Tory robber and rapparee in arms upon his keeping". A further sum of £80 was added to the £20 to encourage "the speedy killing, apprehending or bringing in of… Charles McKaragher". This was a princely sum and served to add to the outlaw's stature among his peers.

The reward, unsurprisingly, remained unclaimed. Big Charlie and his band were by this time so dangerous that anybody attempting to go after them was effectively signing his own death-warrant. A Tory hunter, Mr Arthur Bashford, learned this lesson in costly fashion. In January 1718 he and his associates tracked the outlaw and

BY
The Lord Lieutenant and Council
OF
I R E L A N D,
A
PROCLAMATION.

Bolton,

WHEREAS in pursuance of An Act of Parliament passed in this Kingdom, intitled, *An Act for the better Suppressing Tories, Robbers and Rapparees and for preventing Robberies, Burglaries, and other Heinous Crimes:* The Grand-Jury at a General Assizes and General Goal Delivery Held at *Carrickfergus*, in and for the County of *Antrim*, the Twelfth Day of *August* One thousand seven hundred and seventeen, did Present *Paul Mc. Sevenagh* of *Glenboab*, *Bryan Agnew*, near *Stony-ford*, *Ewar Magee* of *Braid*, *Duncan's Kelly* of *Glenarm Glen*, *Daniel Magee* of *Braid*, *Allister Buoy Mc. Koy* of *Glenelarey*, and *Gilbert Agnew* of *Stony-ford*, all in the County of *Antrim*, Labourers, to be Notorious Rogues and Robbers, and not upon their keeping, and refuse to be brought to justice. And the Grand-Jury at a General Sessions of the Peace Held at *Monaghan*, in, and for the County of *Monaghan*, on *Tuesday* the Eighth Day of *October*, One thousand seven hundred and seventeen, did present *John Lamb*, late of *Cassleboy*, Son to *Patt. Rane Lamb*, late of *Cassra* in the said County, to be a Tory, Robber and Rapparee out in Arms and upon his keeping, Murdering, Plundering and Robbing His Majesty's Subjects, and not Amenable to Law: Which said Presentments are duly Returned, and now remain with the Clerk of the Council of this Kingdom, according to the Directions given by the said Act.

WE therefore the Lord Lieutenant and Council pursuant to the Tenor of the said Act, do by this Our Proclamation give Notice, Publish and Declare, That the said Persons in the said respective Presentments Named and Presented, are Presented as Tories, Robbers and Rapparees, out on their keeping, by the respective Presentments aforesaid, And We do hereby Command and Require all the said Persons so Presented, and in this Our Proclamation herein before named and each, and every of them respectively, forthwith and at farthest, on or before the first Day of *February*, in the Year of our Lord One thousand seven hundred and seventeen, to Render him or themselves respectively to some one or more Justice or Justices of the Peace in the said respective Counties wherein the said several Persons stand Presented as aforesaid, as Prisoners, to Answer all and every the Matters and Charges that shall be Objected to him or them respectively, which said Justice

Justice and Justices of the Peace respectively, are hereby required forthwith to send the said Person or Persons to Kending him or themselves by *Mittimus* to the Goal of the said County, in which *Mittimus* shall be mentioned, That such Prisoner or Prisoners is, or are of the number of the Persons Proclaimed, and shall be thereby Committed without Bail or Mainprize, there to continue till the next General Assizes and General Goal Delivery to be Held for the said County until he or they shall be thence Discharged by due Course of Law; And in Case the said several Persons so Presented, and herein Named as aforesaid, do not, or shall not, on or before the said first Day of *February* One thousand seven hundred and seventeen, Render him or themselves as aforesaid, to some one or more Justice or Justices of the Peace for the said respective Counties named in this Our Proclamation, That then the Person or Persons neglecting, and not Rendring him or themselves as aforesaid, shall from and after the said first Day of *February*, One thousand seven hundred and seventeen, according to the said Statute Convict of High Treason, and Suffer accordingly.

And whereas the Grand-Jury at a General Quarter Sessions of the Peace Held in and for the County of *Louth*, the Eleventh Day of *January* One thousand seven hundred and fourteen, did Present among others, *Charles Mc. Karagher* of *Darcy*, in the County of *Armagh*, and late of the County of *Louth*, to be a Tory, Robber and Rapparee, in Arms upon his keeping.

And whereas by Proclamation bearing Date the Eighth Day of *February* One thousand seven hundred and fourteen, the said *Charles Mc. Karagher* was Proclaimed to be a Tory, Robber and Rapparee, out on his keeping, and required to Surrender himself on or before the Twenty First Day of *March* next ensuing the Date of the said Proclamation, or otherwise be Convict of High Treason, and suffer accordingly; and by the said Proclamation the Sum of Twenty Pounds is promised to such Person or Persons as should Kill, Apprehend, or Bring in the said *Charles Mc. Karagher*, in Case he did not Surrender himself by the time aforesaid, And likewise in pursuance of the said Act, the Grand-Jury at a General Assizes and General Goal Delivery Held at *Cavan*, in and for the County of *Cavan*, the First Day of *April*, One thousand seven hundred and fifteen, did Present *John Reily* of *Mountjeney*, to be a Tory, Robber and Rapparee, and out upon his keeping in Arms.

And by one other Proclamation bearing Date the Twentieth Day of *July* One thousand seven hundred and fifteen, the said *John Reily* was Proclaimed to be a Tory, Robber and Rapparee, out on his keeping, and by the said Proclamation was required to Surrender himself on, or before the twenty Day of *November* next after the Date of the said Proclamation, or otherwise be Convict of High Treason, and suffer accordingly; notwithstanding which said Proclamations, it hath been lately Represented unto Us, that the said *Charles Mc. Karagher* and *John Reily* have been continued in Arms and out upon their keeping, and have been lately Convicted of Murder, and are at present Captains or Chiefs of two several Parties of Rapparees. And whereas *Flan Brody* als. *James Brown* als. *Demis Culligan*, a Popish Prest, was laid Convicted of being a Popish Prest remaining in this Kingdom, contrary to Law, and by Order of the then Justices of Assize and Goal Delivery, was Transmitted to the City of *Limerick*, where he was put on Ship Board in order to be Transported beyond Seas, And whereas We have received Information, That he the said *Flan Brody* als. *James Brown* als. *Demis Culligan*, hath since Escaped from on Board the said Ship, and returned into the said County of *Clare*.

WE therefore the Lord Lieutenant and Council, taking the Premisses into Our serious Consideration, and intending to give all due Encouragement for the speedy Killing, Apprehending, or Bringing in of the said *Charles Mc. Karagher* and *John Reily*, and of the said *Paul Mc. Sevenagh*, *Bryan Agnew Ewar Magee*, *Duncan's Kelly*, *Daniel Magee*, *Allister Buoy Mc. Koy*, *Gilbert Agnew*, and *John Lamb*, in Case they do not Surrender themselves as aforesaid, and also for the speedy Taking and Apprehending the said *Flan Brody* als. *James Brown* als. *Demis Culligan*, do hereby Publish and Declare, That if any Person or Persons whatsoever after this our being Acquainted herewith, shall Kill, Apprehend, or Bring in them or cause to be Killed, Apprehended, or brought in or any of them, to Surrender themselves as aforesaid, shall Kill, Apprehend, or bring them or any of them, that every such Person or Persons to Killing or Bringing in all or any of them

then the said *Paul Mc. Sevenagh*, *Bryan Agnew*, *Ewar Magee Duncan's Kelly*, *Daniel Magee*, *Allister Buoy Mc. Koy*, *Gilbert Agnew* and *John Lamb* shall Receive from Us the Sum of Twenty Pounds for each of them to Killed or brought in, over and above the Rewards to hun or them, Payable by vertue of the Statute in that Case made and provided; And We do hereby likewise Publish and Declare, That We will give the necessary Orders for the Payment of the further Sum of Eighty Pounds *Sterl* over and above the Sum of Twenty Pounds mentioned in the said Recited Proclamation, to any Person or Persons who shall Kill, Apprehend, or Bring in the said *Charles Mc. Karagher*; and also the Sum who shall Kill, Apprehend, or bring in the said *John Reily*.

And We do further by this Our Proclamation Publish and Declare, That We will give the necessary Orders for Payment of the Sum of Twenty Pounds *Sterl.* to such Person or Persons as shall Take and Apprehend the said *Flan Brody* als. *James Brown* als. *Demis Culligan*.

And We do hereby strictly Charge and Command all His Majesty's Good and Loyal Subjects, from henceforth not to Harbour Entertain, Abet, Cherish or Assist the said *Paul Mc. Sevenagh*, *Bryan Agnew*, *Ewar Magee*, *Duncan's Kelly*, *Daniel Magee*, *Allister Buoy Mc. Koy*, *Gilbert Agnew*, and *John Lamb*, *Charles Mc. Karagher*, *John Reiley* and *Flan Brody* als. *James Brown* als. *Demis Culligan*, herein before named in this Our Proclamation as aforesaid, or any of them, nor to permit them or any of them to come into, or Abide or Lodge in their Houses, nor to furnish them or any of them with Provision, Meat, Drink, or other Necessaries or Conveniences whatsoever, under the Pains and Penalties by the said Act, or any other Laws or Statute in Force in this Kingdom.

And We do hereby strictly Charge and Command all Magistrates and Officers, and all other His Majesty's Good Subjects, with their utmost diligence, to be Aiding and Assisting in the Execution of the said Act, and in Taking and Apprehending the said several Persons herein before mentioned, as they shall Answer the contrary at their Peril.

Given at the *Council Chamber* in *Dublin*, the Twenty Fourth Day of *December*, 1717.

Middleton Canc, *Will. Dublin*, *Edw. Tuam*, *Wharton and Catherlogh*, *Abercorn*, *John Gugher*, *Tyrawly*, *St. George*, *Ferrard*, *Newtoun*, *Ralph. Gore*, *Fob. Forster*, *Jeff. Gilbert*, *Oliver St. George*, *Fredrick*, *Hamilton*, *ben. Parry*, *E. Webster.*

God Save the King

Dublin : Printed by *Andrew Crooke*, Printer to the King's Most Excellent Majesty, at the *King's Arms* in Copper-Alley, 1717.

some members of his gang to a safe house near Carrickmacross, County Monaghan. There was a surprise attack and a fierce battle, which resulted in the deaths of the Tory hunter James Boyle and the outlaw James Gilsenan. The other highwaymen, including Big Charlie, escaped into the hills.

It was plain that if Charles Carragher was to be brought to justice, then the services of a professional fighting man were called for. A commission was issued for a Captain Mervyn Pratt to be

"commander of all detachments of the Army quartered at Balleneyhragh, also Ball's Mills, Ballybeach, Carrickmacross, Castleblaney, Cabra, Louth, Virginia, Cross[maglen], Nobber, Drumcowra, Cootehill, Shercock, Slane and Stackallen, to repress Tories and rapparees in counties Armagh, Cavan, Louth and Monaghan who have murdered and robbed… Also commission to Thomas Coote to command all the militia in said counties."

But try as Pratt and Coote might to "repress Tories and rapparees", their quarry remained tantalisingly out of reach. No sooner had the soldiers got wind of Big Charlie's presence in one locality but news reached them that he had carried off a daring robbery in a neighbouring parish. No matter how many troopers were mobilised, Big Charlie invariably found a way to stretch their resources to the limit by means of misinformation.

Treachery

Charles "Collmore" Carragher was invincible from without, but, like many a leader before him and since, he was vulnerable from within. The Judas in his case was John McKeown, a trusted member of his band. Folk-legend tells that he received £80 in blood money as reward for his treachery. Because the full price on Charles' head was £100, we can only surmise that McKeown received a pardon into the bargain. It is not known whether he lived to enjoy it.

Big Charlie was taking his ease in a cottage close to Ball's Mill, on the road between Dundalk and Newtownhamilton. With him were other members of the gang, including his eighteen-year-old nephew, Patrick Carragher.[lxii] They had just executed a successful highway robbery and repaired to the cottage to share the spoils and celebrate their good fortune, believing themselves to be safe. Their enjoyment was short-lived, however; John McKeown had slipped away to alert the authorities. Within the hour the cabin was surrounded by a large force of military and its occupants were called upon to surrender.

Big Charlie was all for attempting to fight his way through the lines of soldiers, even if it meant dying in the affray. He knew that capture and a gruesome death on the gallows was imminent. It was better to die by a musket ball or a blade of cold steel.

But the presence of his young nephew dissuaded him from this suicidal path. The lad had not yet committed a crime that warranted the death penalty. Big Charlie knew that some of the cabin's other occupants might also be spared an early death for this reason, if they surrendered now. The besieged men threw out their weapons and emerged from the cottage. Soon they were all conveyed to Dundalk Gaol, to await their fate.

A Savage Execution

Big Charlie Carragher's trial took place on February 17, 1718. He was charged with a number of murders, rapes and robberies, all committed in County Armagh. The accused denied everything.

A witness was called: one Andrew Thompson, who had known the outlaw in his younger days. Under oath he testified that the man on trial was "the same Charles Carragher who liv'd formerly with Mr Blykes of Darcy in the Fews, and that he stole two Heffers from Alderman Grimes, and was for the same indicted and proclaimed at Ardee".

Big Charlie objected. Thompson, he declared, was an unreliable witness; he had perjured himself in another courtroom. Thompson retaliated by saying that the accused had accosted him late one night as he was going home and allegedly threatened to kill him unless he swore never to "present" in court.

This dramatic hearsay was enough for the jury. Acting only on this witness' word, Big Charlie was found guilty of "Bloody Murthers, Rapes and Robberies". For these crimes he was to be hanged, drawn and quartered.

At this time, around 1718, European culture and art were exploring new heights. For example, English society was praising the wonder of Händel's *Water Music*, performed for their Sovereign the previous summer; in Germany Bach was composing his *Brandenburg Concertos*; and in London Daniel Defoe had just delivered *Robinson Crusoe* to his publishers.

In Dundalk, in stark contrast, on February 18, 1718, a Christian community was wreaking savage revenge on a highwayman. The grisly will of the court was carried out to the letter.[lxiii]

Big Charlie was hanged first, but cut free from the gallows while he was still conscious. According to the custom, the hangman then tore off the prisoner's breeches, and sliced off his genitals. Charlie cried out as this act of barbarousness was taking place. His private parts were burned in a brazier as he looked on in a haze of horror and agony. Next, his belly was slit open and his entrails drawn out. They too were thrown into the brazier, sizzling before the still-living prisoner's eyes.

At last came the *coup de grâce*, or cut of mercy. In Big Charlie's case, the phrase was a misnomer: the hangman's first attempt to cut his throat failed because of the victim's tortured struggles. He tried again and again until at last the unfortunate highwayman was well and truly dead. Carragher was then decapitated. A pamphlet of the time reported that the outlaw's jaw continued to open and close even though the man's head was a yard from his body. As one onlooker put it: "He died very obstinately."

The hangman's axe divided the body into four parts: the "quartering". The heart, liver, spleen and other organs were extracted from the ruined torso and thrown into the flames before the public.

The four parts of Big Charlie's body were removed from Dundalk and each hung on display in a separate place. One quarter was gibbeted at Ball's Mill, his place of capture, while the remaining quarters were exhibited at places where he had committed some of his worst crimes. Big Charlie's head was spiked and joined others above the entrance to Dundalk Gaol, but "two yards higher than any of the rest with his hat and wig on", apparently to demonstrate that even the dandiest of highwaymen would meet this fate.

He went to his death a brave man indeed. Kevin McMahon, a local historian, wrote: "Of Cal Mór himself it can be said: he may have lived a disreputable life but he died an honourable death." He was aware of the form that his execution would take and had in all probability stood and watched many times as others "danced on air".

In his last moments, with nothing more to lose, Big Charlie at last confessed to the more serious crimes he had committed – the murders – but strove to exonerate himself from some others. His last words were eloquent:[lxiv]

"Good People,

Almighty God has by a just Providence brought me to this untimely End. He has been Mercifully pleas'd not to Cut me off in the midst of my Sins, but to allow me some Time to reflect on my unhappy misspent Life, and to Implore Forgiveness for my many Iniquities, which I trust he will graciously Pardon.

And as my Crimes have been of publick crying Nature, so I think my self Bound to make a publick Confession of them both to God and my Country.

THE LAST
SPEECH

And Dying words of *Charles Calahar* alias
Collmore who was Try'd on *Tuesday* the 17th
Inſt. *Feb.* 17$\frac{18}{19}$. at the *Seſſions* of *Dundalk*, for
being a Proclaim'd *Tory*, and was the next Day
Hang'd, Quarter'd and his Intrals burn'd

Deliver'd at the Gallows to Will Moore Eſq;
High Sheriff of the County of Lowth.

Good People,

ALMIGHTY God has by a juſt Providence brought me
to this untimely End, He has been Mercifully pleas'd not
to Cut me off in the midſt of my Sins, but to allow me
ſome Time to reflect on my unhappy mis ſpent Life, and to
Implore Forgiveneſs for my many Iniquities, which I truſt
he will graciouſly Pardon.

And as my Crimes have been of publick crying Nature, ſo I think
my ſelf Bound to make a publick Confeſſion of them both to God and
my Country.

And firſt with Shame and Confuſion of Face, I confeſs I have been
Guilty of many Robberies and Thefts, and have alſo Seduced and Encouraged others to do the like.

I Barbarouſly and Unjuſtly Em bru'd my Hands in the Blood of my
Fellow-Creatures, and in particular I Murder'd Martin Grey and Chri-
ſtopher Betty, and ſuffer'd that worthy honeſt Gent. Mr. Edmond Reily to
be wrongfully Executed at Cavan Aſſizes for the ſaid Murders; He being
no ways Privy or Acceſſary to them, but entirely Innocent of that bloody
Fact which was the ruin of his Wife and ſeveral ſmall Children.

I likewiſe Confeſs I was at the Inhumane Murders and Butchery of *Bryan
O' Hanlan*, and *Mc Gibbin*, for all which I moſt humbly beg the Almighty's
*Pardon, and the Pardon of all whom I have in any way Injur'd, and declare I have
a thorow ſenſe of my former Impietys and an utter Abhorrence and Deteſtation
of them, and hope God will pleaſe to look on me, and accept of my Blood, tho' a
moſt unworthy Offering, ſince my Puniſhment is not half what I deſerve.*

*I die a Member of the Church of Rome, tho' an unworthy one, and do freely for-
give every one that have Injur'd me, eſpecially John Mc Keoine who betray'd
me, and I declare I wou'd have Fought my way thro' the Soldiers who ſurrounded
the Cabbin where I was, and had new Charged and Prim'd my Piſtols in order
to it, but was prevented by the Entreaties of my Nephew, and am now thankful
to God for it ſince I have by that bad opportunity to think of my Soul. I humbly
Recommend into the Hands of my moſt Merciful Redeemer, and beg the Prayers
of all good People.*

After he was Executed there was 3 Kiſhes of Turff lighted, wherein
his Hart, Livers, Lights and Members were Burned, and his Head ſet on
the Goal, Two Yards higher than any of the reſt with His Hat and Wigg
on ; his Nephew James M^c. Garaghar and 3 more are to be Executed
on Saturday 21ſt.

Dublin Printed, by C. Carter, 1718-19.

And first with Shame and Confusion of Face, I confess I have been Guilty of many Robberries and Thefts, and have also Seduced and Encouraged others to do the like.

I Barbarously and Unjustly Embru'd my Hands in the Blood of my Fellow Creatures, and in particular I Murder'd Martin Grey and Christopher Betty, and suffer'd that worthy honest Gent. Mr. Edmond Reily to be wrongfully Executed at Cavan Assizes for the said Murders; He being no ways Privy or Accessary to them, but entirely Innocent of that bloody Fact which was the ruin of his Wife and several small Children.

I likewise confess I was at the Inhumane Murders and Butchery of Bryan O' Hanlan, and Mc Gibbin, for all which I most humbly beg the Almighty's Pardon, and the Pardon of all whom I have in any way Injur'd, and declare I have a thorow sence of my former Impietys and an utter Abhorence and Detestation of them, and hope God will please to look on me, and accept of my Blood, tho' a most unworthy Offering, since my Punishment is not half what I deserve.

I die a Member of the Church of Rome, tho' an unworthy one, and do freely forgive every one that hath Injur'd me, especially John Mc Keoine who betray'd me, and I declare I wou'd have Fought my way thro' the Soldiers who surrounded the Cabbin where I was, and had new Charged and Prim'd my Pistols in order to it, but was prevented by the Entreaties of my Nephew, and am now thankful to God for it since I have by that had opportunity to think of my Soul. I humbly Recommend into the Hands of my most Merciful Redeemer, and beg the Prayers of all good People."

Big Charlie may have died knowing that his surrender to the authorities for the sake of his nephew had been in vain. His belief that the courts would show clemency toward his nephew, who he claimed was innocent of everything except having knowledge of or perhaps being present at a murder or robbery, was misplaced. The young man, together with three other members of Big Charlie's band, was executed just three days after his uncle, on February 21. His last words were moving:

"Dear Christians,
I, Patrick Carragher, am a Nephew of that Collmore who was executed last Wednesday, who was the Ruin of me, who am but eighteen years of Age now. Tho' of these tender Years, I am very sensible of the great Follies and Sins that I have been guilty of. My Father and Mother liv'd in the Place call'd Loghross in the County of Armagh. As for my Father, People may say what they please of him, for

he is still alive, but for my Mother she was never charg'd with anything that was ill and the Neighbours in the Country knew her to be an honest, good Woman. She dy'd when I was very young. Nevertheless I was bound Prentice to a Taylor, but did not serve my Master long, but followed my Uncle, which is the Cause of my coming to this untimely End. Tho' I was try'd for keeping Company and assisting one Gillaspy McCulum, a proclaimed Tory, for my Part I was neither guilty of Murther nor Robbery of my Self, but I have been by when Robbery was committed. I have no more to say but that I die a Roman Catholick, and I beg of thee O my great God to have Mercy on my poor Soul. Dear Christians, pray for me."[lxv]

Local folklore has it that, after Big Charlie's death, the military discovered a cave in a rock, high above a bend on the old road from Dundalk to Armagh, in the parish of Lower Killeavy in the townland of Burren. The cave was reputed to have been one of Big Charlie's most secure hiding places. In order to deter further acts of outlawry and any threat of reprisal, the military removed the head of the dead outlaw from the gates of Dundalk Gaol and placed it above the entrance to the cave. The rock, which was known up to that time as Carraigh Dubh (the Black Rock), was subsequently called Cathal Mór's Rock. It is rumoured that the area around the cave is haunted by the ghost of the highwayman.

In closing, it should not go unrecorded that Andrew Thompson, whose accusations led to Big Charlie's conviction, retracted his testimony after the execution. It was too little, too late.

The Ballad of Big Charlie Carragher

B- e - neath___ the oak bea - med scrag - ging post Stood the lad___ who ga- ve___ us hope_____ Bra- ve Cath - al___ Mor fr - om Dar - cy___ Now shadow - ed by__ a rope._____ They said___ he was_____ a rapp - ar - ee___ An_ out - law_ and_____ a thief, A To - ry and_

But to us who suffered the burdens
That kept us poor and bent;
Weighed down by laws and tithes and dues
And cruel, foul rack-rent,
We looked for his shape in the moonlight
And we listened, young and old,
For the hurry of hoofs, the light in the dark,
The sharer of Saxon gold.

So tonight we remember young Carragher
And the heart which with every beat
Struck a spark, lit a flame which still flickers
And kindles all with its heat.
For each morning around Deburren
Up struts a crowing cock;
To sound the alarm o'er Killeavy
From the crag above Cathal Mor's Rock.

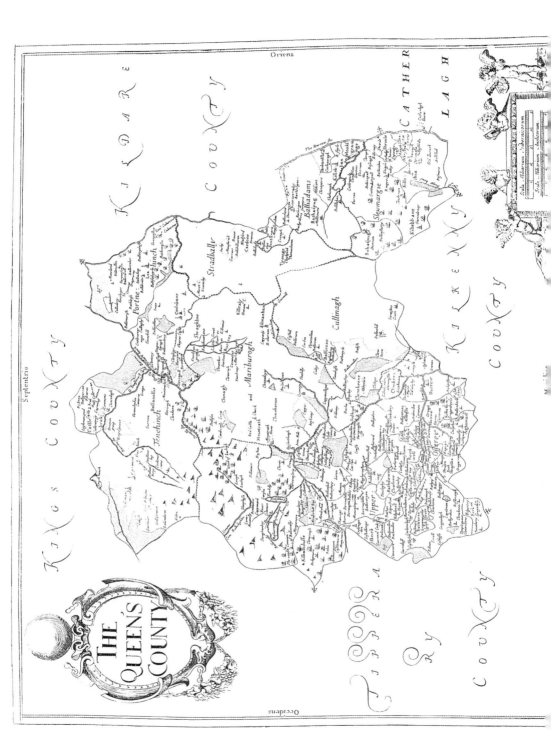

THE QUEEN'S COUNTY

Oriens

Occidens

Septentrio

KINGS COUNTY

KILDARE COUNTY

CATHERLAGH

KILKENNY COUNTY

TIPPERARY COUNTY

Scala Milliarium Hibernicorum.
Scala Milliarium Anglicorum.

Charles Dempsey

Cahir na gCapall (Charles of the Horses)

Galloping Hogan was one of the original rapparees, who earned a respectable name riding with Patrick Sarsfield. However, there followed a less honourable generation of outlaws, many of whom were the sons of those who had defended Limerick against the Williamites. Charles Dempsey, notorious horse-thief and occasional highwayman, was one of them.

He was called Cahir na gCapall (Charles of the Horses) for more or less the same reason Daniel Hogan acquired the sobriquet "Galloping". In a society where every man possessed riding skills to some degree, only a truly exceptional equestrian could have earned such a name.

That he inherited some of his skill from his father is indisputable. Dempsey senior was a brave and fearless warrior who fought as an irregular with the army of James II, and later with Sarsfield. After the fall of Limerick and the Treaty of 1691, he took advantage of the pardon offered and, giving up his arms, returned to farming. His property was little more than a smallholding on the slopes of a hill in what is now County Laois, but was in 1702 named Queen's County.[lxvi] It was in the townland of Lea, now known as Windmill Hill, near Ballybrittas, and had once been part of the old hereditary lands of the O'Dempseys known as Glenmalier.

Dempsey had several sons, three of whom became notorious: Donnell (or Daniel), Feagh (or Luke), and the infamous Cahir (or Charles). Not much is known about Luke except that he was a horse-thief also for a time, but did not possess the cunning or ruthlessness of his other brothers. He fled the country to avoid the gallows.

The Dempsey children were probably typical of the small farmer's family of the time: very little money, lots of hard work, and little or no education. Daniel, the eldest, was the exception. His parents ensured that he received good schooling and the boy became an excellent scholar. It was intended that he would go abroad to finish his studies and join the priesthood; but he had different ideas.

By this time Cahir and his brother Luke were making a name for themselves as highwaymen. Daniel plainly regarded this life as more exciting than that of a clergyman and elected to abandon his studies and join forces with his siblings.

Cahir was undoubtedly the leader of the group. Daniel became his assistant – and accountant. He managed the growing amount of money that the Dempsey brothers were amassing. Cahir also needed a trustworthy partner who could write well and had a good command of English, for his first language was Irish. Although he understood English fully, he spoke it badly and could neither read nor write. Daniel's good education proved invaluable to him.

It was the beginning of a thriving family business.

The Horse Rustlers

If his abilities with language and figures left something to be desired, then his skill with horses certainly compensated for those shortcomings. He was extraordinarily fond of them from a very early age, and before he was five years old he could ride and "stick" on a wild horse as well as a great many men.

The old Irish proverb "He that is born to be hanged will never be drowned" found living proof in Cahir. Tradition has it that when he was four years of age he begged to be allowed to ride a certain colt. It had no saddle or rein – there was only an old collar around the skittish animal's neck – but the plucky youngster implored a man to lift him up onto the animal's back. No sooner was he seated than the horse bolted and galloped headlong into the swollen, flooded waters of the river Barrow. Young Cahir held fast to the wild animal's mane; miraculously, both horse and rider reached the opposite bank, despite the dangerous currents. As the horse tried to clamber out of the river with the child, the soggy bank gave way and the two were plunged again into the swirling rapids. Animal and boy disappeared under water. Long minutes later they surfaced, spluttering, and were swept at least fifty yards down river. The onlookers were powerless to intervene and could only watch helplessly. It seemed to all that the boy must surely drown.

But, eventually, the colt recovered. The animal found its footing and scrambled from the water – young Cahir still clung to its collar and mane. He appeared to be dead; there was a blueness to his skin and no pulse could be detected. He was taken down from the horse and laid in his father's arms. To everyone's astonishment, the boy regained consciousness.

In later years the outlaw was often heard to say that he had no fear of drowning and that even if he were to "go to sea in a turf ketch", he would reach America safely. This fearlessness and close affinity with water was to stand Cahir in good stead on many occasions. In later years he was to make a number of daredevil escapes across the same Barrow river, avoiding the clutches of the sheriff and the military.

At the age of twelve Cahir began to practise the ancient art of decoying and catching horses, and became so accomplished at this craft that even "the wildest colts ever foaled could be tamed by him"; he was, in effect, an eighteenth-century horse-whisperer. Folklore has it that he achieved his amazing success with horses and knowledge of the Canting Language by some form of witchcraft or magic.[lxvii] This assertion alone attests to the high degree of skill he must have possessed. It is said that he received a charm from a witch in County Monaghan, with whom he was very friendly and whom he used to visit when making trips to deal with his confederates in Ulster.[lxviii]

Whatever the truth about how he acquired his skills, Cahir had light hands, a perfect seat, and always kept his temper when dealing with horses. No matter how wicked or obstinate his mount might have been, before they parted he was always its master. Cosgrave, in *Irish Rogues and Rapparees,* relates a story told by a country gentleman concerning Cahir's father: it gives some indication of how the younger Dempsey might have learned to behave with horses.

"... there appeared through the hedge a man before me driving some horses very quietly into a corner, one whereof he took hold of by the near fore leg and held him fast until he threw a short rope about his neck, then he vaulted on him with more agility than I ever saw a miller do on his sacks; in this posture with a long stick in his hand he drove the colt (he was never handled before) across the bog till he got out of my sight, plunging and leaping to such a degree all the way, that one thought if the old boy were on his back he had but a dull chance of coming off without a broken neck, and by the noise they made. I conjectured they might have gone a mile at the same rate before I left the place. I had no notion of rapparees being out at this time and thought it might be some one that owned the colt that had made so free with him, till returning to my friends I told the story, and they all suspected as it really was from the manner of catching the colt, that old Dempsey had come to pay them a visit."

As Cahir grew into adulthood his talents were brought to the notice of a local land-lord, who employed him as an attendant to his groom, a job in which he excelled. Praise of his name was heard widely and it was not long before he had made acquain-tances in most parts of the country. This circle was to prove valuable to him: when he embarked upon his career as an outlaw, he could readily enlist admirers willing and able to assist him.

He employed five or six of his own relatives in Leinster and Munster, and had confederates in counties as far away as Leitrim, Monaghan and Derry. It is said that at the height of his fame he never had fewer than four apprentices working at once. These young men were contracted to him for a fixed term of seven years and charged a hefty sum for the privilege of learning Cahir's art. It seems more than likely that his brother Daniel – he of the fluent English and accountancy skills – would have had a hand in the drawing up of such contracts. Boys from all over the country were sent to learn at what was, in effect, an academy of horse-thieving.

Besides his apprentices and receivers, Cahir employed many spies – one or more in almost every parish in the land – whose sole task was to keep him abreast of any forthcoming sales of horses or cattle. Very little movement of livestock took place without his prior knowledge.

It was an enterprise of staggering complexity and organisation. The spies had no direct communication with Cahir's gang members or their leader. When information was gathered, a runner would be sent to Cahir, who would then pass on a description of the intended targets to his most trusted lieutenants. They in turn would call on their own hirelings and thus obtain the animals. Even though the dogs on the street knew that Cahir was a "receiver general", nothing could be proved against him; his operation was too intricate for that. How Daniel kept account of movements within the web of crime – and he surely did – probably never will be known.

Cahir had various safe houses and hideouts scattered around the countryside. These were remote places where he concealed stolen horses and cattle before dis-posing of them. He had a particularly good arrangement with his cronies in Ulster. He would send stolen horses to them and they would either ship the animals to Scotland or dispose of them at the numerous fairs and sales throughout the province. Sometimes the horses were sold; at other times they were traded. Cahir was only too keenly aware that when horses were swapped, those received in exchange were "legitimate" and could be sold openly – an early form of laundering! Any horses stolen in Ulster on his orders were immediately moved to a hidden location in the south until the time was right for disposal in Munster or Leinster.

The "horse trading" could sometimes go awry. According to an unnamed member of the Dempsey gang, reputed to have told the following story to his gaolers as he awaited the rope in Kilkenny, one evening a member of the network of spies visited Cahir with information on the whereabouts of three fine mounts. The horses were in a park near Clonegal, County Carlow, hard by the Wexford border. There was a black with a star and one white foot; another was a bay gelding that "padded" (was slow-paced); while the third was a white pad with his mane cut short. Cahir and his band acted on the information two nights after the visit, spiriting away the animals and driving them to the vicinity of Glenmalier.

When the rustlers later examined the majestic white horse, it was clear that the beast was too easily identifiable to take to market; therefore, they had to dye it. By mixing brazilet, a brown-red substance, and alum, a white crystalline powder used in the dressing of leather, the robbers made up a flesh-coloured red dye. They stained the animal all over and then proceeded to transport it with the other horses to Monaghan. But they chose a particularly unfortunate time at which to do so: it rained torrentially, the animals were soaked, and the disguising colour washed off the white horse. Notwithstanding this setback, the animals were disposed of without incident or suspicion at a fair in the county. Two sold for £20, while the third, the black mare, fetched £6.

The story has a sequel. Some time after the robbery the rightful owner of the bay gelding was put in contact with Cahir, having been told that he might have the means of getting some information about the horse. The crafty outlaw agreed to make some enquiries, demanding an advance fee of two guineas.

Twelve days later the horse was "lifted" from the park where it was kept by its new owner, and brought to a wood near the river Barrow. Cahir duly informed the rightful owner of the animal's whereabouts. The owner was delighted and went to retrieve his horse that very night – and Cahir pocketed a fat fee for his services.

Shortly afterwards, however, the owner set out for Ulster with the intention of purchasing some linen for his business. He was mounted on the bay. As he was journeying in the vicinity of Monaghan town he was spotted by a party of constables, who recognised the horse as that which had been stolen a week or two before. The man was arrested.

Fortunately, he was carrying documents which included the bay's pedigree; this indicated that he was the horse's breeder. After much questioning, he was freed and allowed to keep the horse – the Monaghan purchaser could only state that he had bought the horse at a fair from an unknown buyer. Once again the trail ran cold; no-one could link Cahir to the theft.

Many stories abounded in County Laois concerning Cahir and his way with horses. One such tale is so persistent that it is still recounted.

An old, eccentric gentleman-landowner living in the county owned a fine, but highly spirited, thoroughbred. He allowed no-one else to ride it, even when he became infirm and unable to mount the beast. If *he* could not sit in the saddle, then nobody would.

The old gentleman's son loved the horse and wished to own it. Try as he might, he could find no way of making his possessive father part with the animal. His thoughts turned to Charles Dempsey, it being an open secret in Laois that the outlaw could "get things done" as far as horses were concerned. The son approached the outlaw, who, in return for a substantial fee, formulated a plan.

Cahir obtained the skin of a horse whose colouring and markings were almost identical to those of the old man's prized steed. He then had some of his trusted handlers spirit the animal away from the demesne under cover of darkness. The elderly gentleman, upon learning of his loss, was very upset; the horse meant the world to him.

Cahir placed the skin of the "ringer" in a bog hole and left it there for a period of time. He brought it to one of the old man's tenants who, in turn and for a fee, presented the skin to his landlord, explaining that it was the hide of his missing horse. It was clear, the tenant said, that the beast had drowned in the bog. The old gentleman had no reason to doubt the story or the "evidence" before him.

Some time later, after a respectable period had elapsed, the son retrieved the horse from Cahir and rode it home. He presented it to his father, pretending to have bought it at the local fair. The old man was flabbergasted.

"If my own splendid mount had not perished in that bog," he cried, "then I'd gladly swear an oath that this horse and mine are one and the same!"

The story enjoyed many a retelling among the local gentry.

Stratagems and Bargains

By this time Cahir was at the height of his career. There was money pouring in, a constant supply of stolen horses and cattle, and the odd mail-coach robbery. He even had business premises, of sorts, where he could be contacted. The invaluable Daniel, a handsome and portly man of seemly behaviour, was in charge there. He kept accounts of all the animals disposed of and the prices they had fetched. He also had a list of all their employees country-wide, records of what they were paid and where they lived. As a result of this the brothers were able to "assist" all individuals who had queries regarding missing horses or other livestock. According to Cosgrave, writing in *A Genuine History*, Cahir had worked out a detailed method of procurement and remuneration.

"If they were to be had at all, he generally demanded a fee in hand for putting the owner in a way of getting his beast, which fee was always proportioned according to the beast's value, or the difficulty that might attend the recovery of it, and if it happened that the beast could not be procured with any safety, he was to return such a part of his fee as was agreed to beforehand, which he seldom refused."[lxix]

Cahir acted as an "honest" broker or mediator in the so-called investigations, never involving himself in the recoveries. When a beast was rediscovered by his men, a series of intricate instructions would be conveyed to the owner, directing him to a certain place where his animal could be found.

On one occasion a gentleman from County Kildare had a herd of cows stolen from his estate. He dispatched one of his servants to Cahir with a request to try and locate the missing animals. The outlaw, as was his custom, demanded and received his advance, and a short time later directions were passed on as to the whereabouts of the herd. The Kildare gentleman acted immediately and managed to apprehend a man who was in the vicinity of the cows. This man turned out to be a minor member of Cahir's extended operation.

Fearing the worst and hoping for clemency – cattle rustling was a capital offence – the prisoner accused Cahir of being the ringleader of a band of notorious outlaws and implicated him in a number of serious crimes. This was a welcome confession: the authorities had been aware of Cahir's illegal activities in the region, but had not been able to gather enough evidence against him. It seemed that their opportunity had at last arrived.

Cahir was arrested immediately and taken into custody at Naas Gaol.[lxx] He turned Crown evidence, impeaching six or seven people in County Kildare who, when they got wind of the betrayal, fled the region. He also struck a bargain with the judges: in return for supplying the name of a prominent outlaw in every county in the province, Cahir would be set free and all charges retracted.

The pact was sealed. The outlaw was taken on a circuit of Leinster and the principal towns visited: Maryborough (Portlaoise), Carlow, Kilkenny, Wexford and Wicklow. At each venue Cahir informed on known rogues, rapparees and highwaymen – none of whom, it must be said, had any prior dealings with him or might be liable to tell stories of their own.

The enterprise worked to Cahir's advantage: he rid the region of his enemies and rivals. Four or five men were hanged, solely on the evidence of Cahir's testimony. As a result of this purge, Cahir escaped the hangman's noose and was free to resume business as usual, having had the foresight not to betray any of his own confederates.

Cahir's Leap

Cahir's liberty was short-lived. Not long after his discharge, a fine, strikingly marked stallion went missing from a local stables. Suspicion fell on Cahir; he was again arrested and imprisoned, to await the assizes. Left in a gaol cell to ponder his position, the outlaw concocted an ingenious plan.

The night before the assizes began he had one of his men enter the place where the stolen horse was impounded – and substitute it for a mare of identical markings and colour. The following morning, with Cahir in the dock, the confident owner swore that the stallion – now tethered outside the court – belonged to him. Cahir challenged this, urging the clerk to examine the animal. It was discovered that the stallion was in fact a *mare*. The case collapsed: Cahir had escaped the gallows once again "by the black of his nail".

But by far the most celebrated of all incidents relating to the outlaw occurred a short time after the switching of the horse. The local sheriff, accompanied by a party of his men, was patrolling the area around the ancient ruins of Lea Castle – the former stronghold of the O'Dempsey clan – when he observed Cahir acting suspiciously. He called on the outlaw to halt, but instead Cahir turned his mount and galloped off in the direction of the castle, hotly pursued by the sheriff and his men.

The gates were open and Cahir clattered into the courtyard. It was then he realised that he had ridden into a trap.

There was one escape route open, though, and the outlaw took it. There was a door in the inner wall, with a staircase visible. Cahir made for it and, remaining in the saddle, mounted the stairs. The sheriff and his men dismounted and followed him on foot. When Cahir had reached the top of the stairs there was no further avenue of escape – apart from a big window.

Cahir did not hesitate; the sheriff and his men were hard on his heels. He spurred his horse and leaped out into space. As his pursuers reached the top of the stairs, Cahir and his horse crashed down onto the bawn below. The animal was killed instantly. Badly injured and shaken, the outlaw managed to crawl to the bank of the nearby Barrow river and swim to safety. The scene of the daring jump is still known as "Cahir na gCapall's Lep".

An Outlaw to the End

In keeping with many Irish outlaws and highwaymen, Charles Dempsey was a genuine and caring friend to those he trusted – and a merciless foe to anybody who crossed him.

Lea Castle near Portarlington. Cahir na gCapall leaped on horseback from the tower at the left.

A man came to County Laois seeking information regarding two of his horses. He claimed that they had been stolen from his farm in a neighbouring county. Two things aroused Cahir's suspicions: the man seemed too eager to hand over the "finder's fee" advance payment, and his knowledge of the local countryside was somewhat too intimate for a genuine stranger to the area. Departing from his customary practice, Cahir had one of his confederates bring the man to meet him in a wood in the dead of night.

The outlaw leader sent some of his men to "locate" the horses while he and the stranger, together with one or two of the gang, remained behind. Cahir just happened to have a couple of bottles of sack (sherry) in his panniers and he plied the stranger with copious amounts of the wine. The more relaxed the stranger grew, the looser his tongue became, and the more well-founded Cahir's suspicions appeared. He became convinced that the man was in league with the authorities.

After discreetly dispatching one of his men to a nearby mill to purloin a large sack, the outlaw turned on the drunken stranger and trussed him hand and foot. He thrust a gag in the captive's mouth and put him into the sack. The remaining space was filled with hay before the top of the sack was secured; a small hole was all the prisoner was left to breathe through. When Cahir stepped back from his work, he observed that the bag looked for all the world like a sack of corn.

In the meantime, the two stolen horses had been brought to the wood. Cahir mounted one, had the sack placed across horse's rump, and took the reins of the second animal. He trotted through the woods for about two miles until he came to the highway, where he dumped the sack and removed the terrified victim's gag. He tethered the horses nearby and stole off through the undergrowth on foot as dawn was breaking.

No-one heard the abandoned man's cries until nine o'clock that morning, when he was released from his confinement by a passer-by. He returned home at the gallop and never ventured into Dempsey territory again.

Another would-be traitor did not get off so lightly, however, principally because he was a member of Cahir's band and the outlaw could not countenance deceit in one of his "own".

It began fairly innocuously. One of the Dempsey gang, an illiterate youth, behaved very foolhardily during a robbery, causing Cahir to slap him. The youth's pride was hurt and he threatened to go to the sheriff and tell all. He relented later, apologised, and the incident was forgotten.

From that time odd occurrences began to plague the gang. Troopers and constables seemed to acquire knowledge of Cahir's plans and were ready for them. The robbers would escape capture by the skin of their teeth. Daniel was convinced that the gang harboured a traitor in its midst. Suspicion centred on the youth Cahir had slapped.

On the pretence of a planned raid, Cahir decoyed the youth to a lonely wood where, with the assistance of some trusted aides, he overpowered and bound him with ropes. They questioned the young man and it soon became obvious that he was indeed the traitor. The outlaws wanted to kill him, but Cahir would not condone murder. Instead, he meted out a brutal punishment. Knowing that the traitor could neither read nor write, and that speech was his sole means of communicating with the authorities, Cahir cut out his tongue.

Yet despite Cahir's ability to sniff out traitors and to escape the clutches of the law, the net was closing about the Dempsey brothers. The authorities were watching them more closely than ever and waiting for the opportunity of catching them red-handed. On more than one occasion the brothers outwitted their pursuers by turning their horses' shoes, thereby frustrating the search.

One day, without warning, Cahir and Daniel were taken into custody, along with an associate known only as Jack. The three were charged with numerous crimes, including a recent spate of mail-coach robberies, and committed to Maryborough Gaol.

But the Dempseys had allies in unexpected places. The landlord of the property on which the Dempsey farm was situated was Hector Graham of Lea Castle[lxxi]. To the utter amazement of the judiciary, he stood as a character witness for the brothers.

The relationship between Graham, landlord and gentleman, and Charles Dempsey, suspected horse thief, was a curious one. It is known that Hector allowed Cahir to stable some of his "unstolen" horses in a large vault that lay beneath the ruins of the old keep at Lea, and local folklore has it that Cahir actually planned and designed the secret vault for him. The landlord had also given him permission to stable horses in a dense wood adjacent to the ruins. The reasons behind this arrangement and the basis of the relationship between the two are a mystery; in any event, Graham's intercession ensured the Dempseys' acquittal.

Not long afterward, however, a serious dispute arose between that landlord and Cahir, one that was to have far-reaching consequences. Graham's immediate response was to evict Cahir's aged parents from their smallholding on the pretext of non-payment of rent. Cahir was outraged that his family should suffer as a result of a personal feud and vowed revenge. He stabled some purloined horses at Lea, and then went to the authorities and accused Graham of being the receiver of stolen goods. The landlord was brought to trial. Only with the greatest difficulty and determination – and after much public derision – did he succeed in escaping the gallows.

The gloves were now well and truly off. Cahir was to bitterly regret having made an enemy of Graham, who vowed that his mission in life was to rid himself and the country of this "lying scoundrel". Graham joined forces with the sheriff; together they enlisted a large body of men to follow Cahir's every move, making it virtually impossible for the highwayman to operate in his normal fashion. Similar pressure was applied to his confederates, hampering their movements.

Cahir found himself having to take unaccustomed risks. He was eventually surprised committing an unlawful deed and only barely escaped arrest. Now he was on the run, hunted like an animal. There followed a protracted and difficult pursuit, in the course of which Cahir swam the flooded Barrow on several occasions, outwitting his pursuers. In the end, in November 1734, Cahir was finally tracked down to a haggard (farmhouse field) in the locality. He was surrounded and captured, having been chivvied by Graham's men with "much resolution".

Cahir was confined in Naas Gaol until the March assizes and then transported to Maryborough for trial. While on remand there Cahir swore oaths against a prominent local gentleman and also implicated many others in serious crimes. Owing to the credibility of his depositions, Cahir's trial was put back until August, while the charges were being investigated. One of those accused by him was a man named Hickey. He admitted to involvement in certain petty crimes but not the grave ones of which he was accused. He was hanged, nevertheless, still protesting his innocence.

Cahir was eventually brought to trial in August 1735 and more than thirty charges were made against him.

"Are you guilty of these charges?" the judge asked in English.

The outlaw pretended not to understand the foreign language. He sought help in Irish from a man in the public gallery, who agreed to act as his interpreter. The judge repeated the question.

"*Níl mé* (I am not)," Cahir answered in his native tongue.

The judge was no fool. He knew full well that, even though Cahir spoke English badly, he understood what was being said. This was not the first time the outlaw had appeared before the judiciary, and the judge was aware that the earlier trials presided over by his peers had been conducted entirely in English. He was determined to catch Cahir out.

The first deposition was taken, then the second, the third – and all the time Cahir spoke in Irish, his interpreter translating.

Then the fourth witness – an Ulsterman – took his place in the box, and began giving evidence about a certain cow, implicating the accused in its theft. Halfway through the speech, Cahir leapt to his feet.

"That's a murder, my Lord!" he shouted at the judge in broken English. "He does not know me at all. He's a lying rogue, for I had that cow wid my shelf ever. She was born'd upon my own ground; my broder here knows it."

"Ah," said the judge in triumph, "you and your brother." Cahir had betrayed himself.

The trial continued in English. Owing to the great number of witnesses produced by the King's Counsel, it lasted a further twelve hours. Among those giving evidence was the young man whose tongue Cahir had cut out. The brutal punishment had not rendered him entirely mute: he was still able to speak after a fashion, and made his meaning clear with a series of signs and grunts.

The outlaw put up a good fight, contradicting the evidence presented, but all in vain; the jury had no hesitation in bringing in a verdict of guilty. Cahir was convicted of horse stealing and other, lesser, crimes. He and Daniel were sentenced to be hanged by the neck until dead.

The brothers went to the gallows together and were executed side by side that same month. The corpses were handed over to their relatives for burial. Charles Dempsey, the outlaw once described as "always having the face of a rogue" and who for so long had been regarded as "the terror of seven counties", was laid to rest inside the east end of the old church ruins of Ballyraddan. No stone marks his grave.

Cahir's name lives on in folklore and even in the names of some landmarks. Apart from Cahir na gCapall's Lep, the (now depleted) wood near Monasterevin, County Kildare, said to have been a favourite hiding place of the outlaw, is known as Cahir na gCapall's Wood. The site of a castle in the townland of Ballymaddock, in the parish of Kilteale, County Laois, is identified on the Ordnance Survey map of the county as the "Ruins of Cahir-na-Coppal's House".

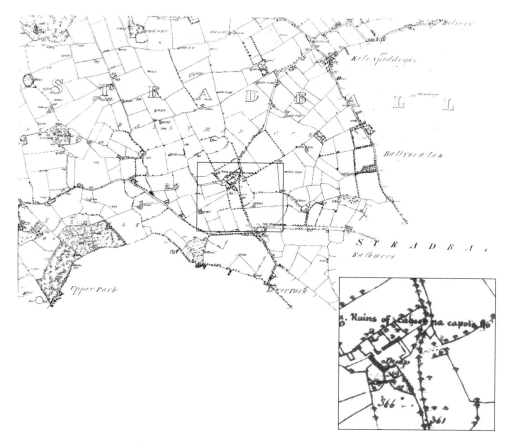

The location of the ruins of Cahir na gCapall's house.

Cahir na gCapall's Lep

The Outlaw Rapparee

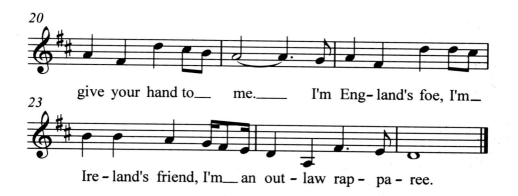

give your hand to— me.— I'm Eng-land's foe, I'm—

Ire-land's friend, I'm— an out-law rap-pa-ree.

The mountain cavern is my home, high up in the crystal air,
My bed is limestone, iron-ribbed, and the brown heath smelling fair.
Let George or William only send his troops to burn and shoot,
We'll meet them here on equal ground, and fight them foot to foot.

Chorus 2: So click your glasses, friends, with mine, the midnight's made for glee,
Stout hearts beat fast in Ireland yet, I'm an outlaw rapparee.

Hunted from out our Father's home, pursued by steel and shot,
And swift the warfare we must wage, or the gibbet be our lot.
Hurrah! The war is welcome work, the hunted outlaw knows,
He steps up to his country's love, o'er the corpses of his foes.

Chorus 3: So click your glasses, friends, with mine, in the coming days I see
Stern labours for our country's weal, I'm an outlaw rapparee.

THE
COUNTY OF
CLARE

George MacNamara

Captain MacNamara of Cong

Dick Turpin is without doubt the most famous highwayman of all time. Many generations have been spellbound by the heroics of the daredevil outlaw and his extraordinary horse, Black Bess.

There was an Irish highwayman, perhaps not as well-known as Turpin but equally audacious in his deeds, who rode a magical mare named Venus. The records show that he – unlike Turpin – was a champion of the poor and oppressed. His name was George MacNamara and he came to be known as MacNamara of Cong.

He was born in County Clare in the year 1690, a descendant of the renowned MacNamaras who owned and occupied lands in that region from the fifth to the seventeenth centuries. Driven from their estates by Oliver Cromwell, the family was scattered to different parts of the country. The MacNamaras were a proud, patriotic and brave clan; many fought and died defending their country from planter and invader.[lxxii]

None, however, gained the fame and notoriety of George MacNamara. Raised as a gentleman and well-educated, George was described as an extremely handsome man, strong, one of Ireland's finest horsemen and, in his time, the finest shot in the land.[lxxiii]

MacNamara married for the first time in September 1740. His wife was Helen Creagh Butler, daughter of Stephen Creagh of Limerick and Cong, and she bore three daughters (Maria, Helen, and Phoebe) before her death. Her Protestant religion appears to have been the only thing they did not share, for by all accounts the couple enjoyed a happy (though short) life together. His second wife was a lady named Honora, but whose family name is unknown. Honora and George had six sons together (James, Charles, Lewis, Marshall, Bartholomew and George).

On his first marriage MacNamara came into possession of a reasonably large estate near the village of Cong. He built a bakery and brewery there and could supply both his own household and the surrounding countryside with fresh bread and good quality beer. He operated a successful fishery on the river and often boasted that he never had to go beyond the walls of the estate for nourishment: the farm provided the beef and the fishery supplied the fish that graced the table; butter and cheese were also produced at home; he even grew the fruits from which his wines, ciders and jams were made. He was a very industrious and fair man who looked after his workers and tenants well and treated all men equally.

MacNamara was also an ambitious man, always ready to add to his possessions and influence. He also enjoyed the power that land ownership brought – even if the land was in his wife's name. As a Catholic he was forbidden by the penal laws from purchasing or holding land.[lxxiv] He began to cast an avaricious eye over the nearby estate of Cong Abbey, with its monastic ruins and great tracts of land. The property was in the hands of the Fellows of Trinity College, and had been since the days of suppression. George had his brother-in-law Stephen Creagh Butler purchase the estate in trust for him. Here he built so fine a house that one distinguished visitor, a Bishop Pococke, described it as "the most delightfully situated residence I had ever seen in the course of my travels".[lxxv]

With the purchase of Cong Abbey began one of the strangest sagas in Irish history. It is the story of a man who led a double life that was almost *larger* than life. It contains the stuff that fanciful tales of superheroes are made of – with this exception: it is not fictitious.

The Secret of Cong Abbey

Cong Abbey held a secret: beneath its ruins was a labyrinth of tunnels, doubtless hewn out by the monks of old as a hiding place in times of persecution. When MacNamara acquired the estate he immediately set about exploring the tunnels in the company of his foster brother and employee, Donal Ruadh ("Red Dan") O'Nolan. MacNamara's interest was not, however, of an archaeological nature. His purpose was both practical and sinister: he wished to make use of the warren of tunnels and extend them so that they would run under the new house he was building.

The truth was that within George MacNamara there burned a hatred of the planter gentry and what they stood for. All about him he saw the cruelty and degradation suffered by the workers and tenants on the estates that adjoined his own. It seemed to MacNamara that this cruelty was mindless: viciousness practised for its own sake. In contrast, the master of Cong treated his own tenants and employees in an exemplary manner, to the great surprise – and sometimes disapproval – of his wealthy neighbours. MacNamara set out to right some of these wrongs.

O'Nolan and he made the ruins their private meeting place and headquarters. They had a concealed forge[lxxvi] built there, where with his own hands the future outlaw made master keys and other tools necessary to the "profession" he was about to join. It was here, too, that he fashioned special shoes for the mare that would become almost as legendary as he: Venus.

Venus, the Magical Horse, and MacNamara's Mysterious Powers

There exists a piece of local folklore which, though it could hardly be taken seriously, nevertheless offers some indication of the awe in which George MacNamara and his mare Venus were held. So successful a highwaymen did he become, and so extraor-

Cong Abbey ruins.

dinary were his exploits, that it was hard for the ordinary people of Mayo to believe
that MacNamara achieved his successes by purely mortal means. In those supersti-
tious times, it was believed that there had to be a supernatural agency involved...

One day MacNamara was fishing off Inis Feenish, an island in Lough Corrib. He
noticed a big raven flying to and from her nest. Being a curious fellow, he climbed up
to the nest and took home the eggs he found there. He boiled them, returned to the
island and replaced them in the nest.

Ravens have the reputation of being very wise birds. This particular one, on dis-
covering that all was not right with her eggs, flew off and returned with a shiny black
pebble in her beak. She rubbed the eggs all over with the pebble and, in no time at
all, a clutch of young ravens hatched, chirping hungrily.

The outlaw was astonished and kept a close watch on the nest. He concluded that
the pebble must have magical powers and decided that he would avail of them.
When the raven left to gather food for her chicks, he climbed up to the nest, took
the magic pebble and rubbed himself all over with it.

Lo, from that instant on, George MacNamara found that he had the gift of second
sight, and was able to foresee any dangers that lay ahead of him! He also acquired the
very useful power to make people do as he commanded.

He hurried back to Cong and into the stable where he kept his favourite mare. He
rubbed her all over with the pebble and she was also given magic gifts. He renamed
her Feenish, or Venus, in honour of the island where he found the magic stone. A
passage in *A Brief Sketch of the Romantic Life of George MacNamara of Cong* relates the
mare's special qualities:

"She would time notes of music with the accuracy and correctness of a stage
performer. She could carry her master on the battlement of a bridge, with the ease
and sure-footedness of a cat. She obeyed the order to go on her knees or
haunches, with the discipline of a life-guard on parade. She could form herself
into an improvised ladder by standing on her hind legs, and so enable her master
to creep up her back, and thus, standing upon this wonderful animal's forehead,
enter an upper stor[e]y, and go through what he himself deemed to be his justifi-
able, because philanthropic, work. On Venus's back he one day jumped in
through the spacious drawing-room window of a country mansion, where a party
of jovial souls were enjoying themselves at table, and flew out again, to the amazement of all, as nimbly as a hare, and without a scratch... She had gone through
so many incredible feats and dangers with the apparent sagacity of a human being,
that she was regarded by many as having something more than horse flesh in her
composition; in other words that she was *enchanted*."

MacNamara's Double Life

It was not long after George built his mansion that a terrifying and very real presence began to appear on the highways of County Mayo. Gentlemen nervously reported that a masked man, dressed in a black cape and a black cocked hat, had robbed them at gunpoint. The magnificent mare he rode seemed to respond to his slightest gesture and carried her rider in a trice far from the scene of his crimes. The authorities were alerted and the Tory hunters mobilised but, try as they might, none could even discover the trail of the mysterious highwayman, let alone catch him. He seemed to appear out of nowhere and to disappear just as quickly.

While leading his double life, George MacNamara played the perfect host to the other landowners in the area, frequently treating them to lavish banquets in his fine home. He was a member of all the hunts in Mayo and Galway and never missed a meet – no matter what nefarious deeds he might have perpetrated the previous night. Of course, he never hunted with his special mare, but kept her hidden for his secret escapades.

MacNamara had a wicked sense of humour. On one memorable occasion he arranged to host a lavish hunt ball at Cong. Invitations went out to all the local gentry and planters, as well as to others from as far afield as County Clare.

A wonderful banquet awaited his guests: fine wines and food, an unlimited supply of beer from the brewery, and an array of brandies and liqueurs. It was a night of great feasting and indulgence. Every excuse was employed to propose a toast, and those present later claimed that George MacNamara raised – and emptied – his glass to each one. It appeared to the gathering that their host was consuming inordinately large amounts of drink. By and by MacNamara fell into a heavy stupor and had to be assisted to his bed. All present believed that "Genial George" had taken a drop too many.

Nothing could have been further from the truth. As the revelry slowed in the early hours of the morning, the last of the intoxicated guests and servants retired and the house fell quiet. A shadowy figure dressed in black riding garb, complete with cape and cocked hat, crept down the stairs.

MacNamara made his way noiselessly to the secret forge. O'Nolan awaited him; Venus was saddled and ready. Arming himself with a brace of pistols and a trusty blunderbuss, the good MacNamara set out. Soon he was galloping hard, the moon on his shoulder guiding him through the Kiltartan countryside, over the border into Galway, then onward into County Clare.

That night MacNamara robbed two mansions in his native county – mansions belonging to two of the guests sleeping contentedly back in the outlaw's home in Cong. Contemporary reports state that only the most valuable items were removed:

quantities of gold, silver and jewellery. No injury was caused to any person in either robbery. He entrusted the spoils to Donal O'Nolan, who later distributed them among the poor in the locality. Before dawn broke, the outlaw was back in his bed, thanks to the speed and stamina of his mare: they had ridden one hundred and twenty miles.

Later that morning MacNamara made a grand entrance for breakfast. Dressed afresh and shaven, but complaining mildly of a slight dizziness, he sat down with his guests and ate a hearty meal. In due course he bade them all Godspeed – and none got a firmer handshake or more enthusiastic farewell than the two unsuspecting land-lords from County Clare he had robbed the night before.

The Masked Captain

The sterling reputation MacNamara had among the people was not one earned lightly; his fight against injustice was one without end. For many years he continued to tor-ment and harass the planters and gentry. He robbed them in their houses, had them "stand and deliver" at pistol-point on the highways, stole their livestock and fodder, or simply taught them a lesson. He was also a master of disguise and was never recognised by any of his victims, even those who came to be entertained at the big house in Cong. Those robbed on the highway knew full well who the culprit was: "The Captain".

If a peasant or tenant was threatened with eviction from his smallholding for non-payment of the outrageous rack-rents, he could always rely on MacNamara or O'Nolan for support. The area around Cong still nurtures stories about the highway-man and his unceasing generosity to the poor. It was said that he had so many locals employed at his estate that not a weed could be found in the perfect lawn.

Yet, while it is true that his victims were principally planters and their descen-dants, it is also fair to say that MacNamara was not averse to robbing the wealthier native Irish when their poorer cousins were in need.

Once, when winter had come and hardship had fallen on the people, MacNamara and O'Nolan left Cong in the dead of night and journeyed into Connemara, the heart of the ferocious O'Flahertys' country. While attempting to relieve the clan of a herd of cattle near Maam Cross, the highwaymen were surprised by a patrol of the O'Flahertys, men known far and wide as brave and fearless warriors. Outnumbered, and knowing that no mercy was shown to cattle thieves, the highwaymen spurred their horses and attempted to escape.

But O'Nolan's mount was no match for the fleet-footed Venus and soon he was lag-ging far behind. Two of his pursuers narrowed the gap, with the rest approaching at speed. There was a flash of light and the roar of gunpowder. O'Nolan's horse stumbled and collapsed under him, mortally wounded. The man recovered quickly, however, getting to his feet and drawing pistol and sabre as the enemy closed in for the kill.

At that moment MacNamara turned in his saddle to check on his comrade and instantly grasped that O'Nolan had only moments left. Without hesitation, he wheeled his mare and galloped back; as he neared his friend, he reached down with an arm outstretched. O'Nolan grabbed it and, in a single motion, was hauled onto the back of the flying Venus.

Before the O'Flahertys could change direction, Captain MacNamara had swung the mare west and was riding full tilt towards a ravine. He did not falter when he reached the edge of the cliff, but urged Venus to jump. The incredible leap – later measured at forty feet – carried the mare and her double burden to the safety of the far side. An 1899 retelling of the story avows that, for many years after this extraordinary feat of horsemanship and daring, four horseshoe prints corresponding with the impressions made by Venus' feet on landing were distinctly visible in the rock.

The O'Flahertys, acknowledging the bravery of the fleeing outlaw, christened the gorge *Leim-Mhicnamara* – MacNamara's Leap. To this day it is known locally by that name and can be found in the vicinity of Maam Cross.

The view over Garromin, Connemara, close by the scene of MacNamara's Leap.

The Trial that Never Was

The problem in apprehending the mercurial Captain was that he took care that every fresh description of him differed from the last. For a time it seemed that Mayo's most successful outlaw would never be brought to justice, but, in the end, MacNamara fell foul of the great scourge of the highwayman: the informer.

Around the time of his fiftieth birthday, the master of Cong Abbey was arrested at his home. The locality was agog with incredulity and excitement. Men and women of the upper classes who had known George MacNamara as a gentleman, genial host and huntsman were simultaneously dumbfounded and indignant at the unmasking.

The prisoner was conveyed in irons to Galway city, flung into gaol, and subsequently brought before the court. Yet, try as they might, the authorities were not able to secure a jury conviction – for they could not get a jury at all. Nobody came to testify; nobody came to sit in judgment upon MacNamara. No man would turn against this great friend of the poor. It was extraordinary. And, for insurance, O'Nolan and his trusted comrades made certain things would continue this way. They spread the word among the gentry and magistrates that a horrible vengeance would be exacted on anyone who dared to swear against the Captain.

Confident of his acquittal, MacNamara kept his composure in the courtroom. The room was empty for the duration of the "trial", save for the judge, two solicitors, the defendant and a military guard. The judge had no choice but to set the prisoner free, but not without warning that his every move would be documented from that day forth.

Upon hearing the decision, MacNamara leaped from the dock, still manacled and shackled, and joyfully requested to be allowed to show the court and the people outside what Venus could do.

"Without delay [he] mounted on the noble beast, trotted down to the bridge at High-Street, got her up on the battlements, where he trotted the nimble and sure-footed animal, which could certainly vie with any mule used in the Alps or mountains of Switzerland; he then got down on the bridge again, and several times got her over the battlement on her hind legs, to the utter astonishment of a crowd of spectators."

Disregarding the judge's warnings, MacNamara continued to ply his "trade" for some years. However, now that his true loyalties were common knowledge, he was shunned and informed upon by his peers, who had not forgiven his duplicity. Despite this, MacNamara gave his open support to the tenants and peasantry and was never convicted of any crime.

Captain George MacNamara of Cong, generous to a fault, died a poor man on January 29, 1760. He passed away in the arms of his dearest and most loyal friend, Donal O'Nolan, while surrounded by family and friends. The number of mourners at his funeral was immense. One chronicler noted:

> "nearly all the gentry and many of the nobility of Mayo, Galway and Clare, were present or represented in the quaint old carriages and vehicles of the period. But the most remarkable spectacle in all that vast Cortége was a numerous cavalcade of Connemara ponies, ridden by those very men who had so furiously chased him for his life but a few short years before! The coffin was carried three times round the Circular Road on the shoulders of the people, and his relatives, the Abbot and Donal Ruadh, acted as chief mourners. While on his last sorrowful journey the procession stopped several times to have his caoiné [or caoineadh: a lament] sung".

MacNamara was buried by the sedilia in the chancel of his beloved Cong Abbey, close to the grave of another champion of the poor in the west: Father Lavelle.

What became of the magic steed Venus has entered the realm of legend. When his beloved mare died, MacNamara was so heartbroken that he held a wake for the animal. Even though the only humans that she had suffered to have near her in life were MacNamara and O'Nolan, people came from far and wide to show their respect for Venus, and those who were unable to attend in Cong waked the mare in their own homes. Venus was placed in an oak coffin before being committed to the earth.

Not even Black Bess had commanded such devotion.

Bold MacNamara

O come all you maids and gen - tle
- men, Come gath - er 'round me do;_____ And I'll
tell a tale of e - x - ploits_____
Where shot and bul - let flew,_____ Of the
mare th-at they call Feen - nish_____ Who's
famed__ in lore and_ song,_____ And__ that
scourge, but no - ble, high - way -
- man   bold MacNa - mar-a of Cong.

He robbed the rich and landlord class,
And stole from the gentry fair.
There wasn't a planter's purse too safe
In Connaught or in Clare;
And the day the Joycemen cornered him,
On yonder high cliff there,
Sure, they never dreamed he'd leap the leap
Upon his faithful mare.

So, the military men did capture him,
Chained him in Galway Gaol.
With a troop of guards around his cell,
This time they would not fail.
Each day they placed him in the dock,
His hands and feet they bound.
And each day the Judge sat silent
For no jury could be found.

So they set him free; they let him go,
No verdict was sent down.
Then the outlaw rode his mighty steed
On the High Bridge in that town.
The soldiers swore they'd catch him
And each chase was hard and long.
But the ranks of redcoats never caught
Bold Mac Namara of Cong.

The Cong Reel

THE
COUNTY OF
LONDONDERY

Shane Crossagh

The Derry Outlaw

Irish historians curse the day in June 1922 that Dublin's Four Courts was shelled. In the conflagration that followed, national treasures were lost for ever: men and women were wiped from history as though they had never existed; records of the deeds of heroes vanished as quickly as the infamy of tyrants. As a result of the fire, it is not known when Shane Crossagh[lxxvii] was born, nor when he was executed (though local tradition gives the year as 1725). We know only that he certainly lived and fought the "good fight". What follows here is the story of a great Ulster highwayman, pieced together from oral tradition, legend, folklore, and scant written record.

He was born John Mullan sometime in the middle of the seventeenth century, near Faughanvale in County Derry. His most vivid childhood memory was of the day he and his family were evicted from their home; they and their meagre belongings were left by the side of the road.

Shane's father took the family into the highlands around Claudy and they eventually settled in a place called Lingwood. The mountains and hills of that area became home to many families who had been cruelly thrown off their property. These people were forced to make way for the planters and British soldiers given Irish land in lieu of wages. The Sperrin Mountains became a hotbed of insurrection and lawlessness, and made an ideal natural fortress for highwaymen and rapparees.

In his youth Shane Crossagh began to display the traits of the natural leader, as well as an instinctive understanding of guerrilla warfare. He made several hugely successful, though minor, forays against local landlords, which attracted the attention of other outlaws. They joined him to form the most feared band of desperados that County Derry had ever seen.

Crossagh's Leaps

Although there is a paucity of written records, Shane Crossagh's deeds and misdeeds have been kept alive by the strong Irish tradition of oral history. *The Benbradagh*, a community magazine published annually in County Derry, recorded Mr Johnny Mc Closkey's recitation of a poem about Crossagh's adventures as recently as 1983.

It's up the heathery mountain,
And down the rushy glen,
Squire Steeple has gone hunting
Seán Crossagh and his men.
With forty mounted yeomen
They followed in their strain
He swears he'll gie them gallows work
'Till he returns again.

Seán Crossagh was a ploughboy
Who lived in Ballinascreen,
But now he is an outlaw
For the wearing of the green.
For the wearing of the green, boys,
For the wearing of the green,
Seán Crossagh is an outlaw
Today in Ballinascreen.

The Squire rode a chestnut,
His brother rode a grey,
And close behind Seán Crossagh
They galloped all the day,
They galloped all the day, boys,
And hunted thus by night,
They never let the outlaw
One moment out of sight.

Beyond the Sperrin mountains
Far, far from Ballinascreen,
They kept the wolfdog on his track
For the wearing of the green,
For the wearing of the green, boys,
For the wearing of the green
They kept the wolfdog on his track
Away from Ballinascreen.

The man then must be wearied,
Who hunted thus has been,
For three long days and fastings,
Since he left Ballinascreen,
Since he left Ballinascreen, boys,
Since he left Ballinascreen.
We'll hang him now for surely
For the wearing of the green.

Seán Crossagh kept a watchdog
That never parted him
And when the bloodhounds neared him
He tore them limb from limb,
"My good friend," cried Seán Crossagh
As the tears began to flow,
"My gallant swift we yet were free,
If we could leap the Roe."

The river Roe is deep, boys,
Its channels twelve yards wide,
Its banks are high and steep, boys,
O'erhanging at each side.
And will he leap the Roe, boys?
And will he leap the Roe?
Squire Steeple soon has parted been
If he can leap the Roe.

Then up the hounds they gave a
    bounce,
Seán Crossagh now I know
And with a leap they all rushed out
And he has leapt the Roe.
And he has leapt the Roe, boys,
And he has leapt the Roe,
Old Ballinascreen may yet be seen
By the man that leapt the Roe.

"A good leap," said the Squire,
When he saw the chase was won,
"Not greater," said the outlaw,
"For such a race I've run,
But mark, my Squire Steeple,
When you come back again.
You'll wish the River Roe between
Seán Crossagh and your men."

The Squire and his yeomen,
Are hurrying down Glenshane,
Right wearied and dejected,
The chase was all in vain.

The chase was all in vain, boys,
The chase was all in vain,
Right well I know they'll meet the green,
'Ere again they pass Glenshane.

Old Feeny bridge is broken,
And on its arch was seen,
To them a fearful token,
A branch of holly green,
And from behind a grey rock
A whistling bullet sped,
And Torrens, the informer,
Fell from his charger, dead.

"O Mercy," cried the Squire
"Seán Crossagh let me live,
And for your sake a thousand pounds,
In yellow gold I'll give.[lxxviii]
I'll lend you arms freely…"
"Lend them singly unto me
For I must bind your yoemen
Each man unto a tree."

The yeomen now consisted
Of seven gallant men,
Of seven gallant men, boys,
Of seven gallant men,
And in despair he tore his hair,
And wept for shame,
Amen.

Stories of Crossagh's capacity for doing good, as well as his thirst for adventure, also live on in the folklore of the region. On one memorable occasion he robbed a worldly priest and handed the spoils to the poor, young curate of the same parish. Crossagh robbed the rich and fed the poor; he made life hell for his planter foes. He led a life that was as harsh and bitter as the winter wind that blows through Glenshane Pass, but it was not, however, a life without its humorous incidents. One such story concerns an occasion when Shane fell foul of the authorities entirely by accident.

Walking through a remote part of the woods one day, he was met by two troopers. Something about his appearance or demeanour aroused their suspicions and they decided that he must be involved in some sort of skulduggery. They arrested him, not knowing that their "catch" was the area's most valuable one, and told him that they were bringing him to Derry Gaol for questioning.

Crossagh became terribly upset and explained to his captors that he had simply been on his way to meet a friend and had come to the woods to retrieve a jug of poteen which was hidden in the whin bushes.

"Give the drink to us," one of the soldiers said, "and we'll let you go."

Crossagh agreed to this proposal and led the troopers to a clump of whin on the outskirts of the woods. He pointed.

"It's in there," he said.

"Well, get it out, then," one of his captors ordered.

Crossagh reached in and, instead of the promised poteen, pulled out a long and fearsome pike. He attacked the two startled soldiers and disarmed them, relieving them not only of their weapons but of their purses as well. After putting the fear of God into the two, Crossagh chased them from the area.

That evening he stopped for a drink of water at a poor farmer's cabin in the hills. The farmer was agitated; it transpired that earlier that day the local landlord, a Protestant clergyman, accompanied by troops, had come to collect tithes. He had taken the farmer's only cow in lieu of cash, which meant certain starvation for his family.

The outlaw reached into a pocket for one of the soldiers' purses and gave the farmer four sovereigns. He then went on to the clergyman's house and robbed him of thirty pounds. In this manner were the tithes returned to the poor.

The robbery of the clergyman was a diabolical, blasphemous deed, and the last straw as far as the authorities were concerned. Shane Crossagh was a thorn in their side and had to be apprehended. To this end, extra troops were drafted into the Sperrins. A reign of terror began: every cottage and farm was searched and people were beaten and intimidated in an effort to find the outlaw.

At last Crossagh was captured. It was rumoured that he gave himself up to prevent any more reprisals being visited on his people – even if untrue, the story indicates the esteem in which he was held by the poor of the area. He was clapped in irons and, under heavy guard, escorted to the city of Derry to await trial.

The journey took his captors over the Sperrins and they stopped to rest on the slopes of Carntogher mountain. As prisoner and soldiers rested on the grass, Crossagh began boasting about what a fine athlete he was. He told his escort that he could show them three jumps they would never forget. The amused soldiers laughed.

Carntogher mountain, where Shane Crossagh leaped to freedom.

"It's the truth," said the outlaw. "But I can't show you unless you take off my manacles."

Nobody foresaw any difficulty with this. They were in open country with nowhere to hide, and the troops greatly outnumbered their lone prisoner. They unchained him for the sport.

Crossagh's first two leaps were astounding – they were equal to two leaps by an ordinary mortal. The soldiers were impressed.

"One more!" the outlaw laughed.

The third leap was even greater than the first two.[lxxix] As the troops looked on in amazement, Crossagh did not turn back, but raced off down the side of the mountain. He must have been an extremely fit man for, keeping out of musket range, the escapee led the soldiers a merry chase for all of four miles, almost to the outskirts of Dungiven, where they lost his trail. The next day an informer told the military that someone answering Shane's description had been seen skulking in the woods near Ballykelly, a good ten miles from Dungiven. By the time the soldiers arrived, however, Crossagh was already on his way to Loughermore.

The fugitive, exhausted and hungry, knew that the soldiers would gain on him. He made his way to the bank of the river only to discover that heavy rainfall had swollen it. The current was strong and swimming was out of the question. As he stood contemplating the best course of action, he heard shouts and, looking around, saw that he had been spotted. With the soldiers on his heels he raced to the cliff at Ness, which overlooked the river. Crossagh launched himself into space in a daredevil jump, landing safely on the opposite bank of the river. From that day this Derry landmark has been called Shane's Leap.

Sons of the Derry Outlaw

We know little about Shane Crossagh's later life apart from the fact that he married and fathered a family. The oral tradition relates that he had two sons – Paudeen and Rory – who followed in their father's footsteps and became highwaymen. The outlaw made sure that the boys would grow up to be fighters, men who could stand on their own two feet.

He was ruthless in this respect. Even when they were very young, Paudeen and Rory were made to fight – not sing – for their supper. Legend has it that Shane used to place a pot of stirabout in the middle of the floor. The boy who was unable to take it by force or by fraud from his father got no supper.

Paudeen – or Paurya Fhad (Young Paddy), as he was sometimes called – was the elder son and by all accounts became as capable and daring a highwayman as his father. Both sons shared many a wild adventure with Shane. The most often reported, and notorious, incident was the one that led to Shane's downfall.

In his latter years, the ageing highwayman often stayed with his sons at Fowler's roadside inn between Dungiven and Carntogher. The landlord was of planter stock; nevertheless, he was friendly with the Crossaghs and, in return for a share of the booty, would often tip off the outlaws about his wealthier guests. There was a special room at the inn which had peepholes and listening posts; this was made available to Shane and his sons, enabling them to eavesdrop on their unsuspecting victims.

One day when the outlaw trio were lodging at the inn, the English General Napier, a man with a reputation for vanity and pomposity, stopped for refreshment on his way to Derry. He was accompanied by several officers and a small detachment of infantry. While the General was having his meal, talk at another table turned to the depredations of Shane Crossagh, the Derry outlaw. In a voice raised loud enough for the General to hear, somebody remarked on the fact that, with so many troops stationed in the county, it showed that the army was incapable of tracking down "a simple peasant brigand".

The remark was enough to provoke Napier into a red rage. He told all present that he would personally get involved in the hunt for "this ruffian".

"A mere Irish thief is no match for a British officer!" he thundered. "I shall track this cur down and he shall hang like the criminal he is."

The promise heartened the travellers at the inn, several of whom had suffered at the hands of Shane and his band. Wine was called for, and the General regaled his audience with tales of his exploits and victories. The day wore on and evening began to fall, but the wine and boasting continued.

Unnoticed by the General and his admirers, Shane and his sons sat in the secret room listening to every word. The more Napier bragged and insulted him, the more incensed the outlaw became. He beckoned to his sons and the three stole silently from the inn. Shane vowed that the General would pay for his pride and vanity – that very evening.

The trio headed off on the road to Derry city, the very road that the good general and his party were certain to take. The place Shane chose to give his lesson in manners was a narrow bridge straddling the river Roe,[lxxx] a short distance from the village of Feeny. The outlaws placed sods of turf and earth on both sides of the bridge, moulding them into the shapes of heads and shoulders. In the dark these models could easily be mistaken for men lying in ambush. To add to the illusion of armed men lying in wait, the Crossaghs pushed sticks into the sods. They then hid in the undergrowth and awaited the arrival of the General and his men.

It was not long before they heard the sound of the soldiers approaching. As soon as they were within range, Shane fired one of his weapons, shooting the General's horse from under him. Panic set in. The startled officers formed a defensive circle around Napier and ordered the men to fall into formation. Like their father, Paudeen and Rory were both armed to the teeth and, without having to reload, fired a few volleys, thereby adding to the confusion and giving the impression of a large body of attackers.

"Lay down your arms," Shane called out, "and surrender to Shane Crossagh, or there'll be a fuller volley the next time!"

The soldiers, thinking themselves surrounded and up against a heavily armed band of men, reluctantly laid down their weapons. Shane then ordered General Napier to come forward and hand over his sword.

Any commander who has to surrender his blade knows that he is a beaten man, but no shame is attached to surrendering thus to a fellow officer and gentleman – a better man on the day. The humiliation of surrendering to a common criminal, however, is another matter entirely. The General blustered and protested, but Shane forced him to hand over the weapon. Next he had Napier order his men to stack their rifles. Keeping the disarmed men under cover, Shane's sons bound the soldiers in pairs and loaded the rifles onto the officers' horses.

But Napier's mortification was not yet complete. Shane forced the furious General to strip down to his undergarments and exchange his splendid uniform for the outlaw's own rough clothes. The greatest indignity of all was when Shane placed his old highwayman's cocked hat squarely on the head of the defeated officer and adjusted it to a jaunty angle.

Shane and his sons then marched their captives twelve miles to Derry's Waterside district, east of the river Foyle. With the walls of the city in sight and with a full moon to guide and expose them, Shane pointed his subdued and embarrassed captives in the direction of the ferry landing stage.[lxxxi] Then, with a wild outlaw's cries, the Crossaghs galloped away into the night on their stolen mounts, laden with British arms and booty.

Napier, not unnaturally, refused to let the matter rest and there is no doubt that the incident hastened Shane Crossagh's capture. No stone was left unturned in the search for the outrageous Derry outlaw.

Crossagh had returned to the hills; he believed that he would enjoy the protection of his own people there. Unfortunately, a weaver in Dungiven, a South Derry man named Torrens, was secretly in the pay of the government. While visiting some friends in the Sperrins he learned of Crossagh's whereabouts and immediately alerted the authorities.

The outlaw and his sons were captured, tried and sentenced to death by hanging.

Shane was offered a pardon because of his advanced age, and on condition that he give up his criminal activities and lead a quiet, law-abiding life. Brave Shane, on hearing that his sons would not be offered the same terms, declined; father and sons would face the gallows united.

He was defiant even at the end. With the noose around his neck and a beloved son on either side, he addressed the onlookers.

"Well, I'm an old man anyhow," he cried, "and can't live long and what use will a pardon be to me? So, with the blessing o' God, I'll shake a foot wi' the boys!"

Shane Crossagh was hanged at The Diamond in Derry, between his two sons and holding on each side one of their hands. Their bones are believed to lie in unmarked ground near the Devlin grave in the Old Churchyard of Banagher, County Derry.

Eavesdropper

The General's Bridge

One even-ing fair three out - laws_

set upon_ their task____ While brave Gene - ral____

Na - pier he o-pened up a cask._ They hid 'neath the

bridge with their bold_ fai-ry band We-ll fixed were_ their

weapons for he-re they would stand_ To-night the old

red - coats would b-e sore and sad___ At the hands of

Shane Cross-agh and__ Paud - een Mc Fad.

One flash of a carbine – the general wheeled 'round
And the steed and his rider both rolled on the ground.
His guardsmen they gaped with panic struck stare
When the voice of Shane Crossagh roared loud in the air
Surrender ye knaves to true Knights of the Pad
The strong hand for ever and Paudeen Mc Fad.

Now oaths wildly sounded and pistols went flashing
And horses high bounding and broadswords all clashing
The demon of plunder in glory did revel
For Shane and stout Rory laid on like the devil
'Till at length fairly routed the whole scarlet squad
Were tied neck and heels by bold Paudeen Mc Fad.

THE COUNTY OF TIPPERARY

William Crotty

The Comeragh Highwayman

In the latter part of the nineteenth century an angler sat by the shore of a mountain lake. He was a Tipperary man from Clonmel who often journeyed at night to fish in the Comeragh Mountains of County Waterford. He was skilled in the art, but too often he would cast his line out into the still, moonlit water of the lake and reel it in empty.

As he was preparing to cast that night, the angler was aware of a dark figure emerging from the shadow of a cliff abutting the lake shore. The figure approached, his feet making no sound on the pebbles. Without a word he wrenched the rod from the alarmed angler's hands and cast out upon the water. No sooner did the hook strike the surface than a fish took it, and was soon landed. Still not uttering a word, the stranger continued fishing for the best part of an hour, and only stopped when the angler's bag was full to the brim. Then he dropped the rod and, as silently as he had arrived, melted back into the shadows lining the shore.

Twenty years after this strange episode, the son of the first nocturnal angler sat fishing at the same lake in the Comeraghs. He cast for hour after hour but could not land a fish, no matter what tricks or tactics he employed. Just as he was about to pack away his tackle and leave, he was approached by a stranger who came out of the mist and grabbed the rod from his shaking hands.

With every cast he made, the silent stranger caught a fish; it was not long before the angler's bag was brimful. The young angler watched wordlessly, too fearful to venture any questions. He had almost summoned the courage to speak when the mysterious stranger turned away and noiselessly disappeared into the shadows.

The confounded young man returned home and was met at the door by his widowed mother. She took one look at the catch and said: "So, like your father before you, you have met the dark stranger."

The dark stranger was none other than the ghost of William Crotty, the outlaw, who had died in 1742.

The men had been fishing in Loch Gorra, more commonly known as Crotty's Lake. Many stories of Crotty's ghost are told in the area: some of the local people claim to have heard the pitiful cries of a woman and the low sorrowful groans of a man, or the clattering of hoofbeats, or the clash of steel echoing around the shores and caves at Coumshingaun Lake and Crotty's Stable. These are the sounds and haunts associated with a highwayman as famous in the Comeraghs as Galloping Hogan was in adjacent County Tipperary.

Crotty's Brigands

William Crotty was born in Russelstown near Clonmel in the year 1712. His early days are virtually unchronicled; we know only that he was the son of a poor farmer who was evicted from his smallholding for non-payment of rent. As a result of this injustice, as did many men of his time in similar circumstances, William became a highwayman. He was, wrote Michael Kavanagh, "one of several refractory spirits who, in the doleful times of the Penal Laws, preferred freedom and outlawry rather than submit to the persecutors of his race".[lxxxii]

At the comparatively tender of age of eighteen the outlaw gathered around him a band of men thirty strong, and for the next twelve years reigned supreme among the lawless of County Waterford. He carried with him always a blunderbuss, two pistols and a dagger, and was a deadly shot using either hand. Yet, far from being a murderous knave shunned by every section of the populace, William Crotty was a particularly popular man around the Comeragh and Monavullagh Mountains. He mixed openly with the people, even though there was a price on his head. It is said that he often frequented the fair green at Kilmacthomas and joined in hurling and football. Handball was also a favourite pastime of his. He was a renowned dancer, often showing up at patterns and wakes to partner the girls. In short, he was an outlaw whose personal charm and social attributes made him unusually welcome in the most respectable of homes.

There is some dispute concerning the composition of Crotty's gang. Some sources submit that they were not run-of-the-mill outlaws; they are described as being, by and large, God-fearing small farmers. Darby Dooley, for example, was a tinsmith, a very respectable occupation in those days. Other sources claim that the gang comprised sheep stealers and cut-throats. There is some suspicion that the latter description was put about by the military and constabulary, in an effort to bring William and his band into disrepute. However, though they showed no mercy to the rich or landlord class, there is no doubt that the gang befriended and helped the poor – it was this characteristic that made Crotty and his men heroes to the ordinary people.

For the record, then, the members of the gang were drawn from many walks of life. Most notable among the members were David Norris, John Cunningham, James Cleary, William Cunningham, Patrick Hickey, and the aforementioned Dooley. William also had outlaw "affiliates", men of influence in the demimonde of Waterford and neighbouring counties, including Richard Power of Churchtown (not to be confused with the Captain Power whose acquaintance we made in Chapter IV). He often supplied William Crotty with food and arms, and even became an accomplice in some schemes, most notably the robbing of the house of Beverly Ussher, a wealthy landowner of Kilmeaden.

There were few places in Ireland more suited to the harbouring of a highwayman than the Comeraghs, in particular the wilder parts that William Crotty favoured. In his time the area from the headwaters of the Nire and Finisk on one side of the hills to Glin and Gurteen on the other was densely wooded, and a man on the run could hide there for days without being detected.

The local yeomen and militia knew that the outlaw had his hideout somewhere in the vicinity, but that knowledge gave them little comfort. William with his band would swoop down from the mountains, carry out a raid, and retreat back the way they had come. Each time the authorities gave chase, the robbers would vanish into dark valleys, caves and other hiding places in the mountains.

William Crotty knew this area like the back of his hand. His principal hideout was so high up that it afforded a commanding view of the surrounding countryside. It was virtually impossible for an interloper to approach the place during daylight without being spotted. An assault in darkness was out of the question: the terrain was too dangerous. As a bolt hole it was virtually impregnable.

It was also a place of eerie beauty and enchantment. The hideout was near a lake called Coumgaura or Loch Gáire (the Lake of Laughter).[lxxxiii] One point, where a rock rises sheer from the water's edge, is known still as Stola Crotaigh (Crotty's Stool). At its foot is an opening in the rock that leads to an underground chamber – Crotty's Den. The only means of access is by rope.

The cave consists of one large chamber from which smaller ones branch off. This is reputed to have been William Crotty's main hideout. He had a number of others, including another cave at Coumshingaun Lake; it is called Crotty's Stable because legend has it that the outlaw stabled stolen horses and cattle here prior to selling them.[lxxxiv] An old Irish song claims that he also had a hideout overlooking the Nire Valley.[lxxxv] At Crough in Kilrossanty is another landmark named after the highwayman. It is a large boulder called Crotty's Rock, which served as a lookout post. From the top of the rock one can look out over most of County Waterford, parts of Tipperary and Kilkenny, and catch a glimpse of County Wexford.

William lived the life of the outlaw more thoroughly than did others of his calling. He married a woman named Mary, who shared his wild existence: where he went, she followed. Mary left the security of a roof and hearth for the rough comforts of cave, fern and bracken. Tradition has it that William never let any of his men enter the cave at Crotty's Lake. This was a private place, which he shared only with his wife. Following an exhausting raid, he would often retire to this particular cave to sleep, while Mary stood guard – she was his most faithful protector. This cave played a central role in an incident known as the Siege of Crotty's Den.

The Siege of Crotty's Den

It happened in the wake of a particularly daring robbery. Hunted by a body of soldiers, the band had split up, each man heading for his own bolt hole in the Comeraghs. Crotty led his pursuers on a wild, circuitous chase that lasted many hours. At last he arrived at his favourite hideout, exhausted. He desperately needed rest but that day there was no-one to stand guard.

The soldiers picked up the trail that led them to the fissure at the base of Crotty's Stool. On peering into the opening, they could just about discern the cavern far below: they suspected that they had the outlaw cornered in his own hiding place. Jubilant, they decided to lay siege and await Crotty's surrender.

It was a long wait. Crotty awoke in the afternoon, in time to see one of the redcoats peering into the cavern; he froze, not making a sound. Neither side would budge. The commanding officer had no wish to return to barracks empty-handed and looking like a fool, so he offered a reward of five guineas – a considerable sum – to any man willing to climb down and search the cavern for the outlaw.

A young trooper volunteered. A rope was secured about his waist, a stout knot tied. In the event of an attack he could be pulled to safety. Armed with a brace of pistols and clutching a lantern, the soldier was lowered underground. No sooner had he reached the bottom than a hand gripped his neck and a razor-sharp blade was pressed to his throat. The terrified soldier whispered a prayer for his life.

William Crotty was not a fool. He knew that killing the soldier would only mean that more reinforcements would be called for and that he might never escape: he would die like a rat in a trap. He thought quickly and arrived at the following proposition. He would spare the young trooper's life if he told his commanding officer that the cave was empty. William reasoned that the soldier, on re-emerging unharmed, would be believed.

"But renege on your word," he warned the young trooper menacingly, "and my men will follow you to the ends of the earth to avenge me. If they fail to find *you*, then they'll surely find your family."

The soldier had no choice but to agree. It was a good bargain: he received his five guineas and William Crotty escaped with his life.

Hearn: the Tory Hunter

Crotty's adventures ensured one close shave after another. Once William and Mary were visiting her brother in the village of Curraheen. The outlaw had performed one of his many errands of mercy that day, giving a poor widow money to pay her rent; that evening, after the agent had been paid, the highwayman waylaid him and retrieved it.

Word got out that the outlaw was in the vicinity and the sub-sheriff, a Mr Hearn, raised a company of cavalry. They set out for Mary's brother's house and arrived when all had retired. But Mary, who was a light sleeper, was roused by the noise of the horses' hoofs. She quickly woke her husband and hid him in the first place they could think of – the middle of a turf stack in the back-yard.

The troopers searched high and low for four hours – the house, the thatch, the outbuildings – but no sign was found of William Crotty. One of them even inspected the stack of turf with sabre and bayonet: one of the thrusts grazed Crotty's shoulder, but he did not flinch or cry out. It was many hours before Crotty was pulled out of the stack and taken to safety.

Crotty's Right-hand Man

David Norris, William's lieutenant, was to play a pivotal role in the outlaw's career. He was the most senior member of the gang; though inferior in strength and agility, it was believed that he was William's superior in ability and cunning. It appears that Norris was the one who thought up the schemes and Crotty the man who executed them.

Crotty and Norris often worked as a pair. Among the more notable instances was their raid on a house near Tramore. The owner was a wealthy widow, a Mrs Rodgers, who happened to be hosting a large dinner party that very evening.

The guests, on seeing two heavily-armed Tories stride into the room, were terrified. Crotty ordered one of the servants, a local lad, to hand over a large silver plate from the sideboard. The outlaws departed without taking anything else.

The shaken hostess and guests immediately accused the servant of being Crotty's accomplice and threatened him with prosecution. Distraught, and knowing he had no other way of proving his innocence, he ran after the outlaws and implored them to return the plate. Crotty took pity on him and returned to Mrs Rodgers' dining room, handing the startled lady back her property. Crotty listened to the lady's profuse thanks – and then ordered her to hand back the silver.

"Now, madam," he said, on accepting it, "remember it was you and not your servant who gave this to me, and do not charge him with the loss."

But events could just as easily take a nasty turn when Crotty was in the company of his right-hand man. There is good cause to believe that David Norris was the more ruthless of the two, often goading his chief into using methods Crotty would not otherwise have considered or committing acts of senseless violence.

One such instance is well documented. One night, as Crotty and Norris were passing by a cottage at Sean Mhichil's Cross, Graiguerush, they noticed a light in the window. On looking in they saw a man and a woman at supper. The man had just peeled a potato and was about to raise it to his mouth. Norris immediately arranged a cruel bet with Crotty.

"I'll wager," he said, "that if you were to fire your pistol as soon as he raises the potato, then your ball will not pass his mouth before the potato touches his lips."

Crotty had only a moment to accept the bet. As the farmer raised the potato, the outlaw fired his pistol – and the ball struck the unfortunate man in the mouth, the savage wound killing him almost instantly.[lxxxvi]

If William Crotty regretted having acted on Norris' suggestion on this occasion, then he would later have cursed the day he ever met the man. It was Norris who, in the end, was his undoing.

The Traitors

On March 21, 1740, Mr White of Waterford city captured Norris and had him incarcerated. We do not know what ensued – perhaps Norris was tortured, threatened or bribed – but it was not long afterwards that some members of his band were ambushed in the Comeraghs. Crotty made a clean getaway thanks to the thick mist which sometimes enveloped that area, yet the authorities counted themselves fortunate. Six men were captured and among them was the tinsmith Darby Dooley, one of

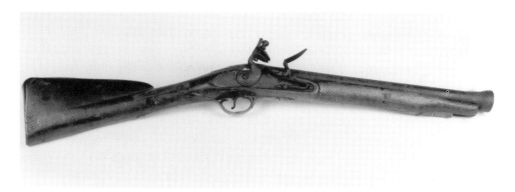

William Crotty's gun (length: 30.5 in.; stock width: 4.5 in.; barrel circumference: approx. 1.5 in.).

Crotty's best men. Dooley, too, was persuaded to provide valuable information about his leader.

Norris escaped from Waterford Gaol shortly after this incident and made his way back to the outlaws' headquarters in the Comeraghs. His return was greeted with a mistrust that bordered on the paranoiac. So grave, in fact, were the gang's suspicions, that Norris decided to throw himself back on the mercy of the authorities rather than risk having his throat cut by his comrades. He returned to custody in October 1741.

Local tradition has it that Mary Crotty always suspected Norris of being an informer, but nobody had ever considered Norris' wife to be a threat. Yet when trouble came, it was from this quarter. Sub-sheriff Hearn bribed Mrs Norris to report on the movements of William Crotty and the remaining gang members. Together they devised code words to communicate snippets of information.

And so it was that Hearn met Mrs Norris on the road one day. She did not greet him but, as he came within earshot, said: "The bird's in the nest."

The sub-sheriff, though alone at the time, made quickly for Crotty's Lake. He crept to the entrance to the cave and called out his adversary's name. The outlaw, thinking it to be one of his accomplices, began to climb up into the daylight.

Hearn was prepared. He guessed that Crotty would be heavily armed, and so had drawn his own weapons. As the highwayman emerged, vulnerable while holding on to the rope, Hearn fired both pistols.[lxxxvii] One bullet found its mark, hitting Crotty in the mouth. Fortunately for the outlaw, he suffered only a flesh wound. Before the sub-sheriff had time to reload, Crotty escaped once again into the sanctuary of the Comeraghs.

Crotty clearly did not suspect Mrs Norris of having betrayed his location to Hearn because she was left free to do so again a few months later, in February 1742. She passed on to Hearn the news that the outlaw would be visiting her home at Ballinafina, Rathgormack, on the sixteenth of the month, alone.

Mary Crotty appears to have been more perceptive than her husband. She had voiced her suspicions about Mrs Norris, yet Crotty steadfastly refused to believe he was in danger and would not accept that the wife of his former lieutenant had turned traitor. He had given Mrs Norris and her children a great deal of help since the time her turncoat husband had given himself up. She could not, he told himself, possibly wish to do him harm.

He arrived at Ballinafina at sundown and found a warm welcome of food and drink at Mrs Norris' home. Everything seemed normal; the children were sleeping; he had no grounds for suspicion. He did not realise that his hostess had laced his drink with a potion provided by Hearn. No sooner had Crotty finished his meal and gone to sit by the hearth than he fell into a drug-induced sleep.

Mrs Norris saw her opportunity. She poured water on the outlaw's pistols, more water into his powder, and carefully removed his dagger to a hiding place. Then she brought a candle to the window and gave the pre-arranged signal.

Moments later the door burst open and in rushed Hearn with a troop of militia. The noise was enough to rouse Crotty, who instinctively went for his weapons. When he tried to discharge his pistols he discovered that the powder refused to ignite; and then he reached for his dagger and found that the sheath was empty. Though still drugged and knowing he was outnumbered, he put up a desperate hand-to-hand struggle.

Crotty was overpowered. Hearn had his man at last. As he was being bound for the journey to the gaol, William turned to the sub-sheriff.

"I knew if I was ever to be arrested, then you'd be the man to do it," he said generously.

"Tell me this," Hearn asked in reply. "You have had plenty of opportunities to kill me. Why did you never try it?"

"I often intended to," the outlaw replied, "and last Christmas I went to shoot you. But through the parlour window I saw you and your wife and children sitting so happily round the fire that, though I had my pistol cocked and you covered, my heart failed me and I could not draw the trigger. I often followed you when you went fishing in the Clodagh. But your son was with you, and if I killed you I felt sure that he would have tried to shoot me – and I could not bring myself to take both your lives."

The Trial

Crotty was brought in irons to Waterford Gaol, and tried in March 1742, together with his captured confederates. Darby Dooley, the tinsmith turned outlaw – now turned

Crown witness – was first to give evidence. He deposed that, under William's leadership, he had taken part in many crimes. He offered chapter and verse on various robberies and described how Crotty had divided up the stolen goods between his men and Mary. For instance, the gang had broken into the house of one John Foley, he said, and stolen a large sum of money, four gold rings, a silver cross and chain, and a wardrobe of clothes. Crotty had given the rings and clothes to his wife. On the fifth of that month they had broken into a house in Ballymorrissey, the property of John Power, where they stole £18 in coin, some linen, and gold and silver jewellery, which Crotty divided up among his men and Mary. Norris later corroborated this account.

Then Dooley gave the testimony that the judge had been waiting for. In February Crotty and Norris had entered the home of George Williams of Clonea with the intention of shooting him dead. Dooley heard three shots before the pair came out of the house. Crotty confessed to the gang waiting outside "that he Crotty had shott the said George Williams".

Mrs Ellen Williams also swore on oath that Crotty was responsible for her brother-in-law's death.

> "She deposes that on 23rd February last at about 10 or 11 o'clock at night two persons entered her house at Clonea and told her to get out of bed and to go to the most distant part of the house as they did not intend to do her any injury. She then heard two shots fired and on coming back found her brother-in-law George Williams dead with a gunshot wound in him. She did not know who the two persons were, but supposes them to be William Crotty and David Norris or two more of that gang of Robbers."

It was David Norris' turn. He deposed that, accompanied by others on occasion but always led by Crotty, he had committed many outrages.[lxxxviii] The outlaw band had, for example, entered the home of David Curran of Cumeen, where at gunpoint they had relieved the panic-stricken occupants of £3 and some clothes. On January 5 he and Crotty had entered yet another residence, the home of Nicholas Hayes of Kilfarrissey, and stolen £12, some silk handkerchiefs, a gold ring and more clothes. Crotty had divided up the spoils between Pierce Walsh, John Murphy and Norris himself.

Norris continued in fine singing voice, implicating both Crotty and others in highway robbery, burglary and mayhem. He swore an oath against James Cleary, another gang member, claiming that Cleary had given himself and Crotty a gun and powder horn, and that the three of them robbed John Neale of Whitechurch, County Kilkenny.

Nor did Norris fail to confess their horse-stealing activities. Crotty, accompanied by John Cunningham, had stolen from Mr Robert Carew of Waterford City a black mare and a sorrel horse which they had transported as far as Curraheen.

Not content with this, he went on to swear an oath against Richard Power, stating that the local Churchtown "gentleman" often helped Crotty and other unnamed outlaws of the area with weapons, shelter and information, knowing them to be "Tories, robbers and rapparees out upon their keeping". He claimed that Power instigated the robbery of Beverley Usher of Killmaidon.

Hammering the decisive nail into Crotty's coffin, Norris corroborated Dooley's evidence concerning the killing of George Williams of Clonea.

It was more than enough for the jury. On March 17, St Patrick's Day, 1742, the foreman made the following summary.

> "We find and present one William Crotty, late of Lyre, County Waterford; a yeo-man, John Cunningham of Waterford city; William Cunningham of Waterford city; and Patrick Hickey of Lower Grawn, County Waterford, a yeoman, to be Tories, robbers and rapparees and out in arms and on their keeping and not amenable to law. We therefore pray Your Lordship to recommend it to the Lords Justice to have them executed."

The judge donned the black cap. William Crotty knew that it was hopeless to plead for a reversal of the verdict. He asked instead for a stay of execution.

"I see no reason for granting it," replied the judge.

Mary Crotty jumped from her seat, distressed. "Oh, my Lord, there is a reason!" she cried. "If only to let him see the face of his child!"

She stood erect and displayed to all present her condition: she was indeed heavily pregnant.

Nevertheless, the request was denied. It was not unusual for the female compan-ions of alleged felons to turn up in court pregnant, begging for clemency for the fathers of their unborn children. Crotty's execution was fixed for the following day.

On March 18, 1742, the Comeragh highwayman was hanged. He was thirty years of age. In accordance with the sentence, he was decapitated and his head placed on a spike over the gate of Waterford County Gaol. A man by the name of O'Meara, a minor member of Crotty's gang, though well implicated, was also hanged on the same day, after nine attempts. Apparently, the rope stuck on the gallows arm every time.

On the same day the Hanging Judge condemned twenty other men to death.

William Crotty's execution had a particularly unsavoury epilogue. It is said that the dead man's hair did not rot with the flesh, but continued growing on the bony cranium, and that the putrescent face of the outlaw frightened as many people in death as its owner had in life. The skull created great interest in Waterford and its surrounding counties and many people came to view it. Such was the temper of the time. The gate his head was spiked upon was a popular meeting place for those farmers who brought their milk to the markets of Waterford. It is recorded that after a few days the head became putrid and drops of foul matter began to fall into the milk-cans below. It was quite a while before anyone noticed – much to the disgust of all who had been drinking the milk.

After her husband's execution Mary Crotty poured out her heart in a *caoineadh* (lament) entitled "Crotty's Lament", which for years afterwards was sung in the Waterford and Tipperary areas.

Despite the fact that she was pregnant, Mary at once took up where her husband had left off and carried out some daring deeds of villainy in her own right. She, too, was proclaimed an outlaw and a price was put on her head.

She gave birth while on the run in the Comeraghs but the unfortunate child died shortly afterwards from malnutrition and fever. Broken-hearted, lonely and demoralised, Mary was hounded night and day, and eventually cornered near Crotty's Lake. Surrounded by troops, the demented widow swore that she would not be taken alive to suffer the same fate as her husband. She climbed to the top of Crotty's Rock and leaped to her death.

The traitor David Norris, the former weaver, was freed in return for informing on his comrades. He died in his own bed a lonely and bitter man, ostracised by the people who had once considered him one of their champions and who revered Crotty's memory.

Crotty's Treasure

William Crotty lived a life that seemed, at times, charmed. It is only fitting, therefore, that he should have left some of this enchantment behind in his beloved Comeragh Mountains. The vicinity Crotty ranged over is rich in stories now passed into legend.

One such tale relates how the outlaw spoke from the gallows in Irish and divulged the whereabouts of his buried treasure to the Comeragh people in the crowd. He is reputed to have said that a fortune in gold and silver lay buried on Tomas Paid's mountain, beneath a stone bearing the mark of a horseshoe. Another local tale would have us believe that a family by the name of Quinlan discovered the treasure. There were reports of large amounts of gold seen in their house.

Rumours still persist of a "shoe of gold" which the outlaw was supposed to have flung into the river at Kilballyquilty.

Not least interesting of the stories still put about are those concerning Crotty's ghost. It is said that those venturing into the Comeraghs in search of the outlaw's gold are confronted by an apparition, dressed and armed like an outlaw, seated on a white horse. Many such sightings have been reported by people travelling through those mountains at night.

Crotty's Lament (Air)

Crotty's Lament

Wil - liam Crot - ty   I

have of - ten told___ you Th-at   Da - vid

Nor - ris would come___ ar - ound___

you, In your bed, when you__ lay

sleep- ing,__ A - nd leave___ me__

here in sor - row_ wee - ping__.

Och___ hone, och___ hone, och__

hone,_____ oh!

He wet your powder, he stole your arms,
And left you helpless amidst alarms,
My bitter curse on him and his,
That brought you to an end like this.

Chorus: Och hone, och hone, och hone, oh!

Oh, the judge but he was cruel,
Refused a long day to my jewel,
Sure I thought that you would maybe
See the face of your poor baby.

Chorus

But temples gold and traitors greedy
Have left the poor and lowly needy;
'Twas you that heard the widow sighing,
'Twas you that heard the orphan crying.

Chorus

Strong, brave and true and kind to woman,
Yet fierce and dread to Saxon foeman,
As thou tonight in gaol you're sleeping,
And oh, I'm left in sorrow weeping.

Chorus

O'er Coumshingaun the dark clouds gather,
You'll sleep no more among the heather,
Through Comeragh's hills night winds are sighing,
Where oft you sent the red coats flying.

Chorus

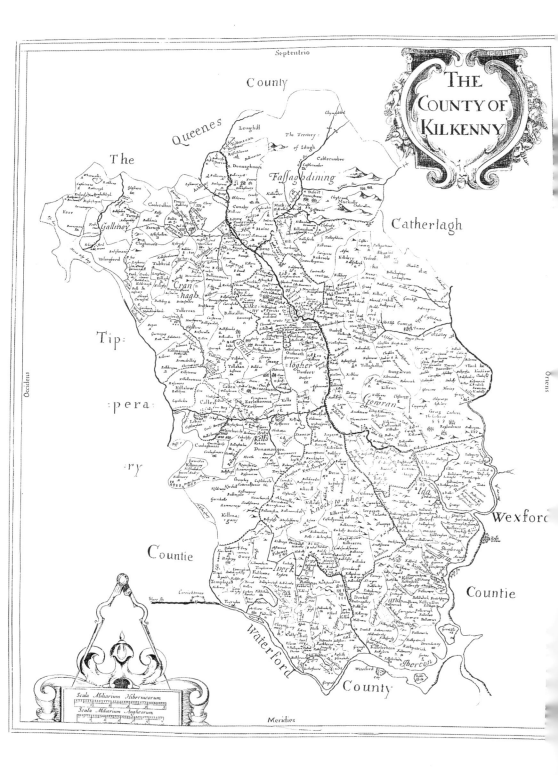

THE
COUNTY OF
KILKENNY

County

Queenes

The

Lewghill

Clogshill

The Territory
of Idogh

Castlecumbr

Faffagodining

Gallmoy

Catherlagh

The

Tip:

Cran-
hagh

:pera:

-logher

Glenran

:ry

Kells

Knock:to:pher

Ida

Wexford

Countie

Iberk

Countie

and

Waterford

Ibercon

County

Occidens

Oriens

Scala Miliarium Hibernicorum
Scala Miliarium Anglicorum

James Freney

Captain Freney

There are at least two Captain Freneys. The first conforms to every cliché involving the Irish highwayman explored so far in these pages. He was an Irish Robin Hood; he robbed the rich and was the champion of the poor. He was a gentleman rogue and a sure shot. In fact, so popular did Freney become that the respected composer Percy French wrote a very successful comic opera in which the outlaw figured as the hero.[lxxxix]

James Freney has been called one of the noblest of all the Irish highwaymen. It is written that he never robbed or harmed the poor, often returning a purse when he discovered its owner faced a sad plight. He never left any traveller stranded on the highway, and always made sure to leave even his wealthy victims with enough money to continue on to their destination.

The other Freney is at huge variance with this noble character. Accounts of the outlaw depict a man who did not have much in the way of gentlemanly behaviour or manners, and whose appearance could not be called dignified. He has been described as a mean-looking fellow, marked by smallpox, and blind in one eye. It is recorded that because of this last injury the name "Freney" became a sobriquet for any unfortunate of the time who had lost an eye.

The real Captain Freney can in all likelihood be found somewhere between these two extremes, yet it can be said with certainty that he was anything but an ordinary man. The life he led was far removed from the commonplace.

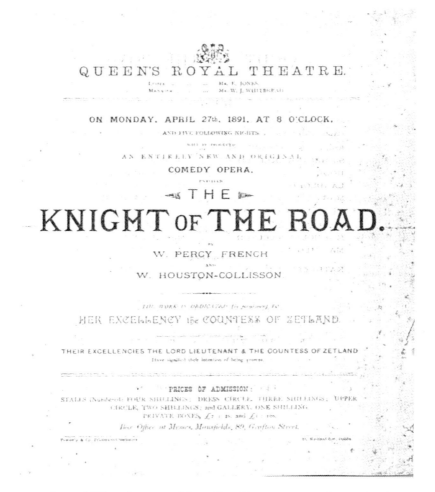

Program cover for an 1891 performance of Percy French's comic opera "The Knight of the Road".

James Freney was born in County Kilkenny, in or about 1730. He is said to have been descended from the aristocratic Anglo-Norman de Freynes of Ballyreddy, a once-powerful Catholic family that had fallen on hard times; however, it is possible that this is a fabrication put about by the outlaw himself.

James' father, an honest and hardworking man, was a servant in the household of a Mr Robbins of Ballyduff, a local landlord. When the boy was old enough to work – and in eighteenth-century Ireland that meant around the age of five or six – he, too, was employed in the Robbins household. It was a life of unrelenting drudgery and, probably, of unpaid labour. The bondage, or villeinage, system still operated at this time throughout Europe; whole families toiled almost as slaves for a "master" in return for holdings of land. James' father would have received some little money in wages from his landlord-employer but his sons would not have been so generously rewarded.

Hard work and a lowly position did not suit young James and, as he grew older and more put upon, he discovered other methods of making a living that did not include blacking boots, scouring pots and pans, or doffing the hat to the local gentry. A youth who led such a miserable existence was apt to turn to anything that would alleviate the tedium. It is known that the young James Freney had a precocious and incorrigible fondness for cock-fighting, hurling and gambling. Possibly his need to fund this last pastime led to his first act of lawlessness, a robbery in Ballyduff. It was to change his life.

It was Christmas 1746 and James could not have been older than sixteen. There was a group of boys involved, most likely all employees of Mr Robbins': James Bulger, who was to become the future Captain Freney's right-hand man, John Stack, John Larissey and Patrick Hackett. The five raided the home of a friend and neighbour of their landlord, a Colonel Palliser, and stole nearly £200 in cash, a quantity of plate and some items of jewellery.[xc] They were masked and armed.

But James Freney bungled it. As he and the lads were making off with the booty, the scarf covering his face slipped. The Colonel, who had often encountered James at the Robbins estate, recognised him at once. The victim hastened to the authorities and provided a detailed description. James and his accomplices were outlawed and had no option but to take to the hills and highways.

Spies, Ransoms and Brave Deeds

The little band of five were forced to learn the "trade" quickly and over time developed into archetypal highwaymen, making the roads unsafe for the prosperous while taking great care never to rob or mistreat the less fortunate. It was not long before James Freney acquired that most coveted of titles: that of "Captain".

The quintet were immensely successful and became more outrageous in their methods with the passing of time. James developed a modus operandi that was intended to induce terror in his victims. The gang would earmark a house for robbing; Freney would then go to a forge in the area and requisition a sledge hammer. Once at the selected house, he would – without warning – batter in the door or windows. Then he and his confederates would rush in and relieve the terrified occupants of their valuables. By all accounts they frightened their victims so much that the robbers rarely encountered any resistance.

Freney was a clever and resourceful man in the Richard Power mould. He employed spies and informants in most of the major business houses in the surrounding counties, who would alert "the Captain" to the transport of large amounts of goods. Primed with such inside information, Captain Freney would plan the ambushes meticulously and pounce suddenly, commandeering the wagons, carts and goods. His favourite ploy was to dispatch a driver back to his employer with a ransom note. A place and time for exchange of monies for the stolen goods would be arranged: it was a very lucrative trade.

It was also a dangerous undertaking, this holding of the victim to ransom. A lesser man than Captain Freney might have contented himself with disposing of the booty among the outlaw fraternity. To continue dealing with the victim after the robbery was to invite trouble. It was inevitable, then, that this was what developed for the Captain and his comrades.

Five heavily laden carts were trundling their way from Waterford city to Thomastown, County Kilkenny, when Freney's gang, having been tipped off about the route, struck. The drivers, not willing to become dead heroes at the hands of Captain Freney and prompted by the sight of an assortment of cocked pistols and blunderbusses, dutifully surrendered their loads.

Freney surveyed the haul with an experienced eye and quickly assessed its value. He sent one of the unhappy drivers back to Waterford with a ransom note demanding the enormous sum of £100. The rest of the outlaws bound the carters and settled down to await the outcome.

What Captain Freney did not know was that one of his spies had been unmasked. The spy had, under duress, revealed the full extent of the Captain's plan – right down to the place and time of the surprise attack. In consequence, the wagon train had set out from Waterford followed at a short distance by a sizeable militia escort and armed local merchants,[xci] all sworn to put an end to the outlawry.

Patrick Hackett was acting as lookout and it was he who spotted the column of heavily armed riders fast approaching. He alerted Captain Freney, who at once issued orders for the gang to split up. Each was to ride off in a different direction, he said, to outfox and divide the oncoming forces.

The Captain was the first to draw the soldiers away from the main group. In full view of the oncoming militia, he emerged from the hiding place and galloped off in the direction of a nearby mountain. The militia commander recognised him and ordered his men to give chase. The highwayman reached the rocky slopes long before his pursuers, dismounted and continued on foot, armed with pistols and musket.

He found a ledge beneath an overhanging boulder, concealed by whin and heather, and decided it was a good place to hide. He crawled in and lay motionless, his musket across his chest. The militia diligently began to comb the area. The day was warm; tired and forced to remain immobile, Captain Freney drifted into sleep. As the search continued, a young trooper examining the undergrowth close to where the fugitive was lying thought he heard the sound of snoring. Listening closely, he found the hiding place and the sleeping outlaw.

But this was the infamous Captain Freney and the young man was a mere raw recruit. Instead of challenging the outlaw himself, the soldier hurried to his commander. The officer flew into action and the crevice was surrounded.

"Open fire!" ordered the commander and a volley was loosed.

James awoke to the reports of musket fire and balls peppering the rock and ground around him. He refused to move and continued to lie quite still, not returning fire.

"Fire!" ordered the officer a second time, and his men obeyed.

Somewhere in the region of forty balls had been fired. The commanding officer, not detecting any movement from within, was satisfied that the target had been put out of commission. He ordered that the highwayman, presumed dead, be dragged from his lair. Two young troopers crawled in and, grabbing a leg apiece, began pulling out Captain Freney.

All of a sudden the "dead" man jumped up, armed with musket and pistol, and lusting for blood. The wildness of his appearance coupled with the fearsomeness of his reputation put the fear of God into the young troopers. As one, they downed arms and fled in terror, much to their commander's disgust. While panic gripped the hunters, the hunted ran at breakneck speed back the way he and the militiamen had come.

There was a horse grazing in a field at the foot of the mountain, perhaps belonging to the officer who had dismounted for the search. Freney quickly cut the horse's ties and sprang onto it, galloping hell for leather towards the nearby river Nore. On reaching its bank, however, he discovered that the river was in flood, swirling with fast and dangerous currents. James was in a dilemma; but his pursuers were close behind and there really was not any other choice. He put spurs to the horse and urged it into the treacherous waters. He had gambled well: horse and rider made it safely to the opposite bank, just as a volley of shots crashed out harmlessly behind them.

The Tailor and the Poet

When considering the career of Captain Freney, it is important to remember that he was a man who lived by his own rules. These could be strange indeed.

He once got word that a Quaker had passed by his area. The Captain, smelling easy game, mounted his horse and soon overtook the traveller. He ordered him to stand and deliver. The Quaker took from his pockets some gold, silver – and a thimble.

The outlaw enquired why the well-dressed gentleman was carrying such an item.

"I am a tailor," the man replied.

The Captain at once returned the money and the thimble.

"You have not been robbed by James Freney," he told the traveller, "for I do not rob tailors, but men."[xcii]

On another occasion it happened that a poet by the name of Eamonn Wall was travelling along the main road between Cork and Kilkenny. As he approached a remote spot he was accosted by Captain Freney, who had his pistol pointed and cocked.

"Hand me any money you have," demanded the highwayman.

"I have not a ha'penny of money, sonny," said the poet. "Come here and search me if you suppose I have."

Freney did not often receive such an invitation and looked at him in surprise. Then he smiled. "Whether you have any money or not, there is not much sign of it on you. But I see you have new boots, wherever you got them."

He looked down at the old worn shoes on his own feet. "I imagine," he said, "that those new boots would suit me. Take them off you."

The poet did as he was bid.

"Now throw them over," instructed Freney, "and draw back a piece."

When the poet had complied and moved away, Freney took off his shoes and put on the man's new boots. He then stood up and tried them out to see how they suited him before pronouncing them lovely altogether.

"They suit me as well as if they were made for me. Here," he said, throwing his old shoes to the poet, "let you have them ones."

The poet put on the old shoes and was allowed to set off about his business. He related the tale of the robbery to another poet, who made this verse:

> "I'm sorry and sad for the fear you took, Eamonn,
> Like a cold-footed yokel with the knees of him caving–
> We were holding the opinion that you'd stand against eighty,
> But here you go and throw over your new boots to Bold Freney."

The story and verse travelled fast from mouth to mouth. When Eamonn himself heard the tongue-in-cheek rhyme, he gave this somewhat more sober answer:

"Your Poetry, young Poet, 'tis cutting you've made it!
It was no fear came o'er me to set my knees quaking,
But a rogue of the road, with a bullet constrained me—
Who set store on my soul as worthless than a ha'penny."

Honour among Thieves

Only the gullible believe in the notion of honour among thieves. Every outlaw had his price and Captain Freney's partners in crime were no exception: avarice got the better of James' once-staunch and true comrades. Stack, Larissey and Hackett informed on one another and on associates of their band. Freney later recounted that when some of the gang were confined in Naas Gaol they forced a bolt on a window and sent a message to him to come to their rescue. Freney believed that this was a ploy to capture him, so he did not answer their entreaty. The prisoners were hanged in succession and the gang disbanded. Only one member remained with Freney: his trusted right-hand man, James Bulger.

The authorities were well satisfied by this rash of executions, believing that the threat was eradicated and that the highways were safe again. They decided to consolidate their success by offering the people's much-admired hero a pardon,[xciii] with one condition attached: Freney must betray his allies and any remaining gang members.

The offer backfired spectacularly. The outlaw scornfully rejected it and became twice as active. He was, however, more vulnerable now, having only the support of James Bulger. The two men were no match for the combined forces of army, militia and yeomanry.

In the year 1748 a sheriff from Kilkenny City, one Henry Burgess, got word from an informer that Freney and Bulger were sojourning in a house near the Desart demesne. Having mobilised a strong, well-armed band of fourteen men, the sheriff set out to capture the great Captain Freney. They almost succeeded, as the outlaw recounted in his autobiography.

"Around nine o'clock, I went and awoke James Bulger, desiring him to get up and guard me whilst I slept, as I had guarded him all night. He said he would and then I went to bed charging him to watch close lest we be surprised. I put my blunderbuss and two cases of pistols under my head and soon fell asleep. Two hours after, the servant girl of the house, seeing an enemy coming into the yard, ran up to the room where we were and said there were a hundred [sic] men coming into

The 18th century rifle known as "Freyney's Blunderbuss".

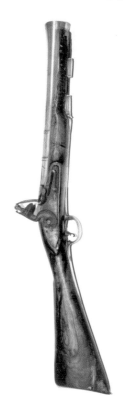

the yard, upon which Bulger awoke me, and taking my blunderbuss, I fired a shot towards the door which wounded Mr Burgess and of which wound he died. They concluded to set the house in fire about us, which they accordingly did; upon which I took my fusee [a short musket] in one hand, and a pistol in the other, and Bulger did the like. As we came out of the door we fired on all sides, imaging it to be the best method of dispersing the enemy who were on both sides of the door. We got through them, but they fired after us, and as Bulger was leaping over a ditch he received a shot in the leg, which rendered him incapable of running; but getting into a field where I had a ditch between me and the enemy, I still walked along with Bulger till I thought the enemy were within shot of the ditch, and then wheeled back to the ditch and presented my fusee to them. They all drew back and went for their horses to ride round the field, which was wide open, and without cover except the ditch."

Captain Freney, knowing that the sheriff's men were closing in, stood bravely by Bulger, who by now was unable to walk. As the enemy bore down, the mud-covered outlaw rushed them, panicking them into a momentary retreat. He seized the opportunity to lift Bulger onto his back and clambered over the demesne wall. He headed for a nearby wood and hid with his wounded comrade in the undergrowth.

The soldiers regrouped and resumed the chase. Freney and Bulger knew that both could not escape while one was seriously wounded, and Bulger insisted on staying behind. He was weak from loss of blood, but determined to keep the hunters at bay until his friend and comrade made good his escape. James Bulger put up a fierce resistance but, inevitably, was captured and brought to Kilkenny Gaol.

When his wounds had healed and he had recovered sufficiently to be tried at court, Bulger was found guilty of the murder of Sheriff Burgess. He was executed and his body gibbeted in chains on the road to Callan, at the very spot where Burgess had breathed his last. Bulger's corpse was stolen the same night; James Freney is believed to have taken the body of his friend to a place where he could be given a decent and dignified burial.

The Noose Denied

It is difficult to know what to make of Captain Freney's account of Bulger's capture, and of the heroism he displayed when trying to save his comrade. Cynics insist that he sacrificed his friend for his own safety and delivered Bulger into the arms of the law in return for a pardon. The awkward fact is that Captain Freney was indeed pardoned. It is, therefore, entirely possible that his version of events was a fabrication designed to mask self-serving treachery.

He obtained his pardon with the assistance of a Lord Carrick, who was said to be returning a favour. Many outlaws of that time ended their lives at the end of a rope or by other violent means, but not the notorious Captain Freney. He lived out the remainder of his days as water-bailiff for New Ross, County Wexford. It is not known whether the degree of salmon poaching in the locality diminished as a result of his appointment.

The erstwhile highwayman lived to be a ripe old age and died a natural death. He is buried in the churchyard of Innistiogue, not far from the place of his birth. His memory has not faded from local lore: on the main road between Clonmel and Kilkenny, the scene of so many of his robberies, stands an elm still known as Freney's Tree.[xciv]

Bold Captain Freney

One—— morn - ing fair, being
free from care, I—— rode a- broad to take the air, 'Twas
my for - tune for to spy A jol - ly Qua- ker
rid - ing—— by; And it's oh, bold Cap - tain Fre-
-ney! Oh, bold Fre - ney, oh!

Said the Quaker – "I'm very glad
That I have met with such a lad;
There is a robber on the way,
Bold Captain Freney, I hear them say."

Chorus: And it's oh, bold Captain Freney!
Oh, bold Freney, oh!

"Captain Freney I disregard,
Although about me I carry my charge;
Because I being so cunning and cute,
It's where I hide, it's within my boot."

Chorus

Says the Quaker – "It is a friend
His secret unto me would lend;
I'll tell you now where my gold does lie –
I have it sewed beneath my thigh."

Chorus

As we rode down towards Thomastown,
Bold Freney bid me to 'light down.
"Kind sir, your breeches you must resign;
Come, quick, strip off, and put on mine,

For I am bold Captain Freney, etc.

Says the Quaker, "I did not think
That you'd play me such a roguish trick
As my breeches I must resign,
I think you are no friend of mine."

Chorus

As we rode a little on the way,
We met a tailor dressed most gay;
I boldly bid him for to stand,
Thinking he was some gentleman.

Chorus

Upon his pockets I laid hold –
The fist thing I got was a purse of gold;
The next thing I found, which did me
surprise,
Was a needle, thimble and chalk
likewise.

Chorus

"Your dirty trifle I disdain."
With that I return'd him his gold again.
"I'll rob no tailor if I can –
I'd rather ten times rob a man."

Chorus

It's time for me to look about;
There's a proclamation just gone out;
There's fifty pounds bid on my head,
To bring me in alive or dead.

Chorus

Come All Ye Fine Ladies

Come, all ye fine lad-ies and

gen-tle-men, too, At - tend to me sing-in' and

I'll tell ye true   A - bout a   brave boy who lived

out in the cold, And the name that he   went by   was

Chorus

"Free - ny   the   Bold." Tur-in-ah,   tur-in-

-ah,____   tur-in-an-the-dan-day. Now

Jack was a rob-ber u - pon the high-way   And

stopped   the   mail   coa - ches   be

night and be day; What he took from the rich he would

give to the poor, So   of Pov-er - ty's bless-in' he

al - ways was sure.

(From "The Knight of The Road" (later called "The Irish Girl"), a Comedy Opera)

One day when the coach had set off for the fair,
It was met be Jack Freeny bestridin' his mare:
Some called for the soldiers, some called for the watch
And one old lady called for two-penn' worth of Scotch.

Chorus: Tur-in-ah, tur-in-ah, tur-in-an-the-dan-day.

The guard held his blunderbuss out on full cock,
Sez he, "Jack, clear out, or you'll know what's o'clock."
Jack flattened him out wid the butt of his gun,
Sez he, "What's o'clock? Well, it's just strikin' one."

Chorus

So the gentlemen pulled out their purses of gold,
And handed them over to Freeny the Bold:
Sez Freeny, "Me boys, ye got off mighty well,
I'd ha' fleeced ye far more if I'd keep an hotel."

Chorus

Now, all ye fine ladies and gintlemen, too,
Ye've heard from my singin'—and I've told ye true,
All about the brave boy who lived out in the cold,
And the name that he went be was "Freeny the Bold."

Chorus

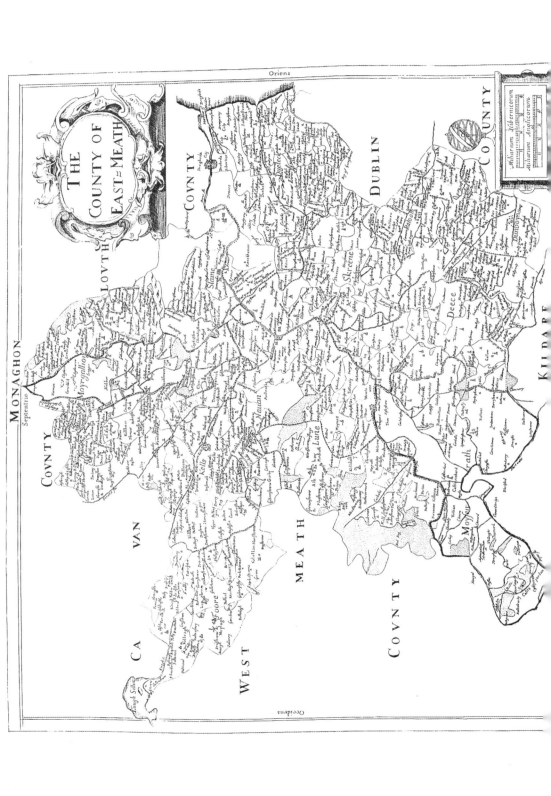

Michael Collier

Collier the Robber

The birth of Michael Collier in 1780 brings the history of Ireland's high-waymen into the modern era. Two years earlier, the Catholic Relief Act had ended many of the gross injustices imposed by the penal laws. No longer would Catholics be required to pay tithes and consideration was being given to the abolition of hearth taxes. Henry Grattan was campaigning for even broader freedoms; there was even talk of Home Rule. Europe was heading for an era of enlightenment; the Americans were fighting for their independence; France was getting set to overthrow her monarchy and before the century ended she would be sending soldiers to help Ireland stage her own rising.

But for Ireland's highwaymen, those men "out upon their keeping", society was not changing for the better. It was growing tougher to stay one step ahead of the law and, before the century ended, it would grow more difficult still. Prior to 1770 there were only about 10,000 British troops stationed in the country; by 1800 the number was close to 60,000, mainly as a result of the 1798 rebellion. Worse, perhaps, for the Catholic outlaw was the fact that by the latter part of the century the British army was actively recruiting from amongst his co-religionists.

Outlying areas of the country remained as remote and inaccessible as they had been in Elizabethan times, but the network of main roads had advanced steadily since the 1730s. New legislation drawn up in 1765 gave the county grand juries the power to levy a tax – the "cess" – on areas served by fresh roads. By 1780 new

market towns had grown up along the routes these roads served, bringing great prosperity to the cities and ports that lay at their termini. Coach roads linked the main
towns and at regular intervals along the routes were post towns and inns.

The rapid expansion in road building was a double-edged sword. If a highwayman robbed a party of travellers outside Carlow in early morning, then there was a
fair chance that Dublin might learn of it before sundown or that, even before this, a
detachment of troopers might have been dispatched from any number of garrisons
and barracks *en route* to hunt down the culprit. The years leading up to the turn of
the century were to give rise to a new breed of highwayman, one who moved – quite
literally – with the times and the spirit of the age.

Michael Collier was born in the townland of Lisdoran, near the hill of Bellewstown,
County Meath. He was the son of a small farmer and at the age of thirteen was sent
to work as a farm servant on the estate of Richard Murtagh, who lived near Pilltown.
Records are scant about this period of his life; it is known only that Michael became
leader of a party of juveniles whose greatest claim to fame was the robbery of fruit
and vegetables from the garden of a local mansion. By this act Michael Collier served
to introduce a caution into the local lexicon: *see what became of Collier after he robbed
the garden.*

From this small beginning came the man who as a highwayman tested the mettle
of the civil and military power in the province of Leinster, and beyond, for many
years afterwards.

Michael outgrew Murtagh's employment, and found work locally as a carter,
travelling to Dublin and Drogheda, transporting goods. That these goods were not
always acquired by legitimate means soon became obvious. Michael had discovered
"an early predilection for other people's property by appropriating sundry ducks,
geese and other fowl to his own use".

It could not last; tongues began to wag and accusations were made. Michael
jumped before he was pushed – or, indeed, flung – into gaol and went to work as a
labourer in the foundry of John O'Farrell of Drogheda. It was while employed here
that he came into contact with characters somewhat more unsavoury than robbers of
orchards and traffickers in stolen fowl. Michael made the acquaintance of several
highwaymen, members of various gangs who rendered the roads around Drogheda
and Dublin unsafe for travel. He had found his true vocation.

Michael Collier related his reasons for embarking on a life of crime to a Drogheda
solicitor in 1849. The lawyer's account of this visit makes for intriguing reading. The
outlaw had been experiencing "wife trouble" and had come to the solicitor for advice.

"Michael Collier, the once notorious highwayman, came to my office, in 1849, for professional advice respecting a charge of bigamy to which he feared he was liable. His first wife (whom he married about thirty-five or thirty-eight years previously) was at the time in the Drogheda poor house; and it seems, notwithstanding, he had married a widow in the town of Navan, who had kept a public house. Whether the whiskey afforded too strong a temptation for Collier, or his drafts on her resources were too often repeated, I cannot recollect, but a quarrel arose between them and Collier had come to Drogheda to get some documents signed by his first wife, that would tend to shield him from any proceedings that might be instituted against him by his new love."

The highwayman was approaching seventy at this time, yet was still a formidable man. The solicitor goes on to give a description of the outlaw, from which we can construe how he might have appeared as a young man.

"Collier, then a dauntless and powerful man, exhibiting all the marks of great muscular powers; and though it was evident his best days had passed away; he yet seemed like an oak that braved the storm and stood the shock of time, defiant as ever. He was upwards of six feet high, and nearly fourteen stone weight, extremely broad in shoulders and made proportionately."

We have another description, written about 1820, that tallies well with this. The author was W.F. Wakeman, the Navan local historian.

"He was a strapping fellow, loose limbed, thin and muscular, and standing over six feet in height. He dressed well, always wore knee-breeches, a blue tail-coat with brass buttons, a canary-coloured vest, and white cravat. In the latter days he became strongly addicted to the bottle."

The Drogheda solicitor's account continued:

"It was the first time I had spoken to him, and I found him of a communicative disposition, relating his adventures as if they were matters of history, for which he could by no means be now made amenable to justice.

He was desirous, however, that he should be looked upon as a member of the social body, rather than an individual beyond the pale of society. He had nothing of the monstraidigeto turn.[xcv] I requested him to sit to a portrait painter (Mr Tumalti, of Drogheda) for me, that I might possess his likeness; but he shrank from the proposition with evident disgust. He said he would not have his likeness paraded in every shop window; and all I could say to the contrary — was without effect, as he still persisted in his refusal.

Being desirous to find out what was the first step he made into that series of crimes which tended to make his name so great a terror, he informed me that it was a woman caused all his trouble, and led him first to violate the law. He had 'taken up' with a young woman of whom he was extremely fond. She had, however, very bad connections, her father and three brothers being professional thieves. Having stolen a horse, and being arrested for the felony, they sent her to Collier, in order to obtain his assistance in regaining their liberty. Urged by her entreaties, he could not refuse; and having accompanied her to a public house, where the parties and their escort were resting on their way to Trim gaol, Collier liberally treated the constables to drink.

Having conveyed files to the prisoners in order that they might free themselves from their handcuffs, and the constables having become intoxicated, they were easily overcome and the prisoners rescued. He had after this to take to the hills, and in a short time he stated that he was enabled, on the booty taken by him, to live like a prince. He related with great bitterness how this very woman afterwards deceived him by going off with another."

Whether or not this was truly how Michael Collier was launched into crime, he took to it as a duck to water and found the life of a highwayman to be more congenial than one of honest toil.

He ranged over the counties Meath, Louth, Kildare and Dublin, and sometimes even farther afield. In his heyday he was the leader of a gang of tough, daredevil outlaws whose deeds were spoken of around the firesides of rich and poor. Huge rewards were offered for his apprehension and he was eventually arrested by Viscount Gormanstown and a party of his yeomanry. Collier's captors delivered him to the authorities in Drogheda. He was tried at the Trim Assizes, found guilty and sentenced to death.

Escape from the Gallows

Michael had once saved two men from the rope with the aid of a file and it was this instrument that enabled his own rescue – along with the help of a young woman. The night before his execution she was allowed to visit him in his cell. Somehow she slipped him the file that he used in the early hours of the morning to free himself from his irons. He next used the tool to remove all but one of the bars of the window and then tore the bedclothes into strips to make a rope.

It was a classic method of escape. He tied the makeshift rope to the only remaining window bar and lowered himself as far as it would allow, before dropping to the ground. The river Boyne flowed adjacent to the gaol and Collier plunged in without hesitation. Despite being shot at by the sentries, he managed to swim safely to the far bank and made good his escape. It was a daring exploit and it endeared the outlaw to the common people, who began to look upon him as a hero.

Undeterred by his brush with death, Michael Collier resumed his career and was soon robbing mail coaches, private carriages, comfortable mansions, and wealthy cattle dealers on their way to fairs and markets. He did not discriminate, but had one proviso: his victims had to be rich.

Depending on the circumstances, Collier would operate alone or with the assistance of his gang. He never committed murder, but did kill one man in an act of self defence. It happened one night while Collier and a number of gang members were robbing the house of a Mathew Ennis of Claristown, County Meath.

Collier always insisted on his men behaving well towards the servants of a household – they were, after all, their "own" people. On this occasion, however, a gang member by the name of Woods mistreated one of the young maids. The leader said nothing about it while the "work" was in progress, but bided his time until they had made good their escape and were heading for the Big Tree inn at Claristown. Collier ordered the men to halt and, going to Woods, struck him a blow, knocking him to the ground.

"You're no longer a member of this gang," he said.

Furious, Woods retorted that he would avenge the insult by informing on Collier and the other gang members. A scuffle broke out between the two outlaws: weapons were drawn and Collier shot Woods dead. The outlaws brought the body to Mullagh Teeling and buried it – a dishonourable man had met an ignominious end. It was not until 1816 that some farmers came across Woods' remains while planting potatoes.

Collier's Noble Heart

In his day Michael Collier robbed thousands of pounds – and spent most of it foolishly. But he was ever mindful of the poor, and had a kind and noble heart. A Carrickmacross public carrier by the name of Hugh Ward could attest to this.

Ward was robbed by a gang of thieves calling themselves Collier's Gang. When the real highwayman heard of this affront he lay in wait for Ward on his next journey. He surprised the carrier and handed him the exact amount stolen by the impostors, telling him that he was the true Collier, who *gave* to the less fortunate, rather than take from them.

The story may not be true, but the account attests to the reputation Michael Collier had acquired; he and his gang were a force to be reckoned with in north Leinster.

History is indebted to another solicitor, a Mr Bell of Dublin, who left an excellent description of how the highwayman went about robbing the Dublin mail coach at The Naul, on the outskirts of the city.

Mr Bell relates that he was on his way to the Armagh and Monaghan Assizes, and was carrying £800. He was acutely aware of the Collier gang's activities in the area and therefore concealed £750 of his money in the bottom of a bag, leaving only £50 in his purse. At the approach to the townland known as The Naul, the coach came to a halt and the passengers saw that their path was barred. Armed men lined the road and, on an order from their leader, the outlaws massed in front of the coach.

"Stand and deliver!" ordered Michael Collier, and a general panic ensued.

Some of the female passengers screamed in terror, while others fainted. To his credit Collier dispelled the travellers' fears, to some extent, by assuring them that no harm would befall them. All he wanted from them, he said, was their valuables.

The outlaws robbed all the male passengers, taking money, jewellery and clothes from their persons and their travelling trunks; the women were left alone on this occasion. Mr Bell handed over his purse containing the £50 but managed to keep his bag with the hidden £750. He told Michael Collier that it contained briefs connected with the trials of poor unfortunate prisoners that he would be defending. The highwayman took the solicitor at his word and was thus deprived of one of the biggest hauls of his career.

It was also one of the last robberies that Collier would commit in Ireland for a long time to come. Having pocketed the spoils from the mail coach, the outlaws split up and made off in different directions. Michael Collier headed north and broke into the house of a Mr Hurst, who lived in the vicinity of Dunleer. He hid out there for a few days until the search for him died down, holding the unfortunate man and his servants prisoner. Despite being intimidated by the outlaw, however, Hurst behaved most civilly.

A few weeks later the same victim was returning from Dunleer with a large sum of money when he was surprised on Glyde Farm Road and robbed by Michael Collier and two of his gang. As the outlaws turned their mounts to leave, Collier recognised his former "host" and remembered the fine hospitality he had enjoyed. Without hesitation he returned the stolen cash and apologised to Mr Hurst. As he was about to take his leave, Hurst invited Collier and his two comrades back to his home. The group passed the night in a most convivial manner.

This show of affability did not dissuade the authorities from declaring the highwayman a public nuisance and demanding his capture at all costs. Collier resolved to depart the area until things settled down.

The Fugitive Abroad

He set his sights on England, funding his passage by disguising himself as a jockey and attending the Ballinasloe fair, where he purchased several thoroughbred horses. They fetched a high price in England and Collier lived for a time very comfortably on the proceeds. The funds were spent all too quickly, however, reportedly on "riotous dissipation", and Collier resumed his profession on the highways of England for a short time.

It appears that the horse trade was to his liking, for he was to cross the Irish Sea for this purpose more than once.[xcvi] For a time Collier made his home in Carlisle, where he kept up a regular trade in stolen horses brought from Ireland.

He met with mixed success. On the one hand he was unknown to the English authorities and could pass as a respectable horse trader, while continuing to indulge in his favourite pursuit: highway robbery. Oddly enough, though, the pickings were not as rich as they were at home. He discovered, too, that security was tighter and more organised than he had been accustomed to facing, and this hampered his efforts. He returned to Ireland to take his chances on more familiar ground.

At home Collier was still a wanted man, however, and before too long he realised that his return to old haunts had been premature. He was not safe anywhere. An acquaintance suggested to him that Scotland might be to his liking. In order to secure the necessary funds for his sojourn there, Collier headed for Dublin to implement a two-step plan. First, he robbed a wealthy Quaker in DunLeary (now Dún Laoghaire), relieving the gentleman of a large quantity of bank notes, which he exchanged for gold with a "fence" in the area. Anxious not to arouse suspicion by his manner of dress, Collier outfitted himself with a whole new wardrobe. When he set out for Belfast to book passage for Scotland, he appeared every inch the gentleman farmer. On his arrival in Belfast, he robbed the city bank in a most fearsome manner, terrifying staff and customers alike and making off with a considerable sum in notes and coin. Thus supplied, Collier then made a quick getaway to Scotland.

Once again Collier's lust for the high life soon made a hole in his "savings". The old ways beckoned and he took to the highways of his adoptive country. Accounts of his life at this time are sketchy, but it appears that he married a woman in Glasgow, left her shortly afterwards, and joined an infantry regiment (though perhaps the cavalry might have been a better choice for a former highwayman). Collier was not long in appreciating his mistake because he deserted soon after, taking with him the bounty granted to him for enlisting.

The next accounts of Collier's exploits find him once more back in Ireland. Evidently, his long absence had lulled the authorities of north Leinster into a false sense of security.

The Return of the Fugitive

Michael did not rush headlong back into his outlaw ways. He settled in the Newry area and lived a relatively peaceful and uneventful life for several months.

His initial crime involved the local excise officer. There was a brisk poteen-distilling trade in the locality, and Michael approached the officer with some "valuable information". All the man need do was proceed to a certain place with a body of military, arrest the culprits and seize their illegal still.

The Newry river.

But Michael followed the authorities at a safe distance and waited until they had tethered their horses near the place in question. While the officer and his men were engaged in the search, the outlaw stole their horses and set off for Monaghan town, where he removed the animals' military insignia and sold them.

Buoyed by this success, Collier gathered together some of his old comrades and set out to rob the Derry mail coach. This was familiar territory; he was accomplished at this type of ambush and expected matters to run smoothly.

One of the coach guards was pluckier than the usual men so assigned. The gang had disarmed their victims and were busy rifling the luggage of the passengers when this particular guard produced a second, concealed, weapon and opened fire. Pandemonium broke out; more weapons were discharged; lead flew and one of Collier's accomplices fell dead. Moments later, the sound of an approaching carriage was heard. Collier gave the order to retreat and the outlaws were forced to leave the body of their comrade behind on the road.

The corpse was brought to Drogheda and left lying in the market square, in full view of all and sundry, in order that it might be identified and claimed. Nobody came forward, but this was not surprising; a person coming to claim the body of a dead outlaw risked being arrested and gaoled as an accomplice. Eventually, a local labourer named Murphy buried the corpse in a lime grave near the town rampart.

Michael Collier had been identified as the leader of the band behind the abortive raid. Now that it was confirmed that he was back in Ireland, large rewards were posted and troops put on full alert.

The outlaw took it all in his stride and thumbed his nose at the authorities. No taking to the hills for him: only a few nights after the robbery he was seen in Drogheda town, drinking in the house of a friend. A couple of mornings after this sighting the highwayman, undoubtedly under the influence of strong drink, proceeded to taunt the forces of law even further. Mounted on an excellent hunter and carrying a long pole with a handkerchief attached, he galloped through the streets of Drogheda.

"Where," he roared at the startled burghers, "is the man who dares arrest Collier?!"

So fast did he gallop that in a few minutes he had passed through Shop Street, West Street and on by the Northern Road, leaving the watchmen and town sentries to stare after him in amazement. There had barely been time to recognise the daring, drunken outlaw, much less the opportunity to saddle up and follow him.

There seemed no end to Collier's impudence. With the region up in arms after the Drogheda escapade, he and some members of his gang robbed the Belfast mail near Dunleer, making off with a large quantity of coin and valuables. One of the passengers had been a man of some influence and news of the crime engendered outrage, especially coming so soon after the Derry mail robbery. The authorities were forced into taking immediate, drastic action.

An official named Armstrong and a regiment of Black Belts were dispatched and garrisoned in Drogheda with one aim: the capture of Michael Collier.[xcvii] They scoured the countryside, leaving no stone unturned in their search for the outlaw and his confederates. Questions were asked of many, palms were greased, and soon Armstrong's persistence was rewarded. News reached him that Collier had been seen at one of his hideouts in the vicinity of Dunleer. Armstrong mobilised the regiment and moved to intercept his prey.

But Collier got wind of their approach; he escaped just before the soldiers arrived and took off across country, making for the Boyne river on foot. The hunters were in hot pursuit, some of them on mounts. The outlaw carried no weapons but, providentially, he had with him the long pole which he had brandished during his daring dash through the streets of Drogheda. The pole enabled him to vault hedges and ditches impossible for the horses to jump. Armstrong and the other riders had to seek out gaps and gates in order to follow him, enabling the fleeing outlaw to put a little distance between himself and his pursuers.

After an hour-long, frenzied chase the exhausted outlaw arrived at a field near Oldbridge, where some labourers were picking potatoes. They immediately recognised the outlaw and, fortunately for Collier, were kindly disposed toward him. They came to the fugitive's aid in an ingenious way. They put him in a potato sack and laid him in a furrow with the others.

"Never did I experience such sensations of fear," said Collier of this adventure. "I heard the sound of approaching men, and the regular tramp of soldiers caused me to tremble. My fate was in the hands of ten or twelve persons, a large reward was offered for my apprehension, a reward that would have made them all rich for life; a nod, or motion of the hand to indicate the place I lay concealed would have been enough to have insured my capture by the crafty man who led the pursuit."

While Collier lay hidden, the soldiers questioned the potato-pickers. One of them volunteered the information that a person fitting the outlaw's description had passed in full flight towards Townly Hall only half an hour before. Armstrong led his men away in that direction and continued the search for the elusive felon. The danger past, Collier shrugged out of his sack and sent some of the workers into Drogheda for whiskey and other refreshments. When the drink was gone, the outlaw divided a sum of money between his saviours, making it the best-paid day's work they had ever done.

While Armstrong continued to comb the highways and byways of Louth and Meath, Michael Collier moved his activities further south. He took to robbing and plundering in Dublin and Kildare.

The Audacious Collier

On the old Great North Road from Dublin to Belfast, between Drumcondra and Swords, is a place called Bloody Hollow. It was the scene of an ambush of British troops by insurgents during the rebellion of 1798 – and it was here that Michael Collier robbed the Dublin-Belfast mail coach, single-handed.

Collier knew that the coach would be heavily guarded, but he also knew that most coach guards were notorious drinkers open to exploitation and intimidation.[xcviii] Drunken guards notwithstanding, to rob a coach alone was a daring, if not foolhardy, undertaking. What prompted him to do so is a mystery.

A certain amount of cunning and deception was called for. Collier gathered together a number of old hats and coats and arranged them in the hedges and ditches on both sides of the steep road rising out of Bloody Hollow. The outlaw knew that the coach had to climb the incline at a snail's pace: it was here that he would swoop. It was the middle of winter and beginning to snow. By the time the coach arrived it would be getting dark. He backed his horse into a place of concealment and awaited the coming of the coach.

The moment came. The post chaise passed through the Hollow and, as it made its slow ascent out the other side, the outlaw appeared on the road. Brandishing a brace of pistols, he demanded that the driver "stand and deliver".

As the coach came to a halt, Collier barked orders to his "men" to cover the guards and passengers. "At the first sign of resistance," he ordered, "you're to let fly with musket, pistol and blunderbuss."

Collier had actually carried out this threat when his gang robbed the Derry mail and one of his men was shot dead; the coach had been peppered with balls and shot. This deed would have been fresh in the minds of both guards and passengers. All weapons were laid aside and no resistance offered. The terrified travellers delivered up their money and valuables to the outlaw who, when his panniers were full, cut the reins of the coach, jauntily wished his victims a safe journey and galloped off in the direction of County Meath.

The following morning the "scarecrow" gang was discovered by a squadron of dragoons from Dublin, much to the embarrassment of all concerned.

Perhaps Michael Collier should have rejoined his gang; there would have been some safety in numbers. He was to learn this truth a few weeks after the mail robbery, though the lesson almost cost him his neck.

On a highway in County Meath he robbed a gentleman of his watch and purse, and repaired to The Cock public house in Gormanstown, where the proceeds of this latest robbery were drunk by one and all. Collier was feeling generous, and he

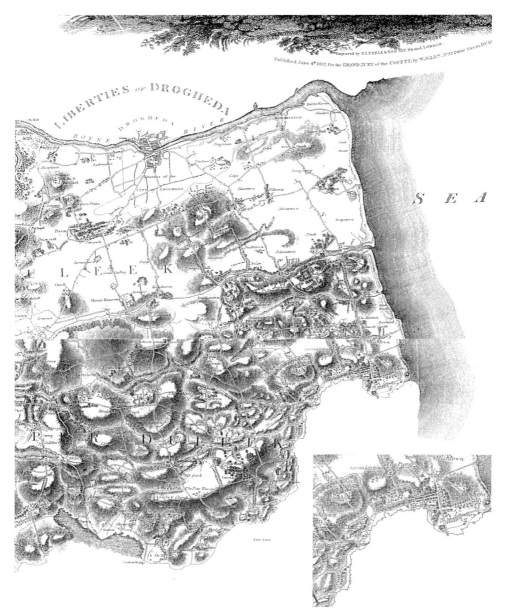

Ireland's oldest pub, The Cock Tavern in Gormanstown, where Michael Collier was captured.

lavished drink and silver on all the patrons. The gentleman's purse had been a deep one and the revelry carried on into the next day. But Gormanstown lay no more than eight miles from Drogheda, the headquarters of Collier's old adversary, Armstrong. When word that the outlaw was carousing nearby reached him, Armstrong saddled up post-haste and, accompanied by a party of constabulary, swooped down on the tavern.

Collier was taken unawares. The first he knew of his predicament was the sound of Armstrong's voice calling on him to surrender. Inebriated and flinging caution to the wind, the outlaw rushed out of the door and made for his tethered horse. He sprang into the saddle and attempted to gallop away. A volley rang out and a musket ball tore into him; he tumbled to the ground.

Despite his wound, Collier was placed in irons and seated on a jaunting car between Armstrong and Sergeant Stephen Strange, one of the constabulary. From Gormanstown he was removed to Trim Gaol, where he was imprisoned under heavy guard. He was allowed no visitors this time; Armstrong had his man at last and would not permit the slightest risk of escape.[xcix]

The Outlaw in Uniform

Collier's wound healed and he duly appeared at the Trim Assizes. He was found guilty of a series of crimes, ranging from burglary to highway robbery and murder. It might have been expected that the death penalty would await a man so judged, but it was not to be. Some say that Collier had influential friends – or perhaps had powerful men in either his debt or his pocket. In any event, he escaped "a meeting with the scrag-boy"[c] and was sentenced instead to seven years' transportation abroad. On appeal this penalty was commuted to allow Collier to enlist in one of the "condemned" regiments on the African coast, on condition that he never return to Ireland. He is also believed to have served on one of the West Indian islands, possibly Santo Domingo.

Collier refused to be drawn on the subject of why he had been allowed to join the army instead of being transported. It is known that somebody of great influence, for reasons undeclared, interceded on his behalf and saved him from the gallows – a fate which befell a number of others in his gang.[ci] Several sources suggest that the clemency was attributable to his giving private information of importance to the government. Terence O'Hanlon, author of *The Highwayman in Irish History*, is in no doubt that Collier ended his days as a "common informer", betraying Young Irelanders.[cii] He goes on to state that W.F. Wakeman, an eminent Irish antiquarian of the times, claimed that he had in his possession an old account book belonging to the County Meath Inspector of the Royal Irish Constabulary, showing payments to Collier for secret information.

Did Collier end his days a turncoat? It is hard to believe it, since all other accounts of his life portray him as a man who would not betray his comrades or countrymen.

Certainly he was no model soldier; he was flogged on a number of occasions and spent a considerable amount of time in the guardhouse.

He did not serve in the army for long. The pervasive peace of 1815 led to a reduction in troop requirements and Collier found himself discharged. Forbidden to return to Ireland, he headed for America where he travelled extensively, eventually settling for a time in South Carolina. Here he became manager and overseer of a plantation, and it was reported that he conducted himself with great humanity. Collier himself often stated that he purchased a farm in South Carolina and in later life attempted to return to the United States, only to squander his travelling funds on drink and other enjoyment. It seems that, no matter how hard he tried, he could not keep money in his pocket.

Collier the Publican

Collier eventually returned to Ireland. Whether he received a pardon in the end or slipped back clandestinely is uncertain, but it is known that he entered the country at Dublin and journeyed on to Drogheda.

It might be thought that such a man would immediately revert to old ways; instead, he became a publican. He rented premises from a friend named Mac Nally, in Ashbourne, County Meath, and soon presided over a thriving business. People would come from all over the county and beyond to marvel at the returned highwayman and enjoy his company. Collier relished the limelight and was not averse to carousing and drinking with anybody who sought him out. Life at home was good for the former exile.

So popular, in fact, did his venture become that Collier decided to celebrate the first anniversary of his return on a grand scale. He had a tent erected on the hill of Bellewstown with a banner proclaiming: *Welcome home, Collier, from America!* Drink was available in large quantities to all who were willing to pay for it.

The enterprise was a resounding success, exceeding even Collier's expectations. Eyewitnesses said that the tent was thronged to suffocation and that the amount of money made would have laid the foundation of any man's fortune. Collier at this time led an extravagant life and his money was spent as quickly as it was earned – he was a man who enjoyed life's pleasures.

Collier's prosperity was briefly interrupted by an involvement with a young servant girl. Fleeing the scandal and recriminations, he again sought refuge in Carlisle, England, and resumed his traffic in stolen horses. But the people were forgiving, in time, and the miscreant eventually returned to Ireland. He was unexpectedly well received and found himself a welcome guest at most firesides in Drogheda and Navan. There were eager audiences, young and old, for the stories of his many deeds and escapades.

Death came to north Leinster's greatest highwayman not by violent means, but by a creeping sickness. He had been to England, America and Africa; such extended travel in the early nineteenth century was not without its perils.

On August 13, 1849 Collier took ill while walking along West Street in Drogheda. He knocked on the nearest door and was admitted by a kind stranger named Edward O'Reilly, who at once recognised the celebrated outlaw. In an act of charity, he carried the sick man upstairs and put him to bed. He sent for help and two doctors, Ellis and Darby, arrived. Both these gentlemen diagnosed a case of Asiatic cholera. They declared that the sickness was spreading through Collier's body at an alarming rate, no doubt as a result of the patient's many years of wild activity and drinking. Every remedy was applied; O'Reilly supplied brandy and everything else suggested by the doctors, but all treatment proved to be of no avail.

Michael Collier died at 10.30 p.m. that evening and was buried on the following day. His remains were brought to their final resting place on an ass cart, followed by only six individuals, including the kind gentleman who had ministered to him at the end.[ciii] Collier was buried in the ancient Cemetery of the Cord, where neither stone, nor cross, nor, indeed, any kind of memorial marks the grave of one of the most celebrated of all the Irish outlaws. He was survived by his wife and daughter.[civ]

It was generally believed in Louth and Meath that, after his discharge from the army and return home, Collier collected "black rent". This was a fixed sum paid to him on a regular basis by landlords and other well-off individuals, in exchange for his protection – and for keeping his mouth shut about matters that would not bear the light of day.

These allegations have a ring of truth. Collier was a spendthrift; he was twice declared bankrupt and confined to Drogheda Gaol for this "crime". He was unscrupulous and would not have suffered pangs of conscience over income derived in this manner. Moreover, to the ordinary people, the taking of black rent was perfectly justified – as justified as robbing a rich man on the highway. Thanks to Michael Collier's famed generosity, they often had a share in both, and for this he is fondly remembered.

Hookey Loughran's Lament

Fare - well to__ you, proud high - way-
man, you rap - par - ee and__ kerne.____ For
you did court the__ bul - le - ts so ___
that the poor might gain_____ With__ pis -
- tols and with sab - re to __ halt the
o - ppress - or's tide,_____ The__ mo - on___ up -
on your sh - oul - der_____ a - n - d__ free - dom_
as_____ your guide.____

Farewell to all the Tory lads, from Navan to Belleek,
And every cabin, field and ditch where the red coat foe did seek,
For we did sit with pipes alit and many a yearn was told,
By the outlaw Michael Collier none braver nor none bold.

Farewell to you, Lisdoran lads, and him that rode the hill,
The music of the Boyne so sweet I recollect it still,
My heart is always with you, though my back is forced to turn,
Adieu to you, stout Collier, the swordsman that I mourn.

Collier's Reel

THE
COUNTY OF
WATERFORD

Willie Brennan

Brennan on the Moor

Willie Brennan is arguably Ireland's best-known highwayman. Not a little of his fame in our time is due to the ballad "Brennan on the Moor",[cv] revived in the 1950s and still enjoying success on the folk circuit. But the persistence of Willie's acclaim is also owing to the kindness and consideration he always showed to the poor and oppressed, and because he never took a life, despite the perils of his "profession".

He was born in the latter part of the eighteenth century. Opinion as to his actual birthplace is divided: some claim he was born in Kilmurray, near Kilworth, County Cork, while others insist that he hailed from the townland of Raspberry Hill in west Waterford. Be that as it may, Brennan plied his "trade" around the Kilworth Mountains, the roads and boreens of north Cork and south Tipperary and, in later years, ventured as far as west Cork and Kerry.

Two things set Willie Brennan apart from most of Ireland's highwaymen: he was not forced into a life of crime by injustice or oppression but began his career as a result of a foolish youthful prank; and although other outlaws favoured the pistol as their weapon of choice – and notwithstanding that Brennan also carried pistol, sabre and dagger – he is famed in song and story for his use of the blunderbuss.

It was a truly menacing weapon. Blunderbusses varied in size, ranging from the ancient artillery piece known as the donderbus (thundergun) to a hand-held gun. The defining features of the hand-held weapon were the bell-shaped muzzle and large bore that could blast many balls at once. It was a short-range weapon and far from accurate, but when brandished by a highwayman it did not need to be. It was insanity, indeed, for a man to challenge a highwayman training a loaded blunderbuss upon him and no wonder that Brennan never killed anybody: the very sight of his firearm was enough to strike terror into his victims' hearts.

The career of "Brennan on the Moor" began lightly. In his youth Willie was employed as a farm labourer by the Grant family at Kilmurry House, a splendid mansion and estate situated on the Fermoy-Ballyduff road. In all likelihood he would have continued to lead an uneventful life had it not been for the visit of a British army officer. A number of the other servant boys wagered that he dared not rob the soldier of his gold watch and chain. Willie accepted the wager and gained the watch and chain, but forfeited his freedom: as a result of this reckless act, he was forced to flee to the hills.

He took refuge in the Kilworth Mountains and made it his permanent hideout. High among the peaks can be found the Goat's Parlour, a barely accessible natural fortress. It is a beautiful, though wild, place and contains the waterfall which gives the area its local name: Poulanasa (the Hole of the Waterfall). It was used frequently by Willie as a hiding place. At the first sign of encroaching troops, he would step behind the cascade and disappear until the danger had passed.

Kilmurry House, Fermoy, County Cork, where Willie Brennan committed his first act of robbery.

Not only could he make himself invisible, but Brennan could gallop his horse backwards as well – or so it must have seemed to the authorities. He was always in possession of fine horses and more often than not was able to out-gallop his pursuers. Having done so, he would give himself some breathing space by reversing his horse's shoes – we must assume that he had a blacksmith's paraphernalia to hand. The tracks heading in the wrong direction would completely baffle those trailing him.

Hard facts about the outlaw are elusive, but a composite picture of his character and life can be formed from the many stories that have survived the passage of years. The tale of how Brennan met the man who was to become his closest accomplice, for example, has become ingrained into local folklore.

One morning Brennan was hiding in the hedge by the side of the road near Leary's Bridge, waiting for an opportunity to plunder. He spied a man approaching on horse-back, leading a pack-horse; he was known locally as the Pedlar Bawn. He was the Georgian equivalent of the travelling salesman. Employed by a well-heeled merchant in Cork city, the pedlar toured the countryside selling a variety of goods to the country people.

As he came alongside, Brennan jumped into the road, aimed his ferocious blunderbuss at the startled traveller and ordered him to "stand and deliver". The quaking victim had no intention of arguing. He handed over his watch and fob, which the outlaw pocketed; he then handed over his cash, which Brennan also gladly received before taking the reins of the traveller's pack-horse and tying them to his own. Brennan was just about to mount up and depart when the pedlar spoke. He asked the outlaw to give him something to prove to his employer in Cork that he had been robbed.

"Tell him Brennan the highwayman robbed you," said Brennan.

But this answer failed to satisfy the pedlar. "They'll throw me in Cork Gaol and try me as a robber unless I have proof – indisputable proof," he protested.

Brennan humoured his frightened victim and enquired what was needed to convince his employer that he had indeed been robbed.

"He'll believe me all right," he answered, "if you were to fire a ball through the side of my greatcoat with your pistol."

Brennan laid his blunderbuss aside and reached for one of his pistols. The pedlar opened his coat and the highwayman fired. The ball sliced through the rough material leaving a gaping hole.

The pedlar asked him to fire another through the opposite side while he held it away from his body. Brennan took out his second pistol and again obliged, firing through the coat before holstering his pistol.

"One more, with your blunderbuss!" cried the pedlar, flinging his hat into the air.

Brennan raised the weapon and blasted the hat, scattering fragments all over the road. He mounted his horse, but as he turned to leave the Pedlar Bawn drew a concealed pocket pistol from his trousers and ordered the outlaw to dismount.

Having discharged his three firearms, and little suspecting a threat from his trembling victim, Brennan had not bothered to reload. Now he acknowledged the cleverness of his adversary and bowed to the pedlar.

"Take me to Cork and I'll suffer my fate," he said. "You have my word on it."

To Brennan's surprise the pedlar put away his weapon.

"I've had enough of traipsing around the country making money for already wealthy merchants," he confessed. "I want to join forces with you and become a highwayman myself."

Brennan, though greatly taken aback, agreed at once. The man had proved his resourcefulness.

Many and great were the adventures that Brennan and the Pedlar Bawn shared together and in the company of other outlaws. They went their separate ways after a series of raids and robberies, only coming together again when the situation demanded their combined ingenuity.

"Bould" Brennan's Adventures

Brennan on the Moor could be immensely kind and compassionate, if the body of legend surrounding him is to be believed. One of the more enduring stories concerns an incident that occurred when he was riding one day near the Cork-Tipperary border.

Being thirsty, he stopped for a drink of water at an isolated cottage, the home of a poor widow and her family. The outlaw's reputation for generosity had preceded him and she told him of her sorrows. It was a heart-rending story. She owed £5 in rent and was unable to pay it. The bailiff was on his way that very day to either collect the debt, or cast the family out onto the side of the road.

Brennan at once opened his purse and counted out the required amount, instructing the widow to obtain a receipt from the bailiff when she paid the rent. He made the woman swear that, while he lived, she would not reveal to anyone where she had obtained the money. Before he departed, Brennan idly enquired when the bailiff was expected to arrive…

That same afternoon the bailiff collected the widow's rent and issued a receipt. The widow's cabin was but one of many tenants' homes he was to call at that day; when his purse was full and his belly empty, he turned his mount for home.

The light was fading when he descended the hills and joined the highway; he was glad of the straight path to shorten his journey. But before he was halfway home, a man emerged from a hiding place next to the road: it was Brennan on the Moor, with his famous and accursed blunderbuss pointing at the bailiff's heart. The outlaw demanded of the bailiff his day's takings, his pistol, and then his horse, and left the enraged man to walk the long, lonely road back to the landlord, empty-handed – but still in pos-session of his receipt book!

Brennan returned to the widow and entrusted all the booty to her, with instructions to share it with her fellow tenants. He kept the prize of the bailiff's fine horse for himself, later selling it to an accomplice in Clonmel.

As a result of this outrage affecting the pocket of a powerful local landlord, a squad of troopers and dragoons was garrisoned in the region for the sole purpose of a putting an end to Brennan's dastardly crimes. They did not meet with much success, however, because records show that in February 1809 Brennan robbed three gentlemen in their homes right under the noses of the military, in the heavily fortified town of Clonmel. Worse, Brennan had the audacity to choose as his targets three individuals bearing the same surname: Jackson. All were extremely wealthy and influential members of society, and had their fortunes substantially lightened.

Brennan's most renowned act, one still celebrated in song, was waylaying the mayor of Cashel a mile outside the town and appropriating a large quantity of his gold. If this incident really did occur, then it would have been viewed as an extremely serious affront to the authorities. No effort would have been spared to track Brennan down.

Yet despite the close attentions of the military, Brennan continued to plunder and rob. That he went uncaptured was due in no small measure to the fact that he never failed to find shelter and sanctuary in the homes of those he always helped: the poor.

Less well-known, but nonetheless audacious, was an incident involving Brennan and his clay pipe.[cvi] It began one summer's day, when the outlaw was at the height of his fame and notoriety. He was surprised while sleeping on a grassy knoll near the Goat's Parlour.

A troop of redcoat infantrymen under the command of a sergeant was patrolling the hills in search of outlaws. The rattling of their buckles and insignia startled Brennan's horse, which was grazing nearby. The horse bolted and, as Brennan rose to chase after it, he found himself staring down the barrels of a line of Brown Bess muskets with fixed bayonets. There was no escape. The sergeant informed their prone captive that he was being arrested on suspicion of being the notorious highwayman Brennan.

"But, gentlemen," he protested, "a poor labouring boy like me could not be the bould Brennan!"

Such dissembling proved useless. Flanked by the troops, Brennan was marched in the direction of the old Dublin Road. After an hour or so the troopers and their still-objecting prisoner came upon an inn. The day being a hot one and the road dusty, prisoner and guards alike adjourned for a drink. The youngest of the troop, a fresh-faced youth, was ordered to keep his musket trained on the captive while the others attended to their ale. Brennan, still trying to convince the unbelieving sergeant of his innocence, was allowed to buy a number of drinks for the soldiers.

As the men quenched their thirst, the outlaw asked the young trooper for permission to light his pipe. The youth deferred to the sergeant who, seeing no danger in the request, consented. The serving girl was called.

Unbeknownst to the troopers, however, she and Brennan were acquainted. The outlaw produced his clay pipe and with a wink gave the girl a secret signal. He then asked her to "put some fire in it". She left the room and returned a short time later with both the lit pipe and a bottle of shrub (fruit cordial laced with whiskey) for the thirsty young guard.

As he grasped the bottle, the guard's attention was momentarily distracted. In this split second the girl slipped Brennan a blunderbuss which she had concealed in the folds of her skirt. In an instant Brennan was on his feet with the deadly weapon – a weapon, moreover, that he was completely at home with.

"Now, gentlemen," shouted the freebooter, covering his captors with the gun, "I *am* the bould Brennan!"

The tables were turned. Brennan had the young trooper stack the soldiers' weapons in a corner and then collect the soldiers' watches, money and sundry items of jewellery. To add insult to injury, the militia were ordered to remove their boots and place them in a pile at the front of the inn. This done, he induced the sergeant to secure his men with lengths of rope commandeered from the inn. Brennan himself then bound the sergeant.

Piling straw around the boots, the outlaw retrieved his still-smouldering clay pipe from the serving girl and dropped it onto the pile of straw and well-seasoned leather. The straw caught fire and, as the pyre burned brightly, Brennan dispatched the embarrassed, bootless and bound troopers back to their quarters.

The incident made the military the laughing stock of the community. Enough was enough: the incensed authorities garrisoned a large force of redcoats in the town of Fermoy and from this secure base sent forth patrols to scour the hills and valleys in search of the outlaw. They also provided dragoons to accompany the mail and stage-coaches on their journeys through the mountains as they made for Dublin. Such a large presence of military in the area made life extremely difficult for Brennan and seriously curtailed his activities. He was forced to turn his attention to the more remote roads of West Cork and Kerry. According to legend, it was on one such lonely road that Brennan on the Moor lost his life.

A Lonely Road

The year was 1812 and the place a point on the road between Millstreet and Killarney at Lisabable. Brennan lay concealed, masked and armed inside the entrance to a quarry, awaiting the approach of some unsuspecting person or coach.

It was not long before he was alerted by the sound of approaching wheels. The traveller was Mr Jeremiah Connor, a solicitor and friend of Daniel O'Connell, the Liberator, returning from a business meeting in Dublin. As his carriage drew close, out sprang Brennan, blunderbuss at the ready.

Connor was well accustomed to travelling the roads of Ireland and was also well acquainted with their dangers. A lone traveller seldom ventured onto the public highway unarmed; Connor was no exception.[cvii]

Without hesitation the solicitor took from his pocket a purse and flung it to the ground, as if surrendering immediately for fear of violence. As Brennan bent to pick it up, Connor drew a pocket pistol from his overcoat and fired. His aim was true: the ball struck the outlaw.

Badly wounded, Brennan dropped his weapon and, unable to return fire, crawled into the dense undergrowth. He did not crawl far, however. The following day the dead body of the outlaw Brennan was discovered behind a ditch a short distance from the road.

This account comes from no less a source and authority than O'Connell himself, who related the incident to his secretary and biographer, O'Neill Daunt. Indeed, when both were journeying together, O'Connell pointed out the exact spot on the road where the outlaw had fallen.

Even in death, the mystery surrounding Brennan invited distortion of the truth. Ballads and some written accounts relate that Brennan was captured in a place called Clonmore, tried and hanged in Clonmel, and his body left hanging in chains from a gibbet. If this is so, then his head would have been spiked on the gates of Clonmel Gaol – still the usual practice for dealing with convicted outlaws.

Local reports of the outlaw's funeral and burial differ greatly, too. One version, for example, has the funeral cortège stretching for two miles, while another says that Brennan received a hurried "funeral", his body being thrown over the cemetery wall in the dead of night and left to rot.

The truth is that Brennan is buried immediately inside the north wall of the old churchyard of Kilcrumper, between Kilworth and Fermoy in the barony of Condons and Clangibbons. The gravestone is now bereft of an epitaph, the words having been worn away by time. Willie Brennan left behind a wife and three children, and it was no doubt they who erected this memorial.

Stories abound of "Brennan's secret treasure", which is reputed to be buried locally on Killeagh Hill. The exact place was known only to the outlaw; regrettably, he took the secret to his grave. The treasure was supposed to have been stolen from a wealthy Cork farmer as he made his way home across the Kilworth mountains. The farmer had won first prize in the Dublin Agricultural Show – a statue of a sow and her six bonhams, fashioned from solid gold.

Brennan had no need of such things to be remembered by. His legacy is the threat he posed to the wealthy who travelled the arterial routes of Cork and Tipperary. While Brennan ranged, those highways were unsafe. In 1855 Charles Bianconi, owner of the famous coach company, boasted that for over forty years his coaches had travelled the roads of Ireland unmolested. What he failed to mention was that Brennan on the Moor had been lying peacefully in his grave for that length of time.

Brennan on the Moor

(an American version)

moor.   Bren- nan on the   moor.   Bold, gay and un-

daunt- ed stood young Bren- nan on   the moor.

It was upon the King's Highway
That Brennan he sat down.
He met the Mayor of Moorland
Five miles outside of town.
Now the Mayor he knew Brennan,
"And I think," says he,
"Your name is Willy Brennan,
You must come along with me."

Chorus: Oh, it's Brennan on the moor,
Brennan on the moor.
Bold, gay and undaunted stood young
Brennan on the moor.

Now Brennan's wife was a-going
downtown
Some provisions for to buy.
When she saw her Willy taken,
She began to weep and cry.
Says he, "Hand me that ten penny,"
And as soon as Willy spoke,
She handed him a blunderbuss
From underneath her cloak.

Chorus

Now Brennan got his blunderbuss,
My story I'll unfold,
He caused the Mayor to tremble
And to deliver up his gold.
Five thousand pounds were offered
For his apprehension there,
But Brennan and the pedlar
To the mountain did repair.

Chorus

Now Brennan is an outlaw
All on some mountain high.
With infantry and cavalry
To take him they did try,
But he laughed at them and he scored
at them
Until it was said
By a false-hearted woman
He was cruelly betrayed.

Chorus

They hung Brennan at the crossroads,
In chains he swung and dried,
But still they say that in the night
Some do see him ride.
They see him with his blunderbuss
In the midnight chill,
Along, along the King's Highway
Rides Willy Brennan still.

Chorus

Brannin on the Moor
(a Scottish version)

As Brannin was walking on yon mountains high,
A coach with four horses he chanced to spy;
He robbed them of their riches, which he gave to the poor;
He's over yon mountains, you'll never see him more.

Chorus: Bold Brannin on the moor, bold Brannin on the moor,
So bold and undaunted stood bold Brannin on the moor.

But Brannin was taken and condemned for to die,
And many a fair maid for Brannin did cry;
But he said all their cries will not save me,
Nor take me down from yon gallows tree.

Chorus

I'm wae from my wife and my children three;
My poor aged mother I never will see;
My poor aged father, with grey locks, he cried—
I wish my bold Brannin in his cradle he had died.

Chorus

A Lament on the Execution of Captain Brennan
(an Irish version)

It's of a famous highwayman a story I will tell;
His name was Willy Brennan, in Ireland he did dwell,
And on the Kilworth mountains he commenced his wild career,
Where many a wealthy gentleman before him shook with fear.

Chorus: Brennan on the moor, Brennan on the moor,
Bold and undaunted stood young Brennan on the moor.

A brace of loaded pistols he carried night and day;
He never robbed a poor man upon the king's highway,
But what he'd taken from the rich, like Turpin and Black Bess,
He always did divide it with the widow in distress.

Chorus

One night he robbed a packman of the name of Pedlar Bawn,
They travelled together 'till the day began to dawn;
The pedlar seeing his money gone likewise his watch and chain
He at once encountered Brennan and robbed him back again.

Chorus

Now Brennan seeing the pedlar as good a man as he,
He says, "My worthy hero, will you come along with me?"
The pedlar being stout hearted, he threw his pack away,
And he proved a loyal comrade until his dying day.

Chorus

One day on the highway, as Willy he sat down,
He met the Mayor of Cashel a mile outside the town;
The Mayor he knew his features: "I think, young man," said he,
"Your name is Willy Brennan, you must come along with me."

Chorus

As Brennan's wife had gone to town some provisions for to buy
When she saw her Willy, she began to cry;
He says, "Give me that tenpenny" — as soon as Willy spoke
She handed him a blunderbus from underneat her cloak.

Chorus

Then with his loaded blunderbus the truth I will unfold
He made the Mayor to tremble and robbed him of his gold.
One hundred pounds was offered for his apprehension there,
He mounted his horse and saddle to the mountains did repair.

Chorus

Then Brennan being an outlaw upon the mountains high
The cavalry and infantry to take him they did try;
He laughed at them with scorn until at length it's said
By a false-hearted woman he basely was betrayed.

Chorus

In the County Tipperary at a place they call Clonmore
Willy Brennan and his comrade that day did suffer sore;
He lay amongst the fern, which was tick upon the field
And nine wonnes he did receive before that he did yield.

Chorus

Ther Brennan and his companion when they were betrayed
They with the mounted cavalry a noble battle maid
He lost his foremost finger which was shot off by a ball
So Brennan and his comrade they were taken after all.

Chorus

So they were prisoners in irons they were bound
And conveyed to Clonmel Jail strong walls did them surround.
They were tried and found guilty the Judge made this reply:
"For robbing on the king's highway you're both condemned to die."

Chorus

When Brennan heard his sentence he made this reply:
"I own that I did rob the rich and the poor supply;
In all the deeds that I have done I took no life away
The Lord have mercy on my soul against the Judgment day."

Chorus

"Farewell unto my wife and to my children three
Likewise my aged father he may shed tears for me;
And to my loving mother who tore her grey locks and cried
Saying I wish Willy Brennan in your cradle you had died."

Chorus

THE
COUNTY OF
TIPPERARY

County Gallway   Kings   Septentrio

Lower Ormond

Lough

Dera

hart

County

Iberine

Queenes

County

The

Owny

Ormond

Teagh

Arra

Elugirh

Killnalongurt

Slew

Countie

dagh

and

Com

ply

of

Lymrick

Killnemana

Terri

tory

Kilken-

Clanwilliam

Mid

dle

third

Offa

ney

and

Countie

Iffa

of

Waterford

The

Countie

Countie

of Cork

The
Mortibes

Scale Miliarum Hibernicorum
Scale Miliarum Anglicorum

Jeremiah Grant

Captain Grant

"The whole country is talking about him; he is a kind of outlaw, a rebel, or robber, all three I daresay; there's a hundred pounds offered for his head... His proper
home, they say, is in the Queen's County where he has a band, but he is a strange
fellow, fond of wandering about by himself amidst the bogs and mountains, and
living in the old castles; occasionally he quarters himself in the peasants' houses,
who let him do just what he pleases; he is free of his money, and often does them
good turns and can be good-humoured enough, so they don't dislike him. Then
he is what they call a fairy man, a person in league with fairies and spirits, and
able to work much harm by supernatural means, on which account they hold him
in great awe; he is moreover, a mighty strong tall fellow."

From George Henry Borrow's novel *Lavengro*[cviii]

Jeremiah Grant was born in the village of Moyne near Thurles in the barony of
Eliogarty, County Tipperary, about the year 1785. His father, Patrick, was the
owner of a comfortable farm and, in Jeremiah's words, "much respected... even
though of a warm temper, tenacious of what he considered his rights, and given to
litigation". His influence over his son was of short duration, however, for Patrick died
while still in his early thirties. His wife Eleanor was left with a young family, the eldest
of whom was nine-year-old Jeremiah.

The boy was adopted by his uncle James, who lived a few miles from Moyne at the Turret of Finner, near Urlingford, County Tipperary. James Grant had no children of his own, so he also declared Jeremiah his heir. He encouraged the boy to continue his education and loved him as if he were his own, indulging his every whim.

Jeremiah grew into a fine young man and developed a taste for country sports and pleasures: hurling, hunting, shooting, horse-racing and gambling, but most especially cock-fighting. He was also fond of "a drop", loved music, and mastered several instruments. He became an ardent "ladies' man", who spent his uncle's money with wild abandon, and gave no thought to the morrow.

Jeremiah was striking in appearance. One of his contemporaries described him as:

> "endowed with strong attractive powers, at least six feet one inch in height, athletic and well proportioned in his person, with a kind, open countenance, an excellent complexion; and his hair which he wore cropped short, was thick, black and shining as jet; his conversation though not refined was good humoured, with engaging manners and cheerful features."

In short, he had all the attributes of a Georgian playboy. At the age of nineteen Jeremiah met and fell madly in love with Anne Dean, the daughter of a wealthy farmer from a neighbouring county. She was a year younger than he, beautiful and intelligent, and had a profound effect on the young buck. James Grant gave the relationship his blessing, but died shortly after the courtship began. Jeremiah inherited his uncle's land and stock. The young lovers married that same year.

Jeremiah gave up his former pastimes and devoted his energies to his new responsibilities. Anne had brought a considerable dowry of gold with her and this, coupled with Jeremiah's recently acquired wealth, ensured that the newly-weds were quite well off.

The couple prospered. Six years later Jeremiah could afford to buy the lease of a fine farm at nearby Loughmore from its owner and landlord, Mr Gilbert Maher. The farm came complete with a grist mill and several acres of prime land. The future looked bright for the Grants, who were by now the proud parents of three small children. So industrious was Jeremiah at this time, and so clever in his business dealings, that he was able to also take care of all the living expenses of his widowed mother, his younger brother John, and his sister Mary. Whatever money he had left went towards running the farm and mill. Anne developed an interest in bee-keeping which proved to be a highly profitable enterprise.

In fact, so successful were the couple at everything they turned their hands to, that Gilbert Maher, the owner of the farm, grew decidedly envious. This envy was to have far-reaching consequences.

Maher was an extremely wealthy man – and unscrupulous. He used every trick "within the law" to oppress his tenants. Jeremiah Grant now owned the lease and Maher was determined to have it back, by fair means or foul. He instigated proceedings against the Grants which, though legally suspect, nevertheless drained all of Jeremiah's finances when he tried to oppose them.

Matters came to a head in August 1809 when the rent was due and Jeremiah was unable to raise it. Maher executed a warrant of distress, which enabled him to publicly auction some stock belonging to the tenant. Anne Grant's lucrative beehives fitted the bill exactly. The arrangements for the sale were organised by a bailiff named Gleeson.

Whether by accident or design, Maher failed to inform Jeremiah of the date of the auction; consequently, he was absent that day. Gleeson went ahead all the same with the sale of the bees, despite the pleas of a very distraught and frightened Anne Grant and her children, who by now numbered seven. The auction was quite successful, with the other local landlords eagerly bidding for the honey and the hives.

Anne's husband returned home to discover that his barn had been turned into an auction room. He was also in time to catch Gleeson verbally abusing his wife with foul language. Jeremiah pushed through the crowd and confronted the bailiff. A fight ensued between the two men and the punches to Gleeson's face resulted in a nose so bloody that the bailiff's "chin and cravat [were stained] incardine". But Jeremiah was overpowered by Gleeson's men, assisted by Nicholas Maher, the landlord's son. Jeremiah fought back furiously, broke free and ran into his home, re-emerging moments later brandishing a loaded pistol. He aimed at Gleeson. The gun misfired.

The frightened bailiff returned to Maher to report the incident. The landlord was outraged. He brought his son and the battered bailiff to the local justice of the peace, who charged Jeremiah Grant with attempted murder, at that time a capital offence. Before he could be arrested, Jeremiah fled to his former homeland of Moyne, where he knew he would be sheltered by friends and relatives, leaving his wife and young family behind in Loughmore. A life of outlawry had begun.

Jeremiah remained for a time in Moyne, moving from one safe house to the next. He sometimes sought concealment in the ruins of an old church, whose many hidden passageways and tunnels offered an impenetrable sanctuary. Occasionally he ventured out at night to visit his wife and family, before slipping away again before dawn.

It was during one of these nocturnal visits that Anne confessed to him that their savings had dwindled to almost nothing; a fresh source of income had to be found. Anne was unable to work the farm, despite the help she received from John, Jeremiah's brother, and her own family. The rent would soon fall due.

Jeremiah returned to Moyne with a heavy heart and much on his mind. He was already an outlaw as a result of shooting at the bailiff and had nothing to lose, so he agreed to became a partner in an illegal poteen distillery. The business flourished and became quite profitable, not least because no taxes were paid.

Not only was Jeremiah Grant able to look after his family, he earned enough money to donate to the local agrarian societies. He and his brother John had become active members of one of these illegal groups. Both men subscribed avidly to the aims of these organisations: to smash landlordism and eradicate the iniquitous tithes levied on Catholics.

Curfews were imposed on the people in an effort to curtail this agrarian agitation. Anyone found breaking the curfew was transported to New South Wales, Australia, without trial. Yet Jeremiah, who risked death if captured, continued to visit his family, while at the same time conducting a campaign of intimidation against local landlords – and Gilbert Maher in particular.

Maher and his son Nicholas made numerous complaints to the authorities concerning these transgressions. They gave evidence which served to convict a number of local men charged with these acts. The Grant brothers remained free, however; nothing could be proved against them – and Jeremiah Grant could not be found, let alone charged.

A Foul and Fatal Seduction

Nicholas Maher was truly his father's son, so energetic was he in his harrying of outlaws. He constantly raided the homes of known rebels and their families, paying particular attention to the house where Jeremiah's widowed mother lived, not a quarter of a mile from the Maher demesne.

On one of these raids Nicholas encountered Jeremiah's sister, Mary, for the first time. Her husband, a man named Costigan, had left her, so she had returned to live with her mother. We do not know for certain why Nicholas Maher took up with Mary. Doubtless he was attracted to this raven-haired beauty, yet there is good evidence for believing that he wished to use the young woman to "get at" her brother, knowing that Jeremiah would be horrified by such a liaison. Mary was vulnerable at this time, freshly disillusioned by her disastrous marriage, and easy prey for a wealthy landlord's son.

Nicholas began his foul seduction. He showered Mary with gifts and compliments, turning her head and heart until she was passionate about him. A liaison began and in no time at all the locality abounded with rumours of the lovers' wild drinking and debauched behaviour. The Grant brothers were greatly distressed by what they heard and their long-suffering mother was distraught. Jeremiah also feared the worst: that the affair was a ruse planned by Gilbert Maher in order to discover his whereabouts. The brothers decided to find out the truth and to put an end once and for all to the relationship.

Nicholas got word from an informer that the Grants were planning to take some sort of action to end his relationship with Mary. Believing herself and Maher to be truly in love, their sister was outraged. Knowing that Jeremiah's movements were already restricted by the threat of arrest, Mary believed that if she could find a way to hinder John Grant's freedom also, then her affair with Nicholas could continue. The pair turned against John. They went to the justice of the peace on March 22, 1810 and swore an oath charging the innocent man with the attempted murder of Nicholas Maher. They swore that John Grant had fired a shot from behind a ditch, and added that he called out after the shot: "Sorry that I missed you."

John was arrested the following day and brought to the Bridewell in Templemore. Mary, meanwhile, encouraged by the Mahers, was informing on Jeremiah's whereabouts. Two days later the outlaw was captured near Borrisoleigh by a strong force of the Templemore Yeomanry under the command of Captain Arthur Carden. They were assisted by Nicholas Maher. Carden described Jeremiah as an "infamous character, a villain and a felon".

The brothers shared the same gaol. It happened that the turnkey was a family friend; he allowed the prisoners to leave their cells on their word of honour that they would return and not run from the town – and *certainly* not go to a local public house. Their parole given, Jeremiah and John headed directly to a drinking establishment, where they were met by several friends. They drank until dawn and then returned to the Bridewell.

Next day they were brought to Clonmel Gaol, guarded by an escort of yeomanry and accompanied by several constables. At about ten in the morning the escort stopped for refreshments at the village of Beloughbee and it was here that Jeremiah decided to make his escape – alone. He knew that his own cause was lost and that he was gallows-bound, but believed that his brother would surely defeat the trumped-up charges. He chose not to involve John in the escape.

When the party entered the inn, Jeremiah produced a full purse and cheerfully called for the best of drink to be made available. The delighted yeomen and constables accepted this unexpected offer… and they accepted again, and again, and again. In no time they were singing and dancing; some were even sleeping, with their weapons resting harmlessly against the wall.

Jeremiah seized his opportunity. He sprang from his seat and raced out of the door, bolting it behind him. By the time the drunken guards broke the door down and interrogated the only passing witness, a country resident who spoke no English, the outlaw had escaped into Jacob's wood.

On arrival at Clonmel, the escort commander informed the governor of the escape. He ordered that John be secured with bolts and bars of iron. The better prize having slipped through his fingers, he was determined to make an example of the lesser. He would see John Grant hang.

But the prosecution could not find enough hard evidence against him and John was remanded in custody. While his brother was thus fortunate, Jeremiah fared badly. He went to visit his wife and children, was spotted by an informer, and promptly rearrested. Once more he found himself in irons in Clonmel Gaol, this time under very heavy guard.

The Spurned Lover

With the Grant brothers secured in gaol, Nicholas Maher had no further need of Mary Grant. As Jeremiah had suspected all along, the man had used and deceived the naïve girl. Now that Nicholas and his father had achieved their goal, Mary's lover refused to have any further contact with her.

Scorned, Mary furiously vowed that Nicholas would pay for his duplicity. On June 6, 1810 she succeeded in enticing him back to her mother's home with seductive promises. Jeremiah's words recount what happened next.

> "Under the pretence of renovating love, she decoyed him to her bed, and when sunk in sleep and inebriety, she became his assassin, and with a heavy stone beat out his devoted brains."

The following morning the body of Nicholas Maher of Loughmore was found in a field near his father's house; it was gruesomely disfigured. Mary, her mother, and a local man named Edward Dunne were arrested on suspicion of murder. At the spring assizes Jeremiah's unfortunate sister was tried and convicted. She went to the scaffold two days later. Her body was delivered over to the surgeons of the County Hospital, to be dissected for the purposes of anatomical study. We can only guess at the extent of Jeremiah's impotent rage upon learning this.

Gilbert Maher, in turn, was incensed at the brutal murder of his son. Not content with Mary's execution, he contrived to implicate the whole Grant family, including Jeremiah's children. He began to stir up resentment among the local gentry against the Grants, and feelings were soon running high. With his connections and influence behind him, Maher foresaw no obstacles in the path to prosecution. The future looked bleak for the Grant family – but Gilbert Maher had not taken Anne's resourcefulness into account.

She wrote a letter to an unnamed gentleman renowned for his service to public justice, outlining the case; he in turn enlisted the support of several other concerned and noted humanitarians. They discovered the falseness of the Mahers' claims and vigorously extracted the truth.

To the consternation of Gilbert Maher, the presiding judge declared that Jeremiah Grant, in the case of bailiff Gleeson, had acted under the influence of passion, having been highly provoked, and the charge of attempted murder was reduced to a misdemeanour with a sentence of twelve months. Anne Grant was acquitted of all crimes; Jeremiah's mother was found guilty of conspiracy to murder Nicholas Maher, but later released.

John, however, was sentenced to death. Jeremiah fought valiantly to save his brother. From Clonmel Gaol he made a secret overture to the Reverend Drought,[cix] a local clergyman who had already shown himself to be compassionate and helpful to the family. Drought wrote a number of letters to William Wellesly Poole, a member of parliament, seeking his intervention and intercession on John's behalf. The death sentence was commuted to one of transportation for life to New South Wales. John Grant was eighteen years of age.

At the beginning of 1811 John Grant was led up the gangplank of the *Providence* in shackles, with 139 other men and 41 women. Of the prisoners on board, 125 had received the minimum seven years; four had received fourteen years; while the remaining 52 were given life sentences.

As the *Providence* embarked on her long voyage to Australia, Jeremiah Grant was beginning his twelve-month gaol sentence. He served his time stoically, fortified by constant visits from his beloved Anne. On his release he discovered to his dismay that whatever money he had accumulated was gone, for he had spent a considerable amount on lawyer's fees. Now he was poverty-stricken, with a near-starving family to support.

Difficult Times

In November he formed a partnership with a horse-thief named Egan, who had connections with the Cartys, a notorious family of rustlers. It was an ill-fated venture.

Business went quite well for a time and many "borrowed" animals passed through the partners' hands, but the Grants were being kept under observation. Their renewed prosperity raised suspicions. It was not long before Jeremiah was betrayed by one of Maher's men. He found himself back in Clonmel Gaol and then Limerick Prison to await the assizes. The case against him collapsed, however, due to lack of evidence and material witnesses; he was acquitted. Tired, he returned to his family and brought them to his native Moyne, determined to live an upright and law-abiding life.

No sooner had they moved house when word reached Jeremiah that one of his former acquaintances, a Carty, had been arrested and was being held in Maryborough Gaol. He was implicating several men in horse stealing, most notably Grant.

Jeremiah fled from Moyne with the military hot on his heels. He went into hiding around Cappawhite and Donohill for six or seven weeks, falling back on horse stealing to make a living. He was again on the run from the authorities, but he was back among the only people he could trust.

This trust was put to the test on May 1, 1812. A troop of soldiers accompanied by a constable marched out from Tipperary to serve a petty criminal named Allis with a warrant. Little did they know that sleeping upstairs in the loft was the notorious outlaw Jeremiah Grant.

Allis was awakened at daybreak by the barking of his dogs. On seeing the troops he immediately alerted Jeremiah who, dressed only in a shirt, leaped straight out of the loft window – and landed on a goose which happened to be sleeping in the yard below.

Leaving the bruised and squawking fowl behind, Jeremiah ran into an orchard at the rear of the house. He scaled the wall, headed for the river and swam to safety.

Tracked down at every turn, Jeremiah decided to emigrate for a time.

After making a night-time farewell visit to his family in Moyne, he travelled to Waterford city, where he booked passage to Newfoundland aboard the brig *Polly*, commanded by a Captain Redmond. He disembarked at St Johns and quickly found employment with a wealthy landowner, Mr Hooan. Jeremiah signed up to work for two summers and a winter, and for this he was to be paid the princely sum of £36. But he failed to read the fine print: the contract effectively made him a slave to his new employer. He soon learned that he had to pay extra for his food, lodgings and "sundries". Within a short time Jeremiah was in debt to this unscrupulous individual.

Relations between the two went from bad to worse, and it appeared to Grant that the longer he worked, the deeper his debt became. He had to get away, but herein lay another dilemma. If Jeremiah absconded leaving behind his debt and was subsequently arrested, he would face a mandatory, lengthy prison term as a felon and possibly never be able to return home. Notwithstanding this threat, Jeremiah relieved his "master" of some money, went to St Johns and booked passage for home. He arrived back in Ireland in December 1812, without the great wealth he had hoped to earn. There was nothing for it but to revert to his former occupation.

Jeremiah renewed his partnership with Egan the horse-thief, who was now living in Waterford, and stayed with him for a number of weeks. Soon Jeremiah was joined surreptitiously in the city by his wife and family. The separation and the constant looking over their shoulders were taking their toll on the couple; they could not go on like this forever.

Jeremiah and Anne approached some of the leading citizens and justices of the peace in Tipperary, imploring them to intercede with the government and beg clemency for the outlaw. Had he received a pardon, Jeremiah would have been quite willing to settle down, either in Ireland or in another country, if the authorities insisted, and lead the life of an honest citizen. This was not to be.

Grant's notoriety coupled with the influence of the embittered landlords ruled out a pardon. Some of the wealthy landowners received threatening letters purporting to be from Jeremiah Grant. These forgeries were counted against him, and his appeal to the authorities was denied. Once again he was thwarted in his efforts to keep to the straight and narrow, and the family had to flee another home in the dead of night. In May 1813 they rented a small house in a remote area near Collena, hoping that the isolation might deter old acquaintances from Jeremiah's criminal past from visiting and drawing attention to them.

It was a forlorn hope. Egan, the horse-thief, soon came calling and, money being as pressing a problem as ever, Jeremiah was persuaded to reunite with his former colleague. Despite Jeremiah's misgivings, the two outlaws dealt in and traded stolen horses with great efficiency, and once again the Grants had money to spend. Unfortunately, the large amount of horse traffic through the area alerted a local man who, in the hope of a reward, betrayed the rustlers. Major Kane, the local magistrate, hoped to make a double arrest: he waited until Egan was present at the Grant home before sending a warrant to the barracks where the North Cork Militia were quartered. In no time a party was on its way to make the arrests.

Jeremiah heard the troops approaching the cabin. He pushed Anne and the children out by the back door and barricaded it with furniture – the family would escape to safety while the troops concentrated on the men. The commander called out for Jeremiah to surrender. Upon receiving no response, he ordered his men to beat down the doors with the stocks of their muskets. Egan crawled under a bed. Jeremiah grabbed a pistol and a handful of ball cartridges. Dressed only in his shirt and hat, he slipped through a small window and into the yard.

With the noise of the splintering doors drowning the sound of his footsteps, he ran across the yard and vaulted over the gate. But he dropped his weapon and, as he bent to retrieve it, was immediately seized by a group of militia stationed outside in anticipation of such an escape attempt. A fierce struggle ensued; Jeremiah fought with the desperation of a cornered man battling for his life. It took twelve men to subdue the outlaw and lead him, bruised and bleeding, back to the cottage.

Once Jeremiah was inside, Constable Fitzmaurice trained two loaded pistols on him. The ever-vigilant prisoner had not given up, however; he waited for a moment when his captor was distracted and seized the opportunity to make a move. Grant struck a well-aimed blow to knock the guard off his feet and, without even grabbing a pistol to defend himself, burst through the cabin door – flooring three troopers who stood guard directly outside, knocking them into a pool of manure. He ran from the yard a second time, while the remainder of the stunned party fired uselessly in his wake.

Meanwhile, the stricken constable had recovered. He rushed to the doorway and spied the escaping outlaw fleeing the yard. Fitzmaurice fired both his pistols, wounding Jeremiah in the right buttock and upper right thigh. But the outlaw, bleeding and with shirt tails flying, did not stop running until he reached a wood about a half-mile distant.

Jeremiah was in considerable pain. He tore strips from his shirt and tightly bandaged and plugged his wounds, stemming the flow of blood. While the authorities desperately continued their search, back at the cabin Egan crept from his hiding place under the bed and slipped away to safety.

Despite a thorough search, the militia failed to locate the escapees and, as dusk approached, they retired for the night. Under cover of darkness Jeremiah left the wood and, in great agony, made his way to a friend's house in Kilmacthomas. His wounds were dressed properly and he was sheltered there until they healed.

Grant was now one of the most wanted outlaws in the land, with a reward of £100 on his head. Military patrols were stepped up and a constant watch was kept on Anne and the children, in the hope that they might lead the authorities to Jeremiah. Astute and inventive, Grant, with the help of his friend in Kilmacthomas, spirited his wife and family away from Collena under the cover of dark. Using backroads and boreens, they made their way to Enniscorthy.

Again Jeremiah tried to live a normal life – and it must be said that no other outlaw in Ireland's history tried so hard to put crime behind him. Despite his best efforts, however, he was unable to find permanent employment in Wexford. The rebellion of 1798 had taken place only fifteen years before; there were heavy concentrations of troops in the county, it having been a hotbed of insurrection. The local people had learned to be suspicious of strangers.

To earn some much-needed money Jeremiah brought two stolen sheep to a fair in Kilkenny; he was to receive a percentage of the price. Unfortunately, he was recognised by a buyer – a man who had been a passenger on the same ship that had brought the outlaw back to Ireland the previous year.

"How do you do, my friend and shipmate, Jeremiah Grant?" he said jovially, for all to hear.

It was as though a bomb had exploded among the fair-goers; the outlaw's name was known and feared far and wide. Jeremiah leaped on board a nearby cart and left Enniscorthy in a hurry, without money or sheep, and with a baying mob at his heels.

He was pursued by mounted men and forced to abandon the cart. He headed across country on foot, losing the hunters in a dense wood. Though he made it home safely, he vowed then to forsake County Wexford for a more hospitable region.

The family moved north under the alias Ryan, settling for a time in Bray, County Wicklow. Jeremiah prudently concentrated his business on neighbouring counties. On one of these excursions he returned to Enniscorthy in disguise to meet up with some former acquaintances. He acquired two cows which had been stolen from a Mr Maguire, well-to-do landowner in the area, and drove the animals back to a field in Bray. He arranged to sell them; meanwhile, Maguire had traced his property to the field and sent the constables after the Grants. As dawn broke, Anne heard the officers approaching the house and immediately awoke her husband. He threw her cloak over his shoulders and escaped to Lord Meath's deer park, where he nearly froze to death hiding in the biting wind and snow. After two days he could bear it no longer and risked going back to his family; fortunately, the house was unguarded and the Grants were able to quietly pack up and head to Dublin. From there they journeyed to Drogheda, where they remained for the best part of a year, living a normal life as Mr Darby Power and family.

In May 1815, confident that he was no longer one of Ireland's most sought-after felons, Jeremiah travelled home to Moyne in order to collect some money owed to him by Fitzpatrick, an old friend who was renting the Grants' former farm. On his arrival, however, he discovered that Fitzpatrick was in Clonmel Gaol for stealing cows. Jeremiah returned to Drogheda penniless, to find that in his absence Anne had pawned whatever bits and pieces the family still possessed.

Great Escapes

The family were in desperate straits. Jeremiah was forced to relieve a gentleman, Mr Steele, of a horse and gig;[cx] he intended to use them to open a business on Blackrock Beach ferrying people up and down the stretches of sand. The gig needed some minor repairs and Jeremiah brought it to a local forge. Unfortunately, the blacksmith recognised the stolen animal and vehicle and, prolonging the repairs, used the borrowed time to raise the alarm. As he stood in the forge, Jeremiah was surprised by Steele and a party of men armed with pistols. He was arrested and spent the night in the lock-up in Rathdowney, before being transferred the following morning to the Bridewell in Thurles, secured in iron manacles.

Somewhere between the forge and Thurles Jeremiah got hold of a nail, which he hid in his clothing. As soon as he was alone in his cell he picked the lock of the hand-cuffs. When the female turnkey arrived with some water, he pushed past her and knocked out the guard on duty outside the cell. But he had not thought out his escape sufficiently and was recaptured before he could even reach the gate. The next day he was escorted to Clonmel Gaol by twenty-one soldiers, his arms secured with irons and a large bolt, which was attached to his leg by a ring. The authorities were taking no chances this time.

Jeremiah spent the next six weeks in gaol, where he was feted as a celebrity by the other inmates. It was not long before he had gathered around him a band of confed-erates and was hatching a plan of escape. An accomplice on the outside managed to smuggle in a quantity of small hacksaws, and Jeremiah and the others set to work.

Each male prisoner was secured by a heavy bolt and ring which encircled one leg just above the ankle and hung suspended from a girdle round the waist. On Jeremiah's instruction, every man began rubbing his manacled leg near the ankle, until the muscles became inflamed and swollen, thus giving the appearance of being irritated by the weight of the iron. A turnkey was alerted and the prison warden noti-fied. He feared that there was a danger of gangrene setting in and gave instructions that the irons should be struck off.

Jeremiah was the first prisoner to be freed. As soon as the other inmates heard his bolts being hammered free, they began cutting through the window bars with the saws, the noise of the hammering drowning out the sawing. They continued in this manner until all the men were unfettered.

Jeremiah's plan entailed the co-operation of the female prisoners, who were housed in another wing. On cue, they created a diversion by staging a mock fight. As the guards rushed to quell the "riot", the male prisoners escaped into the night. The breakout had taken less than four minutes and was not detected until the following morning.

But Jeremiah was destined to see the inside of many gaols. Some months later he was recognised in Drogheda and arrested yet again. This time he was conveyed to Kilmainham Gaol in Dublin. He spent his time planning an escape; he had managed to smuggle in some tools to cut the window bars and he had a rope ladder ready and concealed for the day of the breakout. However, he was informed upon by another prisoner and was transferred to Maryborough. He was met at the gate there by Governor John Clerke, who had every confidence in the security of his prison.

While awaiting trial Jeremiah struck up a friendship with a young inmate named Carol Whelan, who was serving a lengthy sentence for highway robbery. It was not long before the two had gathered about them another escape committee: sixteen men, with Jeremiah as leader.

It was Carol Whelan who devised the escape plan. It involved scalding their guards with boiling water and snatching the keys. Jeremiah opposed the plan because of the brutality of the proposed scalding, but promised his disappointed friends a different and more subtle plan, one which was sure to work.

The scheme was ingenious, and must rank as one of the greatest prison escapes in history. Its success was to earn Jeremiah the nickname of "Captain" – the greatest honour among the outlaw fraternity.

To carry out the audacious plan, the prisoners needed outside help. Jeremiah insisted that everybody who could write should begin corresponding with their families and friends on the outside. The correspondence was to be regular and should not contain any mention or hint of the proposed breakout; all letters, incoming and outgoing, were read by the Governor.

Using code, the outlaws eventually succeeded in telling their accomplices what was needed. Jeremiah got hold of a master key, probably from a sympathiser working in the gaol, and impressed its contours onto the paper his next letter was written on. When the letter reached its destination, it was taken to a blacksmith who fashioned a skeleton key from the impression. The key could not be brought easily into the gaol because both male and female visitors were thoroughly searched – but Jeremiah had already thought of a solution. The prisoners were often brought fresh food by their visitors; the key was smuggled into the gaol in the belly of a herring.

At eight o'clock on the very evening they obtained the key, Jeremiah, Carol Whelan and the rest of the gang made their escape, overpowering and disarming the guards. Breaking open the gates, the convicts rushed out onto the street, causing great panic and confusion amongst the townspeople. Jeremiah added to the mayhem by shouting: "Stop the pickpocket! Stop, thief!" Men, women and children milled about, all trying to catch a glimpse of or seize the imaginary pickpocket and, while they were thus engaged, the escapees slipped away.

The reports of the escape in the newspapers and pamphlets of the day caused great embarrassment to the authorities; the humane Governor Clerke was seriously reprimanded and deemed lucky to keep his job.

The prisoners split up and made off in different directions. Grant, Whelan and some others proceeded without incident to Ballyroan and then to a wood near Ballynakill, where they spent their first night of freedom sleeping under the stars. Early the following morning the fugitives crept under cover of hedges and ditches to the house of a friend of Whelan's about a mile from Ballynakill. After nightfall they set out for Whelan's own cabin near Ballyragget, where they passed the night drinking poteen. News reached them that troops were scouring the countryside and all the outlaws' old haunts, but were being misinformed at every turn by local people loyal to the escapees.

July 13th 1815

I take the Liberty of addressing your Honour your as one of his Majesties Justice of the Peace I Consider my Duty to make this application to your Honour, as I had the Misfortune off falling in to Bad Company, I Wish with all my hart to Lead a Regular Life, as I would have done a Long time aga if I Could but Get aprotection for what had been alledged against me, I never was Guilty of highway robbery house Breaking or Murder, nor any Other offence Only to have the Misfortune of haveing hand in a few horses and Cows, that had been Badly Got, I now offer to Give My Self up to you and will also Give my service for Six months to Government and will youel find Behave a Loyal Subject to his Majesty, there is Many a Bad Member in this Contry whom I will Apprehend and Bring to Justice, after the Six months is Expired, if your Honour Sees that I will be Deserving of Getting Ingaged in Some Imployment under his Majesty I hope youel Recommend one acad =cing as I will merit it, Just Get me Libity to have it in my power to hunt and Bring to Justice the People who Brought me to Misfortune, if your Honour, Does not undertake Me, Please to Let me Know by the bearer who is my wife, that I may apply

apply to some other Magistrate, as I dont wish
to have, them in Readiness any longer, and hope
Your Honour will Consider me and Remain your
Honour My humble Ser't Jerem'n Grant

P'd your Honour May Say and many others to that
only I was in Custody, that I would not ever
Give me Self up, But now I am at Liberty and Ile
Let you See, I only want Some Means to Enable
me to Shew the Contry who was Doing the harm
which I was Blamed for   Jer Grant

*A letter written by Jeremiah Grant to Magistrate Henry Langley on July 13, 1815,
requesting a pardon.*

By now the outlaws were rested and their stomachs full. They left Whelan's cottage and went across country, avoiding the roads and staying close to the woods until they reached the outskirts of Castlecomer, still in County Kilkenny. Here they were joined by a band of local outlaws eager to be led and taught by the now-famous Captain Grant. The new recruits offered information about a local landowner named Kennedy who lived at Ferrodey, who was reputed to have a large quantity of the "ready" in his house, along with some fine plate. Jeremiah agreed to lead the raid.

By the time they arrived at their destination it was nightfall. To their surprise the front door was only on a latch and the outlaws were able to enter without a sound. They stole to the dining-room, where they found the Kennedy family sitting at table. While the rest of the outlaws held them at pistol-point, Jeremiah and Whelan demanded money. Mr Kennedy replied that he had none. It seemed to be the case; the house was ransacked and all that was found was £17, some jewellery and plate, and assorted trinkets.

A disappointed Jeremiah was preparing to leave when the elderly grandmother, who had sat silently throughout the robbery, struggled to her feet.

"A curse upon you all!" she pronounced at the top of her voice. "And you two," she added, pointing at Grant and Whelan, "will swing one day!"

With the curse still ringing in their ears, the outlaws made their way to Boullybawn, where they hid the largest items of their booty. They drank a little fortifying whiskey before paying a visit to the home of a man who had informed on some of the group. Soon after giving the man a beating, Jeremiah and Whelan parted ways with the gang: the bloodthirsty tendencies of the others were not to their taste. The two stole the hunting mare of a Mr Lalor and rode it to Baltinglass, south Wicklow, where they met another of the Drogheda escapees, a man named Crawford.

But the authorities traced the stolen horse to Crawford's father-in-law's home. Without warning the house was surrounded by a party of troopers and the occupants called upon to surrender. Grant and Whelan raced upstairs to the loft where they managed to shut the door behind them just as the soldiers were breaking in downstairs. The outlaws placed themselves on either side of the door with pistols raised, listening as the rooms below were systematically searched. Soon there were footsteps pounding up the stairs. They steeled themselves for a fight.

A sergeant burst into the loft, holding a candle in one hand. As he peered around in the gloom, he heard two pistols being cocked close to his head.

"If you stir hand or foot," Grant told the frightened man, "I will instantly blow out your brains."

The outlaws disarmed the sergeant and marched him back downstairs before them and out onto the street. Then they fired their weapons in the air and, with shouts and screams to intimidate the soldiers, fled to the mountains. They passed the night sheltering in a stack of oats, pulling out some of the sheaves to make sleeping recesses for themselves.

The following morning the outlaws paid a poor family eighteen shillings for breakfast before heading towards the town of Carlow in search of rich pickings. They did not tarry long, for they found that rewards for their capture were posted on the town gaol. The desperadoes prudently decided to journey on to Kilkenny.

There they met yet another fellow-escapee. He had glad tidings concerning a certain Mr Loughman, who was rumoured to have between two and three hundred guineas hidden in his house. All three agreed that the prize was one worth the extra effort.

Jeremiah was mightily weary of the road, the hills, the woods and the deprivations of the outlaw's life. He swore that if the haul was as big as they expected, then he would use his share to take his family to America, never to return.

As they broke in to Mr Loughman's home, they were attacked by a fearsome guard dog. It sprang at Whelan, who loosed off a shot, but missed. Jeremiah took careful aim and, as the snarling dog tried to savage Carol, shot it dead.

The gunfire had roused the house's occupants. Fearing for their lives, they and the servants locked themselves into the drawing-room, barricading the door. This would not do, of course: neither Jeremiah nor his companions knew where the money was hidden. They went to the front of the house, smashed the windows with the butts of their weapons, and clambered into the drawing-room.

Grant questioned Loughman about the large amount of cash supposedly hidden in the house, but the gentleman denied the existence of any such sum. The outlaw threatened to burn down the house; still Loughman refused to hand over his wealth. Jeremiah even had the bloodied corpse of the dog dragged in; the gentleman stuck to his guns.

There was nothing for it, save to make do with £4 and a small amount of plate. The robbers pocketed it and left, going into hiding in the home of another outlaw near Ballyraggat. Jeremiah later learned, much to his chagrin, that Loughman had fooled him.[cxi] In the very room where the family and servants had been held at gunpoint, two hundred guineas in gold were hidden under the carpet and another £50 was concealed behind a picture.

The Captain was determined on robbing his stake for a future in America. Together with Whelan and two others, and acting on information, he raided the mansion of a Captain Stubber, believing him to have £300 in cash hidden in the house. While their comrades kept their weapons trained on the occupants, Jeremiah and Carol ransacked every room in search of the fortune. They failed to find it. The outlaws eventually gave up and left, satisfying themselves with a trunk full of plate, a fine gold watch, some guineas and half-guineas, and a small quantity of silver coins. Grant spotted two cases of fine pistols, which he also took. The robbers relieved the

Stubbers of a fine horse and jaunting car, into which they placed their booty before making their getaway.

Buoyed by this success, the comrades raided the home of a Mr Horan near Maryborough. Jeremiah, on seeing a beautiful piano in the corner, could not resist the opportunity to tinkle the ivories. Seating himself at the instrument, he played some beautiful pieces for the astonished family. Next, the Captain took from his pocket a tin whistle and proceeded to play a few jigs and reels, before bowing and leaving with quite a haul of valuables and cash. Jeremiah and Whelan galloped from the house on stolen mounts and raced to an old abandoned barn near Ballyroan, where they hid some of the booty, before continuing on to Ballynakill before daybreak. They remained in hiding here for a few days, before stealing back to the abandoned barn and retrieving their haul. This they divided among the gang members.

The two desperadoes bade their comrades farewell; there were too many troopers and constables in the vicinity. They left for Kilkenny in grand style, mounted on two fine, "borrowed" hunters, complete with polished saddles and bridles. Each man was armed with three cases of fine pistols and dressed like a gentleman.

Highway Robbery

It was inevitable that when their purses were empty the two outlaws would turn to highway robbery. They set up headquarters close to the main Waterford road and concentrated on the many coaches and private carriages heading to and from the city.

On one of their highway sorties they held up the carriage of a Mr and Mrs MacShane. On the order to "stand and deliver", the lady handed over a paltry £3.

"What time is it?" Jeremiah then asked.

The gentleman unthinkingly produced a fine heavy gold watch – which the outlaw promptly demanded.

"I beg you, sir," the victim pleaded, "do not take this watch. It was a present from a friend."

As chance would have it, Jeremiah knew the brother of the friend in question. He told MacShane that he could redeem the watch at an appointed location some time later. MacShane was delighted and offered to buy it back for £15; to his surprise, the outlaw would accept no more than five guineas.

While the deal was being struck, another gig came trundling down the road towards them. Carol Whelan rode to intercept it, but the driver whipped his horse forward, only halting when Grant fired his pistols into the air. This car was being driven by Brennan, a hearth-money collector from Castlecomer.[cxii] The indignant and outraged lackey was robbed of thirty shillings in coin and his silver watch, and was probably lucky to escape with his life.

As a result of the robbery of one of the government's collectors of taxes, a further reward of £100 was placed on the head of Captain Grant. He decided to head elsewhere with his companion, and the two rode out to a hideout in the Bog of Allen.

Yet even in that wilderness they were not safe from the authorities. They were seen by a small party of dragoons led by a Mr Steele and Constable Fennelly, and called upon to surrender. The outlaws had barely enough time to mount their horses and take to the bog before the dragoons opened fire.

Constable Fennelly raced after the fleeing outlaws and succeeded in firing off a couple of rounds, narrowly missing Grant as he stopped to help Whelan, who had become stuck in the quagmire. Pursued as far as Moyne by the patrol, the outlaws changed horses and, accompanied by a local youth named Fitzpatrick, made good their escape as far as Wexford, where they hid in the dense wood of Killoughraun.

Tired and hungry, the three were in as much need of sustenance and warm clothes as of cash. They robbed a house in the vicinity where, in search of valuables, Carol Whelan came across a fine hat – and it was this seemingly unimportant item that would ultimately lead to the outlaws' downfall.

Unbeknownst to Whelan, the hat had the name of its owner stamped on the inside band. When they left the hat behind during the raid of another property a few days later, it alerted the authorities to the fact that the outlaws were still in the region.

It was June 24, 1816. Almost a year to the day after Napoleon faced Waterloo, Captain Grant was to meet his. As Whelan and he lay asleep in a concealed hideout in the woods, young Fitzpatrick was keeping the first watch. But the youth was weary and failed to observe a party of soldiers and local gentlemen approaching stealthily.

It was the loud snap of a blunderbuss that woke Jeremiah. He jumped to his feet and roused Whelan, who grabbed whatever weapons were to hand. A fierce gunfight ensued, with the outlaws giving as good as they were getting, but it was soon clear that they were completely outgunned and surrounded.

Left with no alternative, they attempted to break suddenly through the cordon of military. As Jeremiah charged, he was felled by one of the soldiers. It was a fierce blow between the shoulders and the musket stock broke with the force of it. Further resistance was useless; Fitzpatrick had already been captured and it was not long before Whelan was also lying disarmed beside his comrades.

So many shots were fired in the battle that it was a miracle no-one was killed that night. Though none of the outlaws suffered injury, seven or eight of the soldiers sustained wounds. The three prisoners were secured with ropes, tied together and bundled into a cart for the journey to the lock-up in Enniscorthy.

Forgiving – not Forgotten

The following day the two notorious highwaymen and their young accomplice were transferred to the more secure confines of Wexford Gaol, where they were incarcerated together to await their fate. Here Jeremiah Grant, veteran of so many breakouts, once more plotted an escape. It was to be his final attempt.

He had hidden a small saw and a sharp piece of metal in the sole of his shoe, and on the first night in the jail managed to saw through the bars of the cell window. But as the three detainees made their way through the window to freedom, they were confronted by Mr Clerke, the son of Maryborough gaoler Governor John Clerke, and a body of armed constables. The prisoners were led to another cell, where they were watched over by armed guards. The following morning they were returned under heavy escort to Maryborough Prison. Each was put into a separate cell, heavily bolted and ironed, with a triple guard placed both inside and outside the walls.

Jeremiah was treated humanely by Mr Clerke, but allowed no freedom. He was kept in his cell at all times; at night his hands were manacled and his feet were secured with heavy bolts. The manacles on his hands were conjoined circles which, when locked on the wrists, formed a figure of eight and were held together by a screw. They were excruciatingly uncomfortable and made sleep impossible.

The authorities were taking no risks with the man who had masterminded the earlier escape from Maryborough Gaol. When he arrived this time, he was thoroughly searched. Numerous small metal items were found in the seams of his clothing and in the soles of his shoes, but his guards had overlooked a copper penny Jeremiah had concealed in his mouth. The prisoner used it to remove a nail from the wall of his cell and, twisting the coin around the nail, fashioned a makeshift screwdriver. The tool enabled him to open his manacles each night in order to get some sleep. He replaced them each morning before his guards entered, concealing the tool in his mouth. In this way he was able to obtain a night's rest.

Captain Grant and Carol Whelan went on trial before the notorious "hanging judge" Lord Norbury at the Maryborough assizes. Jeremiah was defended by Leonard McNally who, thirteen years previously, had defended Robert Emmet. McNally was subsequently discovered to be an informer and spy in the pay of the British authorities. Unsurprisingly, then, Grant and Whelan were convicted of numerous crimes and sentenced to be hanged on August 13, 1816.[cxiii]

Large crowds converged on Maryborough to witness the executions. Many travelled from the surrounding counties, journeying through the night to be present, and every vantage point in the vicinity was requisitioned by the spectators: roofs, windows, and even trees were occupied. When Jeremiah was led to the gallows he received an ovation fit for a king.

After many minutes of prolonged applause he begged the crowd for silence and in a clear and unembarrassed voice delivered a remarkable and lengthy address from the scaffold.[cxiv] He began by asking the gathering for their prayers, "that Almighty God may extend his mercy to my soul that in a few moments must appear before his Divine Presence". He expressed sorrow for his crimes and thanked all those who had been kind to him from the time of his capture.

The man who had triggered his life of crime got a special mention. Of Gilbert Maher he said: "I had a dispute with a county Tipperary gentleman and a lawsuit, and was angry with him for a time – but I long since forgave the injuries he did me." Though Maher was not present, Jeremiah addressed him in person. "I forgive you," he said, "from the bottom of my heart, for the injuries which your malevolence inflicted on me and my family, and it is my hope that God has also forgiven you."

"I never bore malice to any man," Jeremiah continued. "I never laid down on my bed with a wish for revenge. I forgive all who ever injured me as I hope to be forgiven by God and obtain his pardon for my crimes."

When the executioner performed his duties, the board did not drop away suddenly from under the feet of the convicts, but fell to a slanting position, so that the condemned men slipped down to their deaths. But though there was no shock, Captain Grant died without a struggle and, it seemed to spectators, without pain. The bodies of the executed were left hanging for three quarters of an hour before being enclosed in coffins and delivered to their families and friends for internment. Ireland's most dignified highwayman is believed to be buried in the local cemetery of Moyne, County Tipperary.

Captain Grant

My name is   Cap - tain Grant I make bold   for to say, I___

am as worthy a   champ- ion as   ev - er   went the way With a

good _____   case   of   pis -   tols   and   a

trusty_____   broad   sword_____

Stand and   del - iv - er   was the in - stant word.

To commit a mean action I always did scorn,
In robbing the rich I thought it no harm:
Effects and money from them I did secure,
And shared part of the spoil with the languishing poor.

When I met poor travellers hungry and dry,
Their craving wants I always did supply;
And with these poor creatures I divided my store,
When it was gone I went robbing for more.

From Maryborough prison I made my way out
And those who opposed me I put to the route
With my metal bolts, I knocked the centinel down,
And made my escape out of Maryborough town.

In the house of poor Tanner that night I did lie
And for his sad fate I did bitterly cry;
He got sentenced to die for the sheltering of me,
But he never had a hand in any robbery.

Me and my comrade took to the highway,
We then fell a robbing by night and by day;
We robb'd Captain Stubby and a great many more,
On Rum, Gin and Brandy, we spent part of the store.

Straight we took our way to the county of Wexford,
Where we sheltered ourselves in the midst of a wood,
Until a wicked woman did us betray,
She had us surrounded as a sleeping we lay.

On our arms we rested when we awoke,
To our great misfortune our powder [it got wet/was soaked];
We were obliged to give ourselves up,
To that gallant fine hero called Captain Jacob.

The guards did surround us by night and by day,
To Maryborough Prison they marched us away;
And in a short time our trials came on [hand],
We were condemned to die by the laws of the land.

May Heaven pity my wife and children small,
Leave them lamenting my woeful downfall;
All you good people warning take by me,
Shun drinking late hours and bad company.

When that I am dead and laid in the mould,
All you good people pray for my soul,
May Heaven comfort my children and keep them from want,
And Heaven have mercy on the brave Captain Grant.

Endnotes

Dudley Costello

[i] 'THE DE ANGULOS…' One of the original de Angulos (a family who were also known as the Nangles) was named Jocelyn ("Gocelin" in Norman French). This was gaelicised early on as Mac Goisdelbh and, later, Mac Cosdealbha and Mac Coisdeallaigh, and anglicised variously as Mac Custellagh, Mac Guistillo, Mac Costello and, eventually, Costello. A Mayo story gives a different explanation of how the name was derived. Philip, the sixth Lord de Angulo (the original owner of the legendary Toledo Blade) spent some time in Spain and was known as The Castillion. As a result, the family adopted the surname Mac Costillo.

[ii] 'THE FOUR MASTERS…' The four main compilers of *The Annals of The Four Masters* were Micháel O Cleirigh, O Duibhgeanáin of Leitrim, O Maolchonaire of Roscommon, and Cucoigcriche O Cleirigh.

[iii] 'DILLON WAS IN POSSESSION OF 64,195 ACRES…' By 1665 the seventh Viscount Dillon was in possession of 24,454 acres in the barony of Costello alone.

[iv] 'EDWARD "CORNET" NANGLE…' A cornet was a sub-lieutenant in a cavalry regiment.

[v] 'TORY' There had certainly been brigands and outlaws before Dudley Costello's era, most notably County Mayo's Captain Gallagher. In letters and dispatches of the early 1600s the favoured word for the native-bred outlaw was "wood-kerne" or, more simply, "kerne". It was derived from the Irish *ceatharnach*, which Dineen's

dictionary defines as "a foot soldier, kern, yeoman, a tyrant, a bully, a hero". In 1612, for example, the Lord Deputy referred to Armagh as a place which "ever bred kernes". According to T. Crofton Croker, writing in *Researches in the South of Ireland* (London, 1824), the epithet "Tory" originated in the civil wars under Elizabeth and was applied only to a man of the peasantry. Sir Henry Sidney, Lord Lieutenant of Ireland in 1690, "cursed, hated and detested" Ireland above all other countries, because it was most difficult to do any service there, "where a man must struggle with famine and fastnesses, inaccessible bogs and light-footed Tories".

[vi] 'HE LED HIS MEN…' According to another version of this story it was the village of Longford that was attacked and Costello was not present. Nangle is supposed to have led a band of two hundred Tories against the people and been killed in the ensuing skirmish.

[vii] 'A DRAGOON CUT OFF THE DEAD MAN'S HEAD…' Nangle's head was later spiked above the gates of Dublin Castle.

[viii] 'THE CONNIVANCE OF THE LOCAL PEOPLE…' Marshall reports that Lord Kingston, President of Connacht, urged Lord Dillon's steward to employ some of Dillon's tenants to betray Costello. The steward responded that this method had been tried and failed: the men Dillon had recruited had instead become Costello's intelligencers!

[ix] 'A COMMON MURDERER AND TRAITOR…' Dudley's most loyal comrades – Christopher Hill, Thomas Plunkett, Cahir (alias Charles) MacCawel, and Neil O'Neill – were also proclaimed in the same broadsheet.

[x] 'A FORD ON THE RIVER MOY…' Another version of the outlaw's death gives his native Castlemore as the scene of his demise, but a letter written by Captain Theobald Dillon, his killer, specifies the ford on the river Moy as the location. There is yet another local version that insists that Dudley Costello was killed on the slopes of Sliabh Lugha in Barnalyra (*Bárr na Laidre*: the top of the river fork), near his famous hideout (now the site of Connacht Airport).

[xi] 'A REBEL'S HEAD SPIKED ON A POLE…' Peter Somerville-Large in *Dublin* (1979) recounts an Elizabethan poem pointing out that:

> "These Trunckles heddes do playnly show
> Each rebelles fatall end
> And what a haynous crime it is
> The Queen for to offend."

[xii] 'HE TOO BECAME AN OUTLAW.' A local story concerning Dudley's son was recorded in 1874 and included in Maire McDonnell-Garvey's *The Ancient Territory of Sliabh Lugha Mid-Connacht*. Michael Rushe, who became foster-father to the outlaw's

son (also named Dudley), learned that Lord Dillon, in his determination to get rid of the entire Costello clan, had placed a price on the head of the boy. In the dead of night Rushe left the district, taking the young lad with him. Leaving Connacht far behind them, they travelled into Ulster and settled in what is now Lisburn.

They lived there for a number of years, Rushe passing them off as father and son. He worked as a labourer and saw to it that young "Dudley Rushe" was well educated. The plan was that when the boy was old enough he would be told of his true lineage, return to the west to reclaim his title and estates, and avenge the death of his father.

Matters, however, took a different course. While still in adolescence Dudley was involved in a fracas with the manservant of a local planter, who called him "a beggar's brat". Dudley had inherited his father's temper and, with one punch, knocked the fellow into a foaming river. The young planter's father instigated an inquiry into the affair and this worried Michael Rushe. He knew that the tentacles of Lord Dillon reached well outside his domain and that Dudley's identity could be uncovered.

Again he fled with the boy to safety, this time to County Leitrim, where they settled in the vicinity of Carrick-on-Shannon. All about them they could see and hear signs of the immense power wielded by Dillon from his Mayo stronghold, and Rushe feared that so strong was His Lordship's grip that young Dudley would never regain what was rightfully his. For two years the "father and son" lived in the area, the boy still ignorant of his true name and origin.

Dudley grew into a fine young man, strong, brave and educated, with a passion for all things Irish. He was especially skilled at hurling, which at that time was as popular as it is today. At a certain match Dudley played like a demon and was the hero of the day, winning the *sliotar* with ease and scoring at will. He was presented with a yew hurley, which had a silk tassel attached, the highest honour that could be attained at such gatherings. As the crowds of admirers milled around the boy, the referee and judges approached Michael Rushe and began to praise and compliment him and his talented son. Unable to bear his burden any longer, Rushe blurted out his secret and announced to the huge crowd – and to Dudley – that the boy was in reality the son of the outlaw Costello and had been spirited away as a child because of the price placed on his head by Lord Dillon.

Dudley and Michael were brought to a place of safety by some former confederates of the outlaw: a cottage near the decaying ruins of the Costello castle at Tullaghanrock. The inhabitant, an old man who had once worked for the Costellos, still cared for the outlaw's old horse, the steed from which he was shot. He was also in possession of the rapparee's sword, the Toledo Blade, which he presented to the young Dudley. He regaled the lad with stories of his father's deeds and exploits, and his death at the hands of the Dillons.

In the meantime, Lord Dillon had been informed of events and sent word that he would like to meet the young Dudley. They met that very same day, with Dillon professing friendship and extending the olive branch. A peace of sorts was made. The friends of Dudley and Rushe, however, were uneasy and warned the naïve youth to beware of the treachery of "the Sasanaigh" (the English). Shortly afterwards the Earl invited Dudley to a private meeting at a spot called Toby's Bridge. On arrival

Dudley was confronted not by Lord Dillon but by Tobias Dillon, a relative of the Earl and an experienced, keen swordsman.

They set to: Dudley, armed with the Toledo Blade and burning with revenge and disdain, slew Tobias. Like his father before him, he then took to the hills, pursued by the authorities. A short time later he died in a fall from his horse near Ballaghaderreen.

Tomás Costello, brother of Dudley the elder, petitioned the Court of Claims, asserting his right to the family's confiscated lands. The claim was dismissed and the barony of Costello remained in the possession of the Dillons.

Tomás was later ambushed and shot dead by a hired assassin named Ruane, who lay in wait for him behind a turf stack and shot him in the back. Ruane was in the pay of the Dillons. Tomás Láidir, known as Strong Thomas, had also fought against Cromwell and distinguished himself in a fierce battle in the Curlew Mountains (see Douglas Hyde, *Love Songs of Connacht*, Dun Emer Press, 1904).

The same Tomás figured in one of the great Connacht love stories, a tragic love affair with Úna Bán MacDermot. The story goes that Tomás was a guest in the MacDermot home one evening when Úna drank a toast to Tomás instead of to her future bridegroom. Tomás loved Úna, but her father forbade their relationship because there was an enmity between their families. Úna fell ill on her island home in Lough Key and eventually her father gave Tomás permission to visit her. With Tomás beside her bed, Úna slept easily for the first time in some days. Tomás then ventured downstairs; uncomfortable that there was nobody about, he went outside. His servant, meanwhile, was convinced that the MacDermots were only feigning friendship and that there was treachery in the air. Tomás swore an oath that he would never speak to Úna or the MacDermots again unless he was called back before crossing the ford of Donóige. At the ford he hesitated, but crossed over at the urging of his servant. A messenger sent by Úna arrived just as Tomás reached the other side – but Tomás refused to break his vow and would not return to her. Úna was said to have died of a broken heart; tradition has it that Tomás slew his servant.

Tomás is reputed to be buried beside Úna in the graveyard on Castle Island. It is said that ash trees once grew from each grave, reaching and bending toward the other, until the branches met and entwined in the middle to form a natural embrace, a love arch, which could not be parted by human hands. This is also reputed to have happened in the case of Derdriu of the Sorrows and her lover Naoise, except that their graves were at opposite sides of a lake and, instead of ash, two yew trees grew and came together, "never to be separated in this world". Mr Jasper Tully, one time editor of *The Roscommon Herald*, claimed to have seen the trees in 1865 as he made a tour of the area (see Douglas Hyde in *Amhráin Ghrádha*).

Before his murder, the tragic Tomás composed a forty-four verse poem and love song for his beloved Úna, parts of which are still in the repertoires of traditional Irish singers. A translation of one stanza, by J.K. Casey in M.F. Ó Conchúir, *Úna Bhán* (Cló Iar Chonnachta Teo, 1994), reads:

> "I wear within my doublet a bright lock of her hair,
> That she gave me, when we parted, from her tresses curling fair;
> 'Tis all I have to soothe my woe throughout the coming years–
> 'Tis all I have to bear away the traces of my tears."

The Three Brennans

^{xiii} 'REPUTED TO HAVE BEEN THE FOUNDING MEMBERS OF THE KELLYMOUNT GANG...' See Reverend James Graves, *Ancient Tribes and Territories of Ossory* (The Journal Office, Parade St, Kilkenny).

^{xiv} 'THE KELLYMOUNT GANG... CAPTAIN FRENEY...' In the year 1325 in Kilkenny, Lady Alice Kettell was accused by the Bishop of Ossory of being a witch. It was said that she oiled her broomstick with magic ointment; then, mounting it with her accomplice Petronilla, she made a night's journey in a minute, flying to The Devil's Bit in County Tipperary to hold her sabbaths. It was also rumoured that every night from her broomstick Lady Alice supervised a team of demons sweeping the Kilkenny streets, so that her son William Ultan, a greedy land pirate, could use the rubbish to manure his lands. Lady Alice escaped persecution with the help of some powerful friends, who secretly removed her from the area, but Petronilla was burned at the Cross of Kilkenny for her involvement and William Ultan received a long prison sentence. Local folklore has it that Lady Alice had been such an expert on her broomstick that she "beat even Captain Freney the robber, and all his Kellymount gang, in riding amid the darkness of night".

^{xv} 'PRETENDING THAT THEY HAD DISCOVERED IT THEMSELVES IN SOME CAVES...' Lord Chief Justice Keatinge reported scepticism of this story in a letter to Ormonde:

> "The Brennans have much abused Captain Matthew, and cannot to this hour be brought to say how they came to know how the plate was brought to the place where they found it, more than that a spy of theirs brought them word it would be divided there that night; but what that spy's name was, or where he is, or who were to divide it, they know not, though they told Valentine Smyth when they were going to the place, and he questioned them concerning the enemy from whom by dint of sword they were going to rescue it, that he need not fear, for they were a company of pitiful fellows. In this they spoke the truth, though they knew not who they were... so it is believed by all that the Brennans brought the plate thither themselves."

Count Redmond O'Hanlon

^{xvi} 'THE IRISH SCANDERBEG...' The Albanian chief and national hero Scanderbeg, whose real name was George Kastrioti (1403?–68), was the son of an Albanian prince. He was taken as a hostage to Constantinople during the occupation of Albania by the Ottoman Turks. Scanderbeg was educated as a Muslim and enlisted in the Turkish army, where his military skill earned him favour with the Sultan. In

1443, when he learned that Albania had revolted against the Turks, Scanderbeg deserted and returned to his native land. He abjured Islam for Christianity and became leader of the Albanian chiefs. With the aid of Pope Pius II and the governments of Venice, Naples and Hungary, he forced the Turks to accept a 10-year armistice. When Scanderbeg abrogated the armistice in 1463, he was forced to fight Turkey without the aid of his former allies and, shortly after his death, Albania was defeated.

xvii 'AN ANONYMOUS PAMPHLET PUBLISHED...' *The Life and Death of The Incomparable And Indefatigable Tory Redmond O'Hanlon, Commonly Called Count Hanlyn.* It is addressed in letter form to a Mr R. A. in Dublin, dated August 1, 1681, and is now in the possession of the British Library.

xviii 'HE WAS FORCED TO LEAVE THE AREA...' Cosgrave reported that Redmond happened "to be at the killing of a gentleman in a quarrel, and flying for safety, stayed abroad for a long time, still refusing to come to a trial, till he was outlawed".

xix 'DASHING SWORDSMAN...' A swordsman was regarded as someone who had experienced military service, with the armies of O'Neill and O'Donnell in particular.

xx 'A PROTECTION RACKET...' Reverend Lawrence Power, rector of Tandragee, wrote in 1679 of the outlaw and his band:

> "Their chief Redmond O'Hanlon is described as a cunning dangerous fellow, who though proclaimed as an outlaw with the rest of his crew and sums of money on their heads, yet he reigns and keeps all in subjection so far that is credibly reported, he raises more in a year by contribution than the King's Land, Taxes and Chimney-Money come to; and thereby is enabled to bribe Clerks and Officers if not their masters, and makes all too much truckle to him."

xxi 'WORD OF COUNT O'HANLON'S AUDACITY...' Sir Francis Brewster, in a letter to an English newspaper at the time, wrote: "There can be no doubt that in Ireland Redmond O Hanlon has earned unrivalled notoriety as a highwayman." He went on to say that the O'Hanlon gang were so active in Ulster that it was unsafe to travel the roads without an escort, and that O'Hanlon "has evidently great powers of endurance, a capacity for organization and leadership, nimble wits and exceptional cunning. A man of genius he certainly is; but of his personality we know nothing."

xxii 'THE INEBRIATED MEN FIRED A VOLLEY...' In another version of this story Redmond himself dressed as the respectable squire and requested the military escort, which he then plied with wine. On reaching the end of the journey at Mullaghbawn the "squire" handed each trooper a florin and asked the merry men to fire a volley into the air as a celebration of the safe trip. This was the agreed signal for the outlaw's gang to dash forth from their hiding place in some nearby trees and relieve the startled troopers of their weapons, mounts and uniforms. The soldiers were then sent back to Armagh in their underclothes.

xxiii 'HIS MOST TRUSTED MEN…' The following were the most trusted members of O'Hanlon's band: Captain Richard Power (see Chapter IV); Paul Liddy; Manus O'Neill (called the Gold-finder); Charles Dempsey (Cahir na gCapall – see Chapter VIII); "Strong" John Person; Shane Berrah; James Butler; John Mulhone; James Carrick; Quee (Wee) Harry Donahan, also called "The Napper"; Patrick McTeague; John Riley; Arthur O'Neill; "O'Kelly from Kilkenny"; Philip Galloge; Pat Mill; and his brother, Laughlin O'Hanlon.

xxiv 'THIRTY HAND-PICKED MERCENARIES…' Tory hunting was a popular pastime and many adventurers eagerly joined in the chase. Records from July 1649 to November 1656 of all the monies received or paid out of the public purse show that £3,847 and 5 shillings was paid for killing wolves and £2,149, 12 shillings and 6 pence for apprehending notorious rebels and Tories. It was a lucrative business and in June 1676 alone seven known outlaws had been killed.

Two of the most notorious Tory-hunting families in the country were the Cootes of Cootehill and the Johnstons of the Fews, planters infamous for their cruelty and ruthlessness in tracking down and murdering priests. Tradition has it that on one occasion the Johnstons tracked Redmond as far as the shore of Carlingford Lough. With the pursuers at his heels the outlaw was left with no option but to swim the estuary. He was spotted entering the water by the hunters: they unleashed a ferocious hound and the massive animal plunged into the water in pursuit. The dog caught up with Redmond and a fierce struggle ensued, man against beast, with the outlaw proving victorious: he drowned the dog and escaped.

Carlingford Lough, where Redmond O'Hanlon drowned the Tory hunters' dog and swam to safety.

The practice of Tory hunting gave rise to some brutal rhymes, still chanted by children today:

"I'll tell you a story about Johnny Magory
He went to the wood and he shot a Tory;
I'll tell you another about his brother,
He went to the wood and shot another.

He hunted him in and he hunted him out
Three times through bog and about and about
'Till out of the bush he spied a head,
So he levelled his pistol and shot him dead."

xxv 'FOUR LOCAL BUSINESSMEN…' The four were Sir George Ranson, Sir Hans Hamilton, Sir George Acheson and William Hill.

xxvi 'AN ANONYMOUS LETTER…' The letter states that two young men, tenants of a Mrs St John, succeeded in recovering some stolen property which the outlaws had concealed in the locality. That night the Tories burned a house and barn belonging to the young men's father; when the troops garrisoned at Tandragee were alerted, they deliberately delayed the chase until the outlaws were well away, claiming that their informant was lying. The writer remarks:

"It is evident that they had confederates among the soldiers; Sir Toby Poyntz of Poyntzpass, a justice of the peace and his son, Captain Charles Poyntz, who was in charge of the local garrison, were suspect. The one should be removed from commission and the other with his company be replaced by an officer and men with no local connections… [all the passes] between the counties of Armagh and Down, Fathom Castle, Tusker, Poyntzpass, Scarva and Knockbridge should be guarded, and all boats on the river from the mouth of Carlingford Lough to Knockbridge should be taken away."

xxvii 'SIR TOBY POYNTZ OF POYNTZPASS…' How the father and son (Sir Toby and Sir Charles) managed to run with the hare and hunt with the hounds is shown by a letter from Sir Charles Poyntz to Sir William Flower, written shortly after Redmond O'Hanlon's death, in which he gives the impression of being a little resentful of Lucas getting credit for that exploit, and in which he explains how the plot bringing about the downfall of the famous outlaw came about.

"About the beginning of December last (1680) Art McCall, alias Hanlon (who was once a servant to my father), and at that time had no stain on him, but what his surname brought him, came to me and desired to be admitted to my company. I represented to him the unreasonableness of his request, and how it gave occasion for the discourse of malicious rascals that had scandalised my father and me as having too much kindness for the Hanlons, but withal I told him that he might do that service which would serve the King and country, and oblige me and forever make him rich and then proposed the service which he has now performed, as the way to bring all that to pass; at first he boggled at it, but when I laid down several ways to him how it might be performed (and all of them depending on his associating with Redmond), he concluded to undertake it or die in the attempt, upon which I immediately went to Sir Hans Hamilton and gave him an account of what I had done, and desired that he would give him a pass and protection, to prevent his being killed should he meet with any soldiers; which Sir Hans readily consented to, and having made me write it, he signed it, and delivered it to Art's own hand... how he came to be concerned with Mr Lucas I know not but am extremely glad that on any account the service was done... only this much give me leave to say for myself, that had I not on that design first sent him to associate with Redmond he had not been in a capacity to have served Mr Lucas or anyone else."

xxxviii 'BEST DESCRIPTION WE HAVE...' Taken from *Count Hanlan's Downfall, or A True and Exact Account of the Killing of that Arch Traytor and Tory Redmond O Hanlan.*

xxix 'THE TOWN OF LETTERKENNY...' Versions of this story report that Redmond O'Hanlon senior went on to prosper as a merchant in Letterkenny, becoming a highly respected citizen of the town and county.

In 1680, as the O'Hanlon family fled to Donegal to escape the recriminations of the proclamation against them, more troops were poured into Ulster. This was as a result of the discovery of a "Popish plot" to murder the King and to place his brother, the Catholic James II, on the throne. The plot was supposed to have extended to Ireland and the harsh and unjust laws against the people were enforced with renewed vigour. Oliver Plunkett, The Archbishop of Armagh, was arrested and brought in chains to Dundalk. He was accused of conspiring with Catholic rulers abroad to assist with the landing of 70,000 foreign troops at Carlingford Lough and attack England through the "back-door" – a fabrication which enabled the authorities to charge Plunkett with treason. The Archbishop's nationalistic and Catholic outpourings embarrassed and even threatened the establishment. A group of prominent local citizens was to be assembled at the next assizes and asked to swear an oath against the cleric, but the plan failed, as no witnesses of substance were willing to participate. It was said of Plunkett "that he was honoured and respected by Protestant and Catholic alike". Legend has it that an approach was then made to Redmond O'Hanlon, offering him and his men unconditional pardons if he would perjure himself and swear an oath against the prelate. O'Hanlon refused. He protested that no offer could induce him to betray an innocent man, even though the man in question had on numerous occasions denounced outlaws: during the General Synod of the Irish Church in 1670, the Archbishop had ordered priests and preachers to warn all their people "against giving aid to Tories".

Failing in their efforts to produce any substantial evidence against the Archbishop, the authorities had their prisoner transported to London and incarcerated in the Tower. Six months later, after a blatantly unfair trial, Archbishop Plunkett was condemned to death. As he stood in the death cart at Tyburn Oliver, he delivered his last speech to the assembled gallery in which he stated:

"I assure you that a great Peer sent me Notice, that he would save my Life, if I wou'd accuse others, but I answered, that I never knew any Conspirators in Ireland, but such as I said before as were publickly known Outlaws; and to save my Life, I wou'd not falsely accuse any, or prejudice my own Soul."

Archbishop Plunkett was hanged, drawn and quartered on July 1, 1681, some two months after the murder of Redmond O'Hanlon. His execution was greeted with outrage and renewed violent attacks on Government supporters and their property in Ireland.

xxx 'THE TRAITOR SHOT HIM DEAD.' Another account of the murder insists that, after he shot Redmond dead with his carbine, Art discarded the weapon and fled by a rear door of the cottage. He mounted his horse and made his escape to Banbridge, where he alerted the waiting Lucas and his troops to the fact that he had killed the outlaw Count. The traitor and the troops then made their way to the scene of the killing.

Meanwhile, on hearing the shot, William O'Shiel had run into the cottage, to find his leader lying bleeding and dying on the ground; Art had already fled the scene. With his dying breath the outlaw begged his trusted bodyguard to cut off his head and hide it so that the military would be unable to have it spiked on one of their English gaols.

Redmond O'Hanlon died, his head cradled in the lap of O'Shiel. When the last light of life had left the body, and before he himself escaped, O'Shiel obeyed the outlaw's last wish and cut off his friend's head, hiding it in an unused well. The headless body of O'Hanlon was brought into Newry town and handed over to some members his grieving family, who buried it in the Catholic graveyard in Ballynabeck. In due course the head was discovered and spiked above the gates of Downpatrick Gaol.

Richard Power

xxxi 'WILLING TO FIGHT FOR THEIR RIGHTS…' Many years later W.E.H. Lecky was to say about the introduction of the harsh and unjust laws inflicted on the Irish people: "They were not for the persecution of a sect, but the degradation of a nation." In 1641, according to the lowest estimate, there were 8,000 Roman Catholic landowners in Ireland. With the exception of a mere 26, all of them lost their property during the Cromwellian period. A number of the dispossessed received land in compensation to the west of the Shannon river; the Acts of Settlement and Exploration further amended the balance to about 1,300 Catholic owners during the reign of Charles II.

xxxii 'RICHARD RODE BOLDLY UP...' Another version of this story insists that the outlaw was accompanied by some members of his gang, but it seems more likely that he was alone.

xxxiii 'A YOUNG ENGLISH ENSIGN...' A title originally applied to the lowest commissioned officer in the British army, who traditionally carried the ensign or colour. The title was changed in 1871 to Second Lieutenant.

xxxiv 'MEETING OF SOME OF HIS LIEUTENANTS...' They were Patrick MacTigh, John Reilly, Sean Bernagh, Phil Galloge, Patrick Meel, Arthur O'Neal; and the infamous Brian Kelly, lifelong friend and sometime associate of Redmond's, who was later hanged in Armagh.

xxxv 'A SPY IN HIS EMPLOY...' J. Cosgrave in *A Genuine History of the Lives and Actions of the Most Notorious Irish Highwaymen, Tories and Rapparees* asserts that this spy was the serving maid of Richard's brother and was possibly spurned by him.

xxxvi 'GRABBED HIS CARBINE...' A carbine was a shortened form of musket or rifle carried by mounted soldiers, usually attached to the saddle.

Daniel Hogan

xxxvii 'JOHN HOGAN, BLACKSMITH . . .' Local folklore tells us that Daniel was the son of a Tipperary blacksmith. If that tradition is true, then he was more than likely the son of either Donagh O'Hogan, a blacksmith who paid hearth tax in Kilfeacle in 1666, or John Hogan, a blacksmith who paid hearth tax in Goldenbridge in the same year.

xxxviii 'THE DALCASSIANS . . .' The occupants of Dál Cais. Liam de Paor ("The Age of the Viking Wars" in *The Course of Irish History*) wrote:

> "In the second half of the tenth century a new aggressive power emerged in Munster, through the expansion of a hitherto obscure petty kingdom of East Clare, Dál Cais, whose leader Mathgamain captured Cashel from the Eóganachta in 964. Shortly afterwards he defeated the Norse of Limerick at the battle of Sulchoid and sacked their city... Mathgamain himself was killed in 976 but his brother Brian Bóruma (otherwise Boru) within a few years brought first Limerick, then all of Munster, under his control. From Cashel he systematically set about building up power for himself."

xxxix 'NICHOLAS TOLER . . .' He was an ancestor of the infamous John Toler. Born in Ardcroney in 1745, he was better known as the Hanging Judge.

^{xl} 'CHINESE GUERRILLAS…' There's an old Chinese saying which explains the success of guerrilla warfare. To paraphrase: "The people are the water; the warriors are the fish living in the water". The Irish students of war would probably have been familiar with this and other aphorisms.

^{xli} 'REST OF THE RAPPAREES…' The word "rapparee" has an interesting etymology. A *rápaire* or *ropaire* was originally a rapier or a short pike. By a process of metonymy, the name for the weapon came to signify the weapon's user: *ropaire*, "a snatcher or seizer; a cut-purse, a robber or thief". The early definition of "rapparee" was "a treacherous or violent person, a scoundrel".

Interestingly, Alice Curtayne suggests that the word "ropaire" was originally given to the English settlers who had taken their lands and homes. The English themselves then adopted the word, anglicised it, and used "rapparee" to describe the dispossessed and any other kind of lawbreaker.

^{xlii} 'MASSIVE SIEGE TRAIN…' It comprised six 24-pounders, two 18-pounders, 8 brass ordnance of 18 inches, one mortar of 18 inches with 30 shells and 5 cartouches, 6 tin boats, each one in three sections, 800 balls for the 18-pounders, 120 barrels of powder, 1,600 barrels of matches, 500 hand-grenades, 3,000 tools, 94 wool bags, 18 casks of biscuits, a quantity of timber, block wagons, limbers and spare gun carriages, and 153 wagons drawn by 400 draught horses.

^{xliii} 'PATRICK SARSFIELD…' Sarsfield had distinguished himself in England, fighting for James II against the Duke of Monmouth at Sedgemoor in 1685. Curiously, his first commission is said to have been in Monmouth's regiment: soon after 1678 he crossed over to England and entered the service of King Charles II. Sarsfield was created Earl of Lucan in February 1691.

^{xliv} 'THE DUKE OF BERWICK…' Patrick Sarsfield was mortally wounded at the Battle of Landen (Flanders) in 1693. His widow married James Fitzjames, the Duke of Berwick. (1670–1734). Berwick was an illegitimate son of James II. His mother was Arabella Churchill, sister of John Churchill, Duke of Marlborough. He was born and educated in France. He entered the service of Louis XIV and commanded French armies in Spain during the War of the Spanish Succession. His victory over an Anglo-Portuguese army at the Battle of Almansa (1707) helped secure the Spanish throne for Louis' grandson, Philip. Berwick was killed at the siege of Philippsburg in Germany during the War of the Polish Succession.

^{xlv} 'THE BATTLE LASTED BUT A FEW MINUTES…' The Rev. George Story, in his *True and Impartial History…*, describes the destruction in the following manner:

"If they had feared the least danger, it had been easy to draw the guns and everything else within the ruins of that old castle, and then it had been difficult for an army, much more a party, to have touched them. Nay, it was easy to place them and the carriages in such a figure upon the very spot where they stood, that it had been certain death to have come nigh them; but thinking themselves at home, so nigh the camp, and not fearing an enemy in such a place, especially they had no notice sent them of it, they turned most of their horses out to grass, as being wearied with marching before, and the guard they left was but a very slender one, the rest most of them going to sleep. But some of them awoke in the next world, for Sarsfield all that day lurked amongst the mountains, and having notice where and how our men lay, he had those that guided him through byways to the very spot where he fell in amongst them before they were aware, and cut several of them to pieces, with a great many of the wagoners and some country people that were coming to the camp with provisions. The officer commanding-in-chief, when he saw how it was, commanded to sound horse, but those that endeavoured to fetch them up were killed as they went out, or else saw it was too late to return. The officers and others made what resistance they could, but were at last obliged every man to shift for himself, which many of them did, though they lost all their horses and some of them goods of a considerable value...

There was one Lieutenant Bell, and some few more of the troopers killed, with wagoners and country people, to the number of about sixty. Then the Irish got up what horses they could meet withal, belonging either to the troops or train; some broke the boats, and others drew all the carriages and wagons, with the bread, ammunition, and as many of the guns as they could get in so short a time into one heap. The guns they filled with powder and put their mouths in the ground that they might certainly split. What they could pick up in a hurry they took away, and laying a train to the rest, which being fired at their going off, blew all up with an astonishing noise; the guns that were filled with powder flying up from the carriages into the air, and yet two of them received no damage, though two more were split and made unserviceable: everything likewise that would burn was reduced to ashes, before any could prevent it. The Irish took no prisoners only a Lieutenant of Colonel Erle's being sick in a house hard by , was stripped and brought to Sarsfield, who used him very civilly, telling him if he had not succeeded in that enterprise, he had then gone to France."

xlvi 'THE ONLY CASUALTIES SUSTAINED...' A local Hogan family tradition has it that Daniel and several other relatives (possibly Hogan's brothers), fought in that rearguard action, with two being killed and some more wounded. The composer Percy French, in his wonderful poem "Galloping Hogan", suggests that Daniel was wounded in the affray by Colonel Villiers:

> "'To arms! the foe!' Too late, too late,
> Though Villiers' vengeful blade
> Is wet with Hogan's lifeblood,
> As he leads the ambuscade.
> Then foot to foot, and hand to hand,
> They battle round the guns,
> Till victory declares itself
> For Erin's daring sons."

If Hogan was wounded, then it could not have been seriously, and it was not by the blade of Villiers: George Story notes that Colonel Villiers "went with another party of horse towards O'Brien's Bridge but the enemy did not return that way".

xlvii 'THE DECISIVE BATTLE OF THE WAR…' James II had fled the Boyne the previous year, taking with him twelve of the eighteen artillery pieces which the Irish army had and needed, and all before William's troops had even engaged. At Aughrim the Jacobites had virtually no leaders, apart from General St Ruth. His tragic death caused the Irish cavalry to retreat, leaving the infantry behind to be slaughtered by General Van Reede de Ginkel's men. Some 7,000 souls perished needlessly.

xlviii 'SOME SAY HE WAS MURDERED…' *The Journal of the Irish Folk Song*, Vol. 24, Part 2, (1927), records:

> "Daniel Hogan a celebrated Tory was slain near Latteragh in Upper Ormond by some thieves of the name of Burke, to whom he was obnoxious, and buried in Glenmore an adjacent valley."

xlix 'HIDEOUT OF GALLOPING HOGAN…' An old Munster story associates the famous outlaw Edmund O'Ryan (Ned of the Hill) with Galloping Hogan and his hideout. O'Ryan was riding through a remote part of Tipperary when he came upon a gentleman on foot. The man was Captain Thomas Armstrong of Mealiffe, an acquaintance of O'Ryan's and one of the few honourable English officers he knew. Armstrong confided that his best horse saddle and bridle had been stolen earlier by Hogan in an intimidating and daring swoop. O'Ryan was furious with the treatment meted out to this humane officer and gentleman, and immediately went to Hogan's Glen at Labbadiha Bridge, where he confronted his friend and ally. Shortly afterwards he returned to the house of the good captain and handed over the saddle and bridle to their rightful owner, along with an apology from Galloping Hogan.

Edmund O'Ryan

l 'THE GREAT WARRIOR O'RYANS OF KILNALONGURTY…' Many of the O'Ryans lost their lives and property in the plantation of Munster as a result of their support of the Earl of Desmond against Elizabeth. It was a campaign of such butchery that the desolation prevailing afterward could be described by the Four Masters only suggestively: "the low of a cow was not heard from Dún Chaoin to Caiseal Mumhan."

li 'THE DRAGOON TOPPLED FROM HIS SADDLE, MORTALLY WOUNDED…' Local legend has it that the dragoon was buried on the spot. There is a grave at the site, but no indication of who lies in it.

lii 'MR EDWARD SHANAHAN…' It could equally have been Shanahan's brother from Rathmoy, both of whom were known to Ned.

liii 'REUBEN LEE…' Lee's body was buried near his house in Gurtnaskehy by the detachment of troops with whom he had colluded. When the local populace heard of Lee's attempted betrayal of their hero, they were incensed. So great was their rage that the traitor's body was dug up and thrown into the Coumbeg River. Some time later the putrefied body was found by troops on the river bank at a place called Moyaliffe and removed from the area.

liv '"THE BADGER" DWYER…' Local folklore makes Ned the godfather of Dwyer's son.

lv 'A BITTER DISAPPOINTMENT…' Another version of the story insists that Dwyer did indeed receive the £300 for his treachery.

lvi 'SALLY BURIED HER BROTHER WITH DIGNITY…' There is no record of any other family member being present – or another loved one, for that matter.

It is said that, though constantly on the run, Ned still found the opportunity to fall in love. Ned is supposed to have met the lady he afterwards married, Mary Leahy, while roving through the provinces of Leinster and Ulster. He insinuated himself into her affections in the character of a wandering minstrel bard and, at her bridal feast, eloped with her. There are still in existence some beautiful lines of poetry and song of which Ned is said to be the author, including Bean Dubh an Ghleanna, which he may have composed for Mary while he was a suitor (or addressed to Ireland personified).

There is no record of Ned and Mary's marriage, but tradition has it that they formalised their relationship and had a son, who became a successful and wealthy businessman, and whose son in turn – Ned's grandson – went on to become a judge at the Leinster Assizes known by the name of Judge Mountain.

There is another story concerning Ned's son. A lady travelling in her carriage through the Glen of Aherlow was robbed of her money, jewellery and an expensive gold watch by a band of robbers, one of whom represented himself to be Ned of the Hill. Ned happened to pass that place shortly afterward and, seeing the lady in tears, enquired the cause. The lady told him that she had just been cruelly robbed by the outlaw Ned of the Hill and his gang. "Bad enough," Ned sympathised, before asking how much time had passed since the outlaws' departure and which direction they went. The driver of the lady's carriage pointed the robbers out at a short distance: they were making their way up the slope of a nearby mountain.

Ned advised the lady not to leave the area until he returned, which he promised would not be long. Spurring his horse, he galloped away and overtook the outlaws. He shot or slew three of the gang and returned with the booty, bringing another two thieves roped and secured as prisoners to the lady and her coachman.

"These are the scoundrels that robbed you," he said theatrically. "They are not

Ned of the Hill's men, nor is he himself amongst them – for I am the man whom these blackguards had the audacity to charge with this dishonourable robbery!"

The astonished lady apologised for her mistake in falsely charging Ned with the crimes of the bandits and gratefully accepted her restored possessions. She then begged the dashing outlaw to act as her escort until she was safely through the glen. As Ned rode alongside her carriage, the lady engaged him in conversation. She enquired if he had any children and the outlaw confessed that he had a son. As they reached the boundary of the glen, the lady proposed that Ned allow his son to come to her home, in order that he might receive a liberal education along-side her own children. The story goes that Ned consented before departing and that, many years later, the son of this boy became Judge Mountain.

lvii 'HIS REMAINS LIE INTERRED...' There is much confusion over what happened to the body of the famed rapparee after his murder. A version of the story related here adds that Badger Dwyer was hanged for Ned's murder; yet a different version tells that Dwyer was ordered to return to the scene of the crime with his grisly sack and bury the head and body together; and a third account relates that, upon dis-covering there would be no reward, the murderer flung the outlaw's head into the deep waters of the River Suir at Ardmayke Bridge. Some local residents say that the body was buried in Doon, while the head was buried at Foilachluig by Ned's sister. In 1962 Matthew Ryan, a retired American Naval Commander and a descendent of Ned's, in the company of local historian Mainchin Seóighe, discovered that the gravesite in Foilachluig had been dug up. A skull, but no skeleton, had been found. The skull had been taken to the local church, blessed, and reinterred. The Commander was convinced that this was the head of his ancestor and the follow-ing year erected a memorial to the rapparee bearing the following inscription:

> "Edmond Knock Ryan Ned O' The Hill
> Eamann an Chnoic
> His spirit and song live in the hearts of his people"

The grave is marked on sheet number 45 of the Ordnance Survey map of Tipperary. The caption reads: "Emunaknuck's Grave".

Charles Carragher

lviii 'BIG CHARLIE CARRAGHER...' Seldom has a name been subject to more varying interpretation and translation. He was known variously as Charles McKaragher, Charles Carraher, Cathal Mór (Big Charles) Carragher, and Collmore.

lix 'THE FEWS...' The word "fews" is taken from the Irish *fiadha*, pronounced "feeoh", meaning a wood or wilderness. It is on record that during the second part of the seventeenth century a George Blykes was the proprietor of an inn in Dorsey.

[lx] 'AN IRISH SERVANT MAN...' Kolchin went on to make the following indictment of England:

> "Brutal repression of 'rowdy' elements in Britain as well as savage colonization of Ireland preceded the English assault on Native Americans and enslavement of Africans, and demonstrate the insufficiency of race as an explanation of policy towards blacks. If the English regarded Africans as inferior by nature, members of the English gentry regarded their own lower classes – and the Irish – in much the same way: they were ignorant and 'brutish' and required physical repression to keep them in line. The Irish were widely perceived as wild, degraded, and of questionable Christianity, 'more uncivil, more uncleanly, more barbarous and more brutish in their customs and demeanures, than in any other part of the world that is known.'"

W.E.H. Lecky added:

> "[The Irish tenant] was a man destitute of all knowledge and of all capital who found the land the only thing that remained between himself and starvation. The landlord did nothing for them. They built their own mud hovel, planted their hedges, dug their ditches... All real enterprise and industry among Catholic tenants was destroyed by the laws which consigned them to utter ignorance, and still more by the law which placed strict bounds to their progress by providing that if their profits ever exceeded a third of their rent, the first Protestant who could prove the fact might take their farm."

[lxi] 'A REWARD OF £20...' From a proclamation issued by Major Morgan, an officer in Cromwell's army:

> "We have three beasts to destroy that lay burthens upon us. The first is the wolf, on whom we lay five pounds a head if a dog, and ten pounds if a bitch. The second beast is the priest, on whose head we lay ten pounds – if he be eminent, more. The third beast is the tory, on whose head we lay twenty pounds."

[lxii] 'PATRICK CARRAGHER...' He was also called Patrick James McKaragher. Also in the party were Gillaspy McCulum, another proclaimed Tory, and two men named Arthur Quinn.

[lxiii] 'CARRIED OUT TO THE LETTER...' The description of Charles' execution is taken from an old broadsheet pamphlet printed in Dublin: *Document Hib. 0.718.12/14,* Cambridge University Library.

[lxiv] 'HIS LAST WORDS...' From the *Document Hib. 0.718.12,* Bradshaw Collection, Cambridge University Library. The speech was delivered to Will Moore, the high sheriff of County Louth. The misspellings are, of course, attributable to the transcriber of the time.

lxv 'I, PATRICK CARRAGHER...' From *Document Hib. 0.718.14*, Bradshaw Collection, Cambridge University Library.

Charles Dempsey

lxvi 'QUEEN'S COUNTY...' County Laois was formerly known as Queen's County, named after the Protestant Queen Anne (1665–1714), James II's daughter and the last Stuart sovereign. She was queen of England and Scotland from 1707, and of Ireland from 1702 until her death. In 1683 Anne married Prince George of Denmark and became pregnant by him eighteen times. Five children were born alive but none survived childhood.

lxvii 'WITCHCRAFT OR MAGIC...' Superstition was rife among the country people of the time. An old local story has it that at one stage Cahir was extremely anxious to recruit a fit man from Ballybrittas, a miller, into his ranks. He was big and strong, ideal for the work that Cahir was engaged in, and added to that was the fact that the mill would have been a place where folk met and talked – a good place for sympathetic ears. Although the man was willing and eager to join the gang, he had one serious reservation which was preventing him: his great fear of judges. He believed that they possessed supernatural powers and knew the details of every case and crime before they even got to court. The miller believed that if he, by some ill-luck, ended up in court, his fate was a foregone conclusion and he would swing. No amount of persuading would change his mind, and the story goes that Cahir had to take him to the Maryborough Assizes and sit through trial after trial with him until he eventually realised that judges were mortal after all. As a result of this discovery, the miller joined the outlaw ranks.

lxviii 'CONFEDERATES IN ULSTER...' One of these associates is believed to have been Count Redmond O'Hanlon. Cahir is reputed to have been a member of O'Hanlon's gang at one stage.

lxix 'IF THEY WERE TO BE HAD...' From Cosgrave, *A Genuine History of the Lives and Actions of the Most Notorious Irish Highwaymen, Tories and Rapparees* (Belfast, 1750).

lxx 'NAAS GAOL...' Sir Patrick Fitzpatrick described Naas Gaol in the eighteenth century:

"The Gaol of Naas is a strong proof of this assertion [of insecurity], for as the upper parts of it are so insecure, the criminals are confined in the most loathsome dark dungeons, the passage to those is from the street, through a dark entry, guarded by three different strong doors, and so dark are those dungeons that there is no seeing without candles, and are damp and filled with stinking vapours, that candles with difficulty burn; the only passage for either

light or air, is a small window to each of those cells, scarce 14 inches square
and even that small space is in great measure occupied with iron bars; in the
smaller of those dungeons the 29th of last month, there were lying on the
cold damp ground, scarce defended with straw, six double-bolted criminals,
two of them without any sort of covering, save a little straw and mats made
of the same, which they substituted for blankets; in the larger of those dungeons there was but one prisoner, who was confined for his fees; the reason
the gaoler assigned to him for not putting other prisoners into the large dungeon was, that they attempted to cut the bars of the window, and pick the
wall of the prison a few days before; the gaoler humanely permits them every
morning about 10 o'clock to come out of the dungeon on to the street opposite the door, where they generally beg until evening, and then are locked up
in the dungeon until the morning following. There is an excellent situation in
that town to build a gaol, which might be effected at a moderate expense;
there is neither yard nor necessary to this gaol."

lxxi 'HECTOR GRAHAM...' Another source identifies him as Hector Grimes.

George MacNamara

lxxii 'MANY FOUGHT AND DIED...' Next to MacNamara, the most famous was "Old
Fireball" MacNamara, hero of fifty-seven duels, who fought at the battle of Vinegar
Hill in the rebellion of 1798.

lxxiii 'GEORGE WAS DESCRIBED AS...' A vivid description of the outlaw appears in *A
Brief Sketch of the Romantic Life of George MacNamara of Cong Abbey*:

"George Mac Namara was an extremely handsome man, straight as a spear,
and, although supple and lightfooted as a roe, his muscles were of iron, and
his endurance almost miraculous. In manner he was polite and courteous,
but when insulted or provoked by any person – as the mountain torrent was
his wrath! His ingenuity and skill in mechanics were most remarkable, and as
his eventful life truly proves, he was quick and ready of resource in every difficulty and danger. Fear was never a word in his vocabulary, for he was reck-
lessly daring in even the most seemingly hopeless enterprise. MacNamara was
also a thorough sportsman, and prided himself on the excellent quality of his
horses and hounds, of which he kept a goodly number. In horsemanship he
was unsurpassed, and was acknowledged by all to be the best shot of his day
with either pistol or fowling piece. He kept a forge in his yard, in which with
his own hands he shod his horses, forged master-keys and manufactured
every appliance necessary for the perilous role he had resolved upon to follow for the benefit of his less fortunate neighbours, crushed beneath poverty
and the Penal Laws. In fact he possessed every attribute, both mental and
physical, requisite to constitute him past-master in the strange profession he
had laid out for himself."

lxxiv 'PENAL LAWS...' The great statesman Edmund Burke, in *Thoughts on the Present Discontents* (1770), famously described the penal laws as "a machine of elaborate contrivance as well fitted for the oppression, impoverishment and degradation of a people, and the debasement in them of human nature itself, as ever proceeded from the perverted ingenuity of Man."

lxxv 'DELIGHTFULLY SITUATED RESIDENCE...' After MacNamara's death Abbey Lodge was sold to a Mr Lambert and then to Sir Benjamin Guinness. It was allowed to fall into disrepair; the ruins of the house can now be found in the northwest corner of the Abbey grounds.

lxxvi 'A CONCEALED FORGE...' The anvil from the secret forge is said to be still in the village of Cong. Its last known location was the Cong home of the late Michael Foy, sculptor and stonemason.

Shane Crossagh

lxxvii 'SHANE CROSSAGH...' He was also known as Shawn Crossach. The old pronunciation and spelling of his name was Seán Cruthach (Handsome John).

lxxviii 'GOLD...' Tradition has it that Crossagh's gold – a foal skin of it – is buried a gunshot's distance from the site of Fowler's Inn, along the stream running south.

lxxix 'THE THIRD LEAP...' Three cairns (memorial/landmark stones) on Carntogher mountain mark the place and distances of Shane's leaps.

lxxx 'A NARROW BRIDGE...' The bridge is still known locally as the General's Bridge.

lxxxi 'DIRECTION OF THE FERRY LANDING STAGE...' There was not any bridge over the Foyle until the very end of the eighteenth century. A traveller, Arthur Young, made a note in his diary on August 6, 1776: "Reached Derry at night and waited two hours in the dark before the ferry boat came over for me."

William Crotty

lxxxii 'MICHAEL KAVANAGH...' Kavanagh was a Cappoquin man who had a remarkable career as a '48 man and a Fenian writer in America. He wrote a thorough account of Crotty's life and exploits, which appeared in the *Journal of the Waterford Archaeological Society*. Kavanagh spent a lifetime researching the traditions of the Comeragh Mountains.

lxxxiii 'THE LAKE OF LAUGHTER...' It was sometimes called Conn an Ghaire, the Hollow of the Laughter, and is now known as Crotty's Lake.

lxxxiv 'HE STABLED STOLEN HORSES...' A story was put about by the authorities, presumably for the purpose of besmirching the outlaw's reputation, that Crotty was a cannibal who filled the recesses of his caves with stores of human flesh. Yet Crotty did become known as "the Irish Sawney Bean" after a Scottish Highland robber of that name, who is said to have been a cannibal.

lxxxv 'AN OLD IRISH SONG...' From a traditional Waterford song, recorded in *Waterford Heroes, Poets and Villains*:

> "Is breá é an Radharch a chím óm Leaphan.
> Cnoc Maoldomhnaig agus Cnoc an Bhainne
> Cnocán Bhrandán agus Sean Baile Anna,
> Mol ab Staighre agus Gleann Dá Lachainn
> Agus Tuairín Luachra ar Bruach an ghLeanna."

lxxxvi 'THE FARMER RAISED THE POTATO...' Crotty was himself shot in the mouth in a fight later on and the begrudgers of the time said that it was God's judgment on the highwayman for his careless act of cruelty that night at Sean Mhichil's Cross.

lxxxvii 'HEARN FIRED, HITTING HIM...' The gun that sub-sheriff Hearn used to shoot Crotty was preserved and shown as a trophy at Shankill House; it was labelled Crotty's Gun and is now in the possession of the Marquis of Waterford. Lord Waterford attests that the gun was not Hearn's, as has been consistently reported, but Crotty's own.

lxxxviii 'DAVID NORRIS SWORE...' Here follows affidavit sworn by David Norris on March 14, 1740, as compiled by Butler, "Crotty the Robber: Some Original Documents" in *Journal of Waterford and South East of Ireland Archaeological Society* (Vol. 18, 1915).

"David Norris informeth upon oath that some time before Christmas last, he this inform^t joyned Wm Crotty & Pierce Walsh and saith that some few days before Christmas, but what particular day inform^t cannot recollect, at night, said Crotty, Thomas Mara & inform^t burglariously broke open the dwelling house of Michael Ling of Knockatorenore in said county, dairyman to Robert Power of Dungarvan in said County gent., & entred the same and thence feloniously stole about three pounds in money; & this inform^t saith that the night after said robbery said Wm Crotty, Mara & this inform^t at night burglariously broke open the dwelling house of David Curreen of Cumeene in said County, dairyman to John Keily, Esq., entred the same and felon^y stole thereout about three pounds in money & some wearing apparell; and further saith that on or about the fifth of January last said Wm Crotty, John Murphy, P[ie]rce Walsh & this inform^t at night of said day burglariously broke open the dwelling house of Nich^s Hays of Killfarrissy in the County of Waterford & feloniously stole thereout about twelve pounds in money, two silk hand kerchiefs & one gold ring & some apparell; & saith that the same was divided between said Crotty, Murphy, Walsh and inform^t & that the same amounted to ab^t three pounds to each man, and this inform^t further saith that said Crotty, Walsh, John Cunnigain, William Cunnagain, John Power, Darby Dooley, & this inform^t on or about the fifth day of March inst. at night of said day burglari-ously broke open the dwellinghouse of John Power of Ballymorrissey in the said County of Waterford & entered the same & thence feloniously stole about eighteen pounds in money, one gold ring & two silk handkerchiefs & saith that the same was divided amongst this inform^t said Crotty, John Cunnagain, Wm Cunnagain, John Power and Darby Dooley, & said that Mary Crotty wife of s^d Wm Crotty got said gold ring & that she most commonly received the apparell which was taken at the above robberys, knowing them to have been stolen; and further saith that some time before the said robbery of John Power, Richard Power of Churchtown in the said County harbour'd, entertained & abetted said Wm Crotty & this inform^t knowing the said Wm Crotty & this inform^t to be Tories, Robbers and Rapparees at the time he the said Richd Power entertained said Crotty & inform^t; and saith that said Richard Power told said Crotty & inform^t that it would be an easy matter to rob the dwelling house of Beverley Usher, Esq., at Killmaidon in said County; & saith that about the latter end of January or the beginning of February last James Cleary gave said Wm Crotty and inform^t a gunn, a powder horn with some powder in it & a turn screw & saith that said James Cleary was con-cerned with said Crotty and inform^t in the robbing of John Neal of Whitechurch in the County Kilkenny; & this inform^t saith that said Crotty & this inform^t feloniously stole out of the dwelling house of William Veal of Kellanaspegg in said County of Waterford on or about the seventh day of February last one gunn & two cases of pistolls & this inform^t saith that on the eight day of March inst. at night of said day said Crotty, John Cunnagain & this inf^t feloniously stole out of a parke in the liberties of the City of Waterford one black mare, and one sorrell horse the property of Robt Carew, Gent., and carried the same to Currihine in s^d County of Waterford."

James Freney

lxxxix 'A COMIC OPERA...' Percy French, the well known painter and composer, wrote a comic opera in the latter part of the nineteenth century (music by Houston Collisson) entitled *The Knight of the Road* or *The Irish Girl* in which the Freney character was the hero.

xc 'NEARLY £200 IN CASH...' The haul comprised a purse containing ninety guineas, a £4 piece, two moidores (an old Portuguese gold coin in use in Britain and Ireland and worth twenty-seven shillings), some small gold coins, and a large glove containing twenty-eight guineas in silver.

xci 'ARMED LOCAL MERCHANTS...' Among his chief pursuers was his former employer, Mr Robbins. It is said that Captain Freney had him in his sights on several occasions but spared his life each time.

xcii 'I DO NOT ROB TAILORS...' A ballad was later written commemorating this strange encounter, possibly by the outlaw himself.

xciii 'THE PEOPLE'S MUCH-ADMIRED HERO...' So troublesome had Freney become to the wealthy inhabitants of the area, so elusive, and so much of a hero to the local people, that it was suggested by one of the well-to-do citizens that a subscription be raised to enable the outlaw to quit the country; the community would be rid of Freney once and for all. This idea, abandoned when the landed gentlemen of the region refused to subscribe, may have been put forward after a most audacious robbery by Freney and his gang, when with primed pistols and blackened faces they relieved a terrified Mrs Archbold of Castledermot of £400 in plate and cash. Another story, which Freney told himself, much to the amusement of the people and the embarrassment of the authorities, was that in the midst of the great hue and cry about him the outlaw was escaping to the Isle of Man when a huge storm blew up and forced the ship back to Dublin. Freney disguised himself as a woman and made his way back to Kilkenny unhindered.

xciv 'NOT FADED FROM LOCAL LORE...' It is believed that Freney used to hide out in Hollywood glen and that he buried some of his treasure there. Other booty is said to be concealed beneath the bridge at Annalecky. His blunderbuss and mask were found in a hideout above the Carrigower river, along with his bed (made of planks and built on stilts which straddled the water, the only dry spot in the damp refuge). There is a local story which fuses the story of Freney with another outlaw named O'Connor. Both the highwaymen are said to have buried a large cache of gold and valuables on The Scalp mountain not far from Hollywood, County Wicklow. It is said that when the sun attained a certain position in the sky, it would reflect on a silver plate placed on a dresser in a house across the valley and the resulting shaft of light would pinpoint the exact location of the treasure.

Michael Collier

xcv 'THE MONSTRAIDIGETO TURN...' This is either a stunt word or one which long ago became archaic.

xcvi 'HE WAS TO CROSS THE IRISH SEA... MORE THAN ONCE...' On several occasions Collier visited a man named Coleman, who had been arrested for highway robbery and was languishing in Lancaster Gaol under sentence of death. Coleman was pretending to be insane and Collier aided him in this ruse, telling the turnkeys and gaolers that the prisoner was so mad he did not even recognise him, one of his best friends. Coleman was not hanged but eventually released as insane, and returned to Ireland where he gave his account of being visited by Collier. He emigrated to America with funds given to him by his ex-wife (but probably from the proceeds of one of his robberies) who had now remarried and wanted rid of him. Coleman died in poverty in America, without friends – and very possibly insane.

xcvii 'A REGIMENT OF BLACK BELTS…' In the late seventeenth, eighteenth and into the nineteenth centuries there were 263 barracks in use throughout the country. As the century rolled on there were 34 regiments of foot, horse and dragoons quartered and garrisoned in 69 towns and villages. An English regiment in Ireland at the time consisted of 280 men, as opposed to 500 in England. Most were concentrated in Leinster, Connacht and Munster. Ordinarily, Irish Catholics were not encouraged to join the British Army, and when they did they were viewed with suspicion by their officers. Although Protestants were welcomed into the ranks and the officer corps, it was not until 1793 that the Catholic Irish were allowed to become officers. The role of the army in Ireland was principally to defend the country from invasion; to be a reserve force for the main English army; to enforce the stringent form of law and order laid down by the magistrates; and to suppress any attempt at rebellion by the Catholic population. The Lord Lieutenant was to all intents and purposes the Commander in Chief of the army who commissioned, promoted and appointed at will.

Because the troops were dispersed throughout the remote hamlets and garrisons, with higher-ranking officers absent for most of the time "being occupied in the social whirl of Dublin", discipline amongst the bored rank and file troops was bad. It was generally believed that even in the large garrison cities like Dublin, Galway, Limerick, Cork and Waterford basic training and drilling were neglected.

xcviii 'COACH GUARDS WERE NOTORIOUS DRINKERS…' Here follows a description of Irish coach guards in 1803, taken from the anonymous diary of an English gentleman traveller in Ireland.

"The Irish stage-coaches are a most uneasy and unsafe mode of conveyance. The roads are very unequal; and those vehicles move up hill with the tedious pace of a funeral procession, and fly down like a hawk pouncing on its prey. The mail is attended for two stages out of Dublin by two dragoons, who ride one on each side with pistols, exclusively of the guards who carry two blunderbusses and four pair of horse-pistols. One of the guards being taken ill, the other ascribed his indisposition entirely to an abstinence from spirits; which he said, were the only article of diet capable of enabling a man to lead the life of a guard. He was very lavish in his praise of this beverage, saying that he had once given it up for three months upon trial, at the end of which time he had become so thin that another week of the same forbearance would have laid him in his grave. He recounted many instances of longevity, attended with a habit of drinking spirits; and hence agreed more to his own satisfaction than mine, that the one was a consequence of the other. On being asked how much whiskey he had ever drunk in one day, he assured me he had once gone the length of thirty-six glasses."

[xcix] 'RISK OF ESCAPE…' The English army garrisoned in Ireland during the eighteenth and nineteenth centuries appears to have been a body of men much given to alcohol abuse. This appears to have been a genuine problem and the accounts of bored officers joining with their men in wild bouts of drunkenness and revelry are plentiful. In 1750 General Parker, a respected and decorated soldier, was inspecting 4,000 troops on manoeuvres near Kilkenny. He was so disgusted at what he saw that he ordered his carriage driver to take him home immediately, saying that "such a managed exercise would make a dog spew". Later in the same year a regiment marched into Limerick City and it was noted that some of the soldiers were leading greyhounds, pointers, setters, spaniels, and cardogs, and that some of the ranks carried fishing rods and fowling pieces. Some time later in the year, on the evening preceding Bragg's Regiment leaving the same city, so much alcohol was consumed that it caused rioting in the streets. On the following morning the drummers were still so drunk that they could not beat out a march in time, and the regiment staggered and lurched out of the city gates carrying their inebriated commanding officer on a cart of straw.

It is no surprise, then, that clever outlaws like Michael Collier took full advantage of the disorganisation and lack of discipline within the army and used it to escape arrest or free their comrades by plying the all-too-willing troops with copious amounts of "drink".

[c] 'A MEETING WITH THE SCRAG-BOY…' The one near-certainty that faced most convicted highwaymen and outlaws was a meeting with the "scrag-boy", as the hangman was known. Executions in Ireland in the eighteenth and nineteenth centuries were a contradiction: although their purpose was to deter crime, they turned terrible scenes of death into welcome, diverting spectacles. Central to the show was the hangman, who was generally disguised in a fantastic manner, ill-suited to the occasion. He wore a grotesque mask and an enormous hump on his back. The apparent levity of this original design had another purpose, namely to protect the executioner by disguising him, and it was to some degree necessary.

The use he made of the hump was curious. It was formed of a large wooden bowl/dish, laid between the shoulders, and covered by clothing. When the condemned was turned off, i.e. when the trapdoor was opened or the board pulled from underneath the victim, and the "dusting of the scrag-boy" began, the hangman was assailed, not merely with shouts and curses, but often with showers of stones. To escape the latter, he ducked down his head and opposed his hump as a shield, from which the missiles rebounded with a force that showed how soon his skull would have been fractured if exposed to them. After some antics, the finisher of the law dived among the sheriff's attendants and disappeared. The grotesque victim, surrounded by two or more human beings, struggling in the awful agonies of a violent and horrible death, was regarded by the mob as an amusing figure.

One of the most infamous scrag-boys plying his trade at the close of the eighteenth and beginning of the nineteenth centuries was Tom Galvin. When an old man he was visited regularly at Kilmainham Gaol by people curious to see him and the rope with which he had hanged all his victims – and most of his own relatives. A favourite trick of his was to slip the noose around the neck of one of his visitors and give it a sudden jerk, which would cause the sensation of strangling.

By all accounts he was a brutal and uncaring man. When some poor wretch was reprieved, Galvin would nearly cry with disappointment at the loss of his fee. He was notoriously impatient with his victims. An unfortunate named Jemmy O'Brien was about to be executed and the terrified man, mindful of his impending fate, lingered over his prayers in an effort to prolong his life for a few more minutes. "Mr O Brien, jewel," the hangman said, "long life to you. Make haste with your prayers; the people is getting tired under the swing-swong".

[ci] 'A FATE WHICH BEFELL...' Most of the twenty-four desperadoes said to have been involved with Collier met unhappy fates:

Hanged at Cookle Bridge, Garristown:	Griffin of Lisdoran; Carroll of Drogheda; Carroll of Garristown; Boulger
Hanged at different places:	McDaniel of The Naul and his two brothers; Maguire; Flinn (hanged at Drogheda)
Hanged at Trim:	Dixon of Drogheda; Grimes; McGenna; H—?; Brett
Shot by the gang:	Arnold; Loughran (brother of Hookey Loughran); Woods (killed by Collier)
Shot by a mail coach guard:	Murray; —? (unnamed)
Shot while robbing a barn:	Ludlow
Pardoned:	—? (unnamed)
Emigrated:	Harry the Smasher (so called because of his boxing prowess)
Transported:	The Bubberer Carter (so called because he conveyed the plunder); Hookey Loughran (so called because of a clubbed foot)

[cii] 'THE YOUNG IRELANDERS...' The Young Ireland movement was part of the agitation for the repeal of the Act of Union of 1799. The principals included Thomas Davis, John Blake Dillon and Charles Gavan Duffy, and their mouthpiece was the *Nation* newspaper, founded in 1842, which became a huge success. A later recruit was John Mitchel, the transportee who wrote the classic example of prison literature, *Jail Journal*. At first the Young Irelanders supported Daniel O'Connell but later opposed him. An ill-fated rising in 1848 brought the movement to an end and put the leaders behind bars.

ciii 'FOLLOWED BY ONLY SIX INDIVIDUALS...' Namely: Mr B. Reilly, Mr Thomas Rowe, Mr Johnson, Mr Hugh O'Neill, Mr William Reynolds, and Mr James Fitzpatrick.

civ 'HE WAS SURVIVED BY HIS WIFE AND DAUGHTER...' Collier's son predeceased his father while attending The Patrician School, Drogheda.

Willie Brennan

cv 'THE BALLAD...' A version of the ballad "Brennan on the Moor" emerged in Scotland as "Brannin on the Moor". It was described by an eminent detective in Edinburgh in the 1880s, a Mr McLevy, as being a favourite amongst "the thieving community".

cvi 'AN INCIDENT INVOLVING BRENNAN AND HIS CLAY PIPE...' An account of the incident appeared thirty-two years after Brennan's death in J.R. O'Flanagan, *Guide to the River Blackwater* (1844):

> "Brennan was an outlaw of The Rob Roy School, and most popular; he robbed the rich and gave to the poor. His depredations had always something of a chivalrous cast and no blood sullied his exploits. Once he was near being captured by two officers who sallied forth in quest of him. They came up to him on the mountain, and knew by the description they received; he in vain tried to persuade them that 'A poor labouring boy like him could not be the bould Brennan'; but they insisted on his accompanying them. Passing a shebeen-house they halted for rest and refreshment; the captive begged to have the indulgence of his pipe, which was granted; he reached the dhudeen [pipe] to the barelegged girl who attended as barmaid, and nodding significantly, bade her 'Put fire in that'. She understood the hint, and presently returned with his blunderbuss (concealed beneath her apron), which she managed to hand him under the table. 'Now, gentlemen,' shouted the freebooter, covering his captors with the formidable weapon as he rose, 'I am the bould Brennan.' The tables were completely turned; the captors became captive, yielded their money and arms, and were suffered to return to their quarters quite crestfallen. Brennan was hanged at Clonmel, and the gang broken up."

cvii 'A LONE TRAVELLER SELDOM VENTURED ONTO THE PUBLIC HIGHWAY UNARMED...' Brennan's reputation was so great and such was the fear of outlaw attacks on travellers that even O'Connell, a man known to have been courageous, has put on record that he never travelled the roads of the south of Ireland without loaded pistols.

Jeremiah Grant

[cviii] 'HIS PROPER HOME...' George Henry Borrow (1803–1881) was an English author and traveller. He spent a good part of his boyhood in Tipperary and Clonmel; both his father and brother were army men whose regiments were serving in Ireland at the time Jeremiah Grant was riding the highways. It appears that the outlaw made a great impression on Borrow, because he included him in the novel *Lavengro*, published in 1851. His most famous work is *The Bible in Spain* (1843).

[cix] 'A SECRET OVERTURE TO THE REVEREND DROUGHT...' On August 25, 1810 Jeremiah wrote:

> "Honoured Sir,
>   From the tender feeling I judged you had for my situation at present – induces me to trouble your Goodness again as my hopes is still in the almighty God – that from the Knowledge the Gentlemen of the County has Got of our Business Concerning the Murder of Nichl Maher – I real[l]y do hope the[y] will Intercede to respite my One Only brother and I have a good promise from Colonel Bagwill to Intercede for the rest of us – and if he or the Gentlemen of this nation Knew or Could be Insured of the Designation of my mind this present moment – they would bring from the Gallo[w]s for me fifty if I requested it – But I hope in short I will proove it for them – you may know what I main – But on your Life Don[']t Let the Least hint to any Person breathing – unless in the slightest manner – for if My name was spoke of I was Just settled – as I intend to be of some service to Both your [—?] and my own and in fact to the Kingdom By keeping business sacred to be sacred till I give the Proper and preserved open to Put an end to Badnys which I consider it now – nothing Else – and I am not in the Least Doubt But Both me and my family will be Protected after – I would wish to here or see you With out any Delay – But I would be afeard if you were seen talking to me that there might Be Some thing suspected as the people of this Goal are as sharp and as suspicious as any Ever you knew – So if you would have the Goodnys as to write a few Lines to me to mention to me What Ever news you have for me – as I think worse of my Brother than I do of all the whole world – I will Be uneasy till I here from you – and remain Sir with respect your
>   Most humble and obt Servant
>   Jirrimi Grant".

[cx] 'A HORSE AND GIG...' A gig was a light two-wheeled carriage drawn by a single horse. It had no cover. Already in 1815 the wealthy were discovering the delights of visits to the seaside. Such excursions were not, however, for leisure alone. Physicians at the time were prescribing sea bathing for many ailments. The doctors' advice was also much concerned with diet. In the towns and cities water was not usually safe to drink; it had to be treated in some way. Beer was a common

substitute in northern Europe and North America, while wine was drunk in southern Europe. Tea, however, had yet to be approved by many medical men. One called it "a destroyer of health, an enfeebler of the frame, an engender of effeminacy and laziness, a debaucher of youth and a maker of misery in old age."

cxi 'LOUGHMAN HAD FOOLED HIM…' A few weeks later in Kilkenny, Grant and Whelan, dressed like gentlemen, fell into conversation with Messrs Kennedy and Loughman. The innocent and unsuspecting gentlemen failed to recognise the outlaws, who only a short time earlier had robbed them, masked and wielding pistols, in their homes. Mr Kennedy actually confided to Jeremiah that he had been recently robbed by "the rascal, Captain Grant".

cxii 'HEARTH MONEY…' Hearth money, colloquially known as "Smoke Silver", was initially a tax of two shillings on every hearth and fireplace in the country. Established by an Act of Parliament in the reign of Charles II, the first collection was made on Lady Day, 1663, by the sheriff in each county.

cxiii 'HANGED ON AUGUST 13, 1816…' A third man, Michael Fanning from Ballynakill, was also hanged on this occasion, having been found in possession of some stolen plate. The unfortunate Fanning had been neither a highwayman nor an outlaw, and had never taken part in any raid or robbery. Jeremiah testified to this fact but failed to save the man.

cxiv 'LENGTHY ADDRESS FROM THE SCAFFOLD…' Recorded in *The Life and Adventures of Jeremiah Grant, commonly called Captain Grant* (1816):

> "It is customary, and indeed expected, that on an awful occasion like the present, the convict about to be delivered, by the sentence of the law, to the hands of the executioner, should express something in vindication of his innocence, or in acknowledgment of his guilt—
>
> Before I address you, I crave your prayers, that almighty God may extend his mercy to my soul, that in a few moments must appear before his Divine presence. — [A dead silence for a few moments.] —
>
> I cannot, with ease to my mind, leave this world, without making a last public declaration in your presence. I have not in this county a single relation; notwithstanding which, I have many friends. I have often been told, the gentlemen of the Queen's county were blood-thirsty, rigorous, and vindictive, and that a Queen's county jury had neither tenderness nor compassion. In respect to those circumstances, I declare, before my God, I don't believe any man had a more fair, cool, or impartial trial than I had. I had no money, and for some time was apprehensive I should want the aid of lawyers; but I have been as ably defended as if I possessed the riches of a kingdom. I have been found guilty, on the clearest evidence, by an honest jury of my country. The Judge who presided, acted to me as an upright and humane man. As to the gentlemen of the county, may God, in his mercy, preserve them from injury; they have visited me in my affliction, and relieved me in my distress. I have

in particular to bequeath my blessings on Mr Thomas Parnell. If ever a sanctified man walked on the earth, he is a saint, and will yet rest in the arms of his Creator. I regret much that I have lived to cause to him so much suffering in his mind — that a wretch such as I am, should, by bad example, and infamous conduct, hurt the delicate feelings of that amiable gentleman, the religious friend to mankind. He will, however, do justice to my character, since I have been a convert, when my precious soul shall be wafted to another place — a place of happiness, I hope...

May God bless Mr Bell of Abbeyleix, and Mr Horan of Woodville. I cannot mention Mr Horan, without declaring of him, and his amiable family, that I, with my fellow sufferer, Carrol Whelan, was at his house, and robbed him. His house was very badly used; I am heartily sorry for it; he little deserved it from me. I went to his house with Whelan, and two other men; found him with his stepdaughter, Miss Flood, returning from his stable — I secured and made a prisoner of him. I observed him somewhat agitated, and desired him not to be alarmed. He said, I am in your power, but not alarmed — I am a soldier, and expect you will treat me with honor. I assured him he should not be deceived; and, I trust, he will so far be just to say I kept my word; as to personal injury, he received none. I collected all the valuables articles in the house, and when put together, I considered, and I proposed to him, whether I should take away his plate, or that he should pass his word to me for fifty pounds; well aware, had he given his word of honour, he would, as a soldier, fulfil his promise. I carried away this honourable gentleman's property. I would have returned it, on receiving the fifty pounds — and I fervently wish to God, with a repenting mind, it was in my power now to restore his property: but after I had conveyed it for safety to a distant part of the neighbourhood, it was taken from my possession by some of my accomplices.

Mr Horan's servant I must clear; he did not assist us in the robbery; on the contrary, he strove, as much as possible, to preserve his master's property, and to conceal it from us; and I commend him for his honesty. And I think it just to state, on the word of a dying man, his innocence; as I have been given to understand it was reported he was concerned in the plot. I again declare, he was not.

I mentioned at Mr Horan's, that I made my escape from the gaol of Maryborough, by the means of Mr Thomas Clerke, the Gaoler's son. I said so; but it was not true.

The unfortunate Michael Fanning, who now suffers death with me, was never complicated in any of our (including Whelan) nefarious acts of depredation. Michael Fanning was not in the robbery with us. (*Very loud*)

[Here Fanning would have spoken, but Grant prevented him.]

I never saw the gentleman who was accused, and tried with us for being concerned in the robbery, until I saw him in the prison, after I was brought to Maryborough; he had no concern with us whatever.

Many persons knew what was going forward. We flew from the neighbourhood of Ballinakill; having judged, and I believe rightly, that four or five persons who knew of the robberies, and received part of the booty, would set, and betray us. I have now to declare, that after all the perils and dangers I have undergone, I had not as much left as would bury me.

Mr George Steele, whom it was often asserted was my utter enemy, has given me the means of procuring a coffin. He was an active magistrate, doing his duty; I, the leader of a banditti, offending the law. We were often opposed to each other; at times had some sharp shooting — (here he smiled) but a mutual forgiveness has taken place — he condescended to shake me by the hand. I never bore malice to any man — never lay down in my bed, with a wish for revenge. I forgive the world — and hope the world will forgive me. May Almighty God pardon my sins!

I had a dispute with a county Tipperary gentleman (his landlord) and a law-suit; and was angry with him for a time — but I long since forgave the injuries he did me. He is dead; and I wish it was in my power to restore to his family, some papers that were taken from his house; they are buried in the ground, and I understand they are of material consequence to his heir."

Bibliography

General

James Carty, ed., *Ireland from Grattan's Parliament to the Great Famine* (Dublin, C.J. Fallon Ltd, 1949)

A Christian Brother, *Flowers from many Gardens: A New Anthology* (M.H. Gill & Son Ltd)

L.M. Cullen, *Life in Ireland* (London, B. Batsford Ltd, 1968)

Alice Curtayne, *Irish Story: A Survey of Irish History and Culture* (Dublin, Clonmore and Reynolds Ltd, 1962)

The Dictionary of National Biography, Vol. 13 (Dublin, Oxford University Press, 1992)

Reverend Patrick S. Dinneen, *Irish-English Dictionary* (Dublin, Educational Co. of Ireland, 1927)

J.E. Doherty and D.J. Hickey, *A Chronology of Irish History since 1500* (Dublin, Gill and Macmillan, 1989)

R.F. Foster, *Modern Ireland 1600–1972* (London, Allen Lane, 1988; Penguin Books, 1989)

Mr and Mrs S.C. Hall, *Halls' Ireland Vols 1–3* (London, Sphere Books, 1984)

Peter Harbison, *Guide to the National Monuments in the Republic of Ireland* (Dublin, Gill and Macmillan, 1970)

R. J. Hayes, ed., *History of Irish Civilisation* (Boston, G.K. Hall and Company)

Robert Hughes, *The Fatal Shore* (London, Collins Harvill, 1987)

Journal of The Irish Folk Song Society, Vol. 3 (ref. Irish Traditional Music Archive)

Joan Keefe, ed. and translator, *Irish Poems from Cromwell to the Famine, A Miscellany* (Associated University Presses, Inc., 1977)

Oliver Knox, *Rebels and Informers: Stirrings of Irish Independence* (London, John Murray, 1997)

T.W. Moody and F.X. Martin, eds., *The Course of Irish History* (Cork, Mercier Press, 1967)

T.W. Moody, F.X. Martin, F.J. Byrne, eds., *A New History of Ireland, Vol. 8* (Oxford, Clarendon Press, 1982)

Edward MacLysaght, *Irish Life in the Eighteenth Century* (Dublin, Irish Academic Press, 1979)

Anthony North and Ian V. Hogg, *The Book of Guns and Gunsmiths* (William Collins, A Quarto Book, 1977)

Manus O Baoill, *Ceolta Gael* (Mercier, 1986)

T.S. O'Cahan, *Owen Roe O'Neill* (London, T. Joseph Keane, 1968)

Peter O Leary, *My Story: Reminiscences of a Life in Ireland from the great Hunger to the Gaelic League* (Oxford, Oxford University Press, 1987)

Colm O Lochlainn, *More Irish Street Ballads* (Dublin, Three Candles Press, 1965)

Seán Ó Tuama and Thomas Kinsella eds., *An Duanaire 1600–1900, Poems of the Dispossessed* (Dublin, The Dolmen Press, 1981)

Patrick C. Power, *A History of Waterford City and County* (Mercier Press, 1990)

Francis Roche, ed., *The Roche Collection of Traditional Irish Music, Vols 1–3* (Dublin, Pigott & Co.)

J.G. Simms in T.W. Moody, J.C. Beckett and T.D. Williams, eds, *Jacobite Ireland 1685–1691* (London, Routledge and Kegan Paul, 1969)

J. Stirling Coyne and N.P. Willis, *The Scenery and Antiquities of Ireland, Vol. 2* (London, James S. Virtue)

John Stocks Powell, *Huguenots, Planters, Portarlington* (Frenchurch Press, 1994)

Dudley Costello

Echoes of Ballaghaderreen (Ballaghaderreen: ref. Roscommon County Library, 1992)

Sean Henry, *Tales from the West of Ireland* (Cork, The Mercier Press, 1980)

Maire MacDonnell-Garvey, *The Ancient Territory of Sliabh Lugha, Mid-Connacht* (Manorhamilton, Drumlin Publications, 1995)

John J. Marshall, *Irish Tories, Rapparees and Robbers* (Dungannon, 1927)

Patrick, "Tall" James and "Little" James Brennan

Thomas A. Brennan Jr, *A History of the Brennans of Idough, County Kilkenny* (New Hampshire, Whitman Press, 1975)

J. Stirling Coyne and N.P. Willis, *The Scenery and Antiquities of Ireland, Vol. 2* (London, James S. Virtue/City Road)

Dan Dowling, *Tory, Rapparee and Highwayman: Social Unrest in the 17th and 18th Centuries* (ref. Kilkenny Library, 1990)

John J. Marshall, *Irish Tories, Rapparees and Robbers* (Dungannon, 1927)

Redmond O'Hanlon

Sam Fleming, *Count Redmond O'Hanlon* (Letterkenny, Donegal Democrat Ballyshannon)

P.O. Gallachair, "Who was Redmond Hanlen of Letterkenny?", *Donegal Annual* (Letterkenny, Donegal Ancestry, 1962)

P.O. Gallachair, "Letterkenny Legend Crosses the Atlantic", *Donegal Annual* (Letterkenny, Donegal Ancestry, 1965)

"Historical Associations", *Donegal Annual* (Letterkenny, Donegal Ancestry, 1951)

Life and Death of the Incomparable and Indefatigable Tory Redmond O Hanlyn, commonly called Count Hanlyn (Dublin: ref. The British Library (G5580/1), 1682)

Leslie W. Lucas, *Mevagh down the Years* (Belfast, Appletree Press, 1983)

John J. Marshall, *Irish Tories, Rapparees and Robbers* (Dungannon, 1927)

Rev. Canon McGuire, *Letterkenny Past and Present* (Letterkenny, 1917)

Art O Hanlan, *Count Hanlan's Downfall, or A True and Exact Account of the Killing of that Arch Traytor and Tory Redmond O Hanlan* (Dublin, 1681; British Library: G5580/2)

Rev. Laurence Power, "The Righteous Man's Portion", delivered in a Sermon at the Obsequies of the Noble and Renowned Gentleman, Henry St John, Esquire (London, 1680; National Library of Ireland: Lo P14, item 12)

Richard Power

J. Cosgrave, *A Genuine History of the Lives and Actions of the Most Notorious Irish Highwaymen, Tories and Rapparees; from Redmond O'Hanlon, the Famous Gentleman Robber, to Cahir na Cappul, the Great Horse-catcher, Who was Executed at Maryborough, in August, 1695* [sic] (Belfast, 1750)

John J. Marshall, *Irish Tories, Rapparees and Robbers* (Dungannon, 1927)

F.C. McDermott, *Taking the Long Perspective: Democracy and 'Terrorism' in Ireland* (Dublin, Glendale Publishing, 1991)

Daniel Hogan

James Carty, *Ireland from the Flight of the Earls to Grattan's Parliament 1607–1782* (Dublin, C.J. Fallon Ltd, 1949)

Mathew J. Culligan-Hogan, *The Quest for The Galloping Hogan* (New York, Crown Publishers Inc., 1979)

Alice Curtayne, *Life of Patrick Sarsfield* (Dublin, Talbot Press, 1934)

Eamonn De Stafort, "Two Nights To Remember", *Tipperary Association Yearbook 81/82* (Carlton Publications Co. Ltd, 1982)

Tim Lehan, "Echoes Of Galloping Hogan", *The Old Limerick Journal: 1690 Siege Edition,* (Limerick, *The Limerick Journal*, 1991), p. 206

John J. Marshall, *Irish Tories, Rapparees and Robbers* (Dungannon, 1927)

Michael McCarthy, "Sarsfield's Ride", *The Old Limerick Journal: 1690 Siege Edition,* (Limerick, *The Limerick Journal*, 1991), p. 202

Máirtín Ó Corrbuí, *Tipperary* (Dingle, Brandon Books, 1991)

Reverend George Story, *A True and Impartial History of the Most Material Occurrences in the Kingdom of Ireland During the Last Two Years* (London, 1691)

Reverend George Story, *A Continuation of The Impartial History of the Wars of Ireland 1693* (London, 1689–1691)

Edmund O'Ryan

Máirtín Ó Corrbuí, *Tipperary* (Dingle, Brandon Books, 1991)

T. O'Hanlon, *The Highwayman in Irish History* (Dublin, M.H. Gill and Son, 1932)

D.J. O'Sullivan, ed., "Andrew O'Ryan's account of Eamonn on Chnuic" in *The Journal of the Irish Folk Song, Vol. 24, part 2* (Dublin, The Irish Folk Song Society, 1930)

Charles Carragher

Carraher Family History Society Journal (ref. The National Library (Ir 9292 C28 1–4), November 1983)

John Donaldson, *A Historical and Statistical Account of the Barony of Upper Fews* (1838)

Peter Kolchin, *American Slavery: 1619–1877* (Scarborough, HarperCollins Canada, 1993)

"Louth Rapparees" in *Dublin Gazette No. 1081* (February 19, 1714)

Kevin McMahon, ed., *The Creggan Local History Society No. 4* (1990)

Delivered at the gallows to Will Moore, Esq., High Sheriff of the County of Lowth, *The Last Speech and Dying Words of Charles Calaher alias Collmore* (February 18, 1718: ref. Bradshaw Collection, Cambridge University Library (Hib.O.718.12))

T. O'Hanlon, *The Highwayman in Irish History* (Dublin, M.H. Gill and Son, 1932)

Charles Dempsey

J. Cosgrave, *A Genuine History of the Lives and Actions of the most notorious Irish Rogues and Raparees* (Belfast, 1750: ref. Durham University)

Edward O'Lear P.P. and Mathew Lalor P.P., *History of The Queen's County, from 1556–1900: Compiled from the papers of V. Rev John Canon O'Hanlon, P.P., M.R.I.A.* (Dublin, Sealy Bryers and Walker, 1914)

T.F. O'Sullivan, *Goodly Barrow: A Voyage on an Irish River* (Dublin, Ward River Press, 1983)

Edward Ponsonby, "Cahir na Coppal", *Journal of the County Kildare Archaeological Society and Surrounding Districts, Vol. 4, July* (Dublin, 1903–05)

John Stocks Powell, *Huguenots, Planters, Portarlington* (Frenchchurch Press, 1994)

Shamrock, Vols 2 and 11 (Dublin: ref. University College Dublin, Folklore Department)

George MacNamara

J.A. Fahy, *The Glory of Cong* (J.A. Fahy, Mayo County Library, 1978)

Richard Hayward, *The Corrib County* (Dundalk, Dundalgan Press, 1968)

Patrick Higgins, *A Brief Sketch of the Romantic Life of George Macnamara of Cong Abbey or Startling Incidents in The Strange Career of a Daring and Adventurous Philanthropist of the Eighteenth Century* (Ennis, Clare Journal, 1899)

Shane Crossagh

Seamus Hasson, ed., *The Benbradagh* (Dungiven, County Derry, 1983)
John J. Marshall, *Irish Tories, Rapparees and Robbers* (Dungannon, 1927)
T. O'Hanlon, *The Highwayman in Irish History* (Dublin, M.H. Gill and Son, 1932)

William Crotty

M. Butler, "Crotty the Robber" in *Journal of Waterford and South East of Ireland Archaeological Society, Vol. 18* (Waterford, N. Harvey and Co., 1915)
Michael Kavanagh, "William Crotty: Outlaw and Popular Hero" in *Journal of Waterford and South East of Ireland Archaeological Society, Vol. 18* (Waterford, N. Harvey and Co., 1909)
James Maher, ed., *Chief of the Comeraghs: A John O'Mahony Anthology* (Mullinahone, 1957)
P.—, "Extracts from an Antiquary's Notebook" in *Journal of Waterford and South East of Ireland Archaeological Society, Vol. 13* (Waterford, N. Harvey and Co., 1910)
Seán and Síle Murphy, *Waterford Heroes, Poets and Villains* (Waterford, Comeragh Publications, 1999)
The National Dictionary of Biography, Vol. 13 (Dublin, Oxford University Press, 1992)
Charles Smith, *Ancient and Present State of the County and City of Waterford* (Dublin, A. Reilly, 1766)
John Edward Walsh, *Ireland Sixty Years Ago* (Dublin, James McGlashan, 1847)

James Freney

Houston Collisson, *In and Out of Ireland: Diary of a Tour with Personal Anecdotes, Notes, Autobiographies and Impressions* (London, Robert Sutton, 1908)
Con Costello, *Kildare – Saints, Soldiers and Horses* (Leinster Leader Ltd, Naas, 1991)
James N. Healy, *Percy French and His Songs* (Cork, Mercier Press, 1966)
The Journal of the Kilkenny and South east of Ireland Archaeological Society, Vol. 1, (Kilkenny, Journal Office, 1856–57)
Frank McEvoy, ed., *Life and Adventures of James Freney* (Kilkenny, Hebron Books, 1988)

Michael Collier

"The Life and Adventures of Michael Collier (The celebrated Leinster Highwayman)" in *The Argus* (Dundalk)
Patrick Cooney and Enda O'Boyle, "The Life and Adventures of Michael Collier" (Navan: ref. Meath County Library)
Seamus Grimes, ed., *Ireland in 1804* (Dublin, Four Courts Press, 1980)
W.A. Maguire, ed., *Kings in Conflict: The Revolutionary War in Ireland and its Aftermath 1689–1750* (Belfast, The Blackstaff Press, 1990)

Obituary of Michael Collier, *The Meath Herald and Advertiser* (September 15, 1849: ref. Meath County Library)

John Edward Walsh, *Ireland Sixty Years Ago* (Dublin, James McGlashan, 1847; revised as *Ireland Ninety Years Ago* (1877) and *Ireland One Hundred and Twenty Years Ago* (1911)

Willie Brennan

B.—, "Brenan on The Moor" in *The Cork Historical and Archaeological Society*, *Vol. 2A* (Cork, Guys and Co., 1893)

J.C. —, in *The Cork Historical and Archaeological Society*, *Vol. 3A* (Cork, Guys and Co., 1894)

Edward Garner, "'Brennan on the Moor' in Fact and Fancy" in *Evening Echo* (Cork, The Examiner Group, March 14, 1978)

Elizabeth Mathew, "Cork Street Ballads" in *The Cork Historical and Archaeological Society*, *Vol. 1A* (Cork, Guys and Co., 1892)

Máirtín Ó Corrbuí, *Tipperary* (Dingle, Brandon Books, 1991)

Rev. Patrick Power, with notes by Seamus Ó Cassaide and J.S. Crone, "Brennan on The Moor" in *Journal of Waterford and South East of Ireland Archaeological Society*, *Vol. 14* (Waterford, N. Harvey and Co., 1911)

Rev. Patrick Power, with notes by Seamus Ó Cassaide and J.S. Crone, "Brennan on The Moor" in *Journal of Waterford and South East of Ireland Archaeological Society*, *Vol. 15* (Waterford, N. Harvey and Co., 1912)

Jeremiah Grant

Charles Bateson, *The Convict Ships: 1787–1868* (Glasgow, Brown, Son and Ferguson, 1969)

James Duffy, *The Life and Adventures of Jeremiah Grant, commonly called Captain Grant* (Dublin, A. O'Neill, 1816)

Jacqueline Grant, *Providence: The Life and Times of John Grant (1792–1866)*, (Mitchell, Bathurst, Charles Sturt University, 1994)

Music and Song Lyrics

Acknowledgments

NB. Every effort has been made to trace copyright owners of material reproduced in this book. The publisher would be grateful for any corrections or additions to the information given below for use in future editions.

Title		Source Document/s
Brennan on the Moor (an American version)	Music: Traditional; arr. S. Dunford/D. Munnelly	*Universal Irish Song Book: The Complete Collection of the Songs and Ballads of Ireland* (New York, P.J. Kennedy, 1884)
	Lyrics: Traditional	
Brannin on the Moor (a Scottish version)	Lyrics: Traditional	From Cork History & AS, vol. III A (1894)
A Lament on the Execution of Captain Brennan (an Irish version)	Lyrics: Traditional	19th century ballad sheet: ref. The National Library of Ireland (Irish Traditional Music Archive)

Title		Source Document/s
The Ballad of Big Charlie Carragher	Music: S. Dunford/D. Munnelly	—
	Lyrics: S. Dunford/D. Munnelly	
Lament for Dudley Costello	Music: S. Dunford/D. Munnelly	—
	Lyrics: S. Dunford/D. Munnelly	
Castle Costello	Music: Traditional; arr. S. Dunford/D. Munnelly	George Petrie and George Villiers, eds, *The Complete Collection of Irish Music: The Petrie Collection of Irish Music* (London and New York, Boosey & Co., 1902)
Bold Captain Power	Music: S. Dunford/G. Ralston	—
	Lyrics: S. Dunford/G. Ralston	
Ned of the Hill	Music: Traditional; arr. S. Dunford/D. Munnelly	T. O'Hanlon, *The Highwayman in Irish History* (Dublin, M.H. Gill and Son, 1932)
	Lyrics: Trans. Thomas McDonagh	
Éamonn An Chnuic (an Irish version)	Lyrics: Edmund O'Ryan; arr. S. Dunford/D. Munnelly	D.J. O'Sullivan, ed., "Andrew O'Ryan's Account of Eamonn on Chnuic" in *The Journal of the Irish Folk Song*, Vol. 24, part 2 (Dublin, The Irish Folk Song Society, 1930)

Title		Source Document/s
Edmund of the Hill (an English translation)	Lyrics: Edmund O'Ryan	D.J. O'Sullivan, ed., "Andrew O'Ryan's Account of Eamonn on Chnuic" in *The Journal of the Irish Folk Song*, Vol. 24, part 2 (Dublin, The Irish Folk Song Society, 1930)
Bean Dubh An Ghleanna	Music and Lyrics: (Edmund O'Ryan?); arr. S. Dunford/D. Munnelly	Seán Óg and Manus O Baoill, Ceolta Gael (Cló Mercier (Mercier Press), 1975)
Crotty's Lament	Music: Traditional; arr. S. Dunford/D. Munnelly Lyrics: Mary Crotty (1742)	John Edward Walsh, *Ireland Sixty Years Ago* (Dublin, James McGlashan, 1847)
Crotty's Lament	Music: Traditional; arr. S. Dunford/D. Munnelly	*O'Farrell's Pocket Companion* (Dublin, Goulding, D'Almaine, Potter & Co.)
Hookey Loughran's Lament	Music: S. Dunford/D. Munnelly Lyrics: S. Dunford/D. Munnelly	—
Collier's Reel	Music: Traditional; arr. S. Dunford/D. Munnelly	Captain Francis O'Neill, *O'Neill's Music of Ireland* (New York, Lyon & Healy, 1903)
Bold Mac Namara	Music: S. Dunford/D. Munnelly Lyrics: S. Dunford/D. Munnelly	—

Title		Source Document/s
The Cong Reel	Music: Traditional; arr. S. Dunford/D. Munnelly	*Journal of the Irish Folk Song Society, Vol. 3, Nos 3 and 4* (Dublin/London, Figgis, Hodges & Co. and David Knutt, 1905)
Bold Captain Freney	Music and Lyrics: Traditional (18th c.); arr. S. Dunford/D. Munnelly	P.W. Joyce, *Old Irish Folk Music and Songs* (London/Dublin, Hodges Figgis & Co., 1900)
Come All Ye Fine Ladies	Music: H. Collisson Lyrics: P. French	James N. Healy, *Percy French and His Songs* (Dublin and Cork, Mercier Press, 1966)
Captain Grant	Music: S. Dunford/D. Munnelly Lyrics: Traditional	19th century ballad sheet (London, J. Catnach: ref. Irish Traditional Music Archive)
Galloping Hogan	Music: S. Dunford/D. Munnelly Lyrics: Traditional	Turlough Faolain, *Blood on the Harp: Irish Rebel History in Ballad (The Heritage)* (New York, Whitson Publishing Co., 1983)
Galloping Hogan Jig	Music: Traditional; arr. S. Dunford/D. Munnelly	J.M. Crofts, *Walton's Irish Dance Music, Part 3* (Dublin, Walton's)
Redmond O'Hanlon	Music: Traditional air: "Moll Roe"; arr. S. Dunford/D. Munnelly Lyrics: P. J. McCall	An tAthair Pádruig Breathnach, *Songs of the Gael* (Browne and Nolan, 1915)
Ballad of Douglas Bridge	Music: S. Dunford/D. Munnelly Lyrics: F. Carlin	*Songs and Recitations of Ireland, Book 3* (Cork, Coiste Foilseacháin Náisiúnta, 1961)

Title		Source Document/s
The General's Bridge	Music: S. Dunford/D. Munnelly Lyrics: Traditional	—
Eavesdropper	Music: Traditional; arr. S. Dunford/D. Munnelly	Captain Francis O'Neill, *Dance Music of Ireland, Book 1* (Chicago, Irish Music Corporation of America, 1959)
The Brennans' Jig	Music: S. Dunford/G. Ralston	—
Cahir Na gCapall's Lep	Music: S. Dunford/G. Ralston	—
The Outlaw Rapparee	Music and Lyrics: Traditional; arr. S. Dunford/D. Munnelly	Danny Doyle and Terence Folan, *The Gold Sun of Irish Freedom* (Mercier Press, 1998)
There's Whiskey in the Jar	Music: Traditional; arr. S. Dunford/D. Munnelly Lyrics: Traditional	—
The Felons of our Land	Music: Traditional; arr. S. Dunford/D. Munnelly Lyrics: Traditional	Danny Doyle and Terence Folan, *The Gold Sun of Irish Freedom* (Mercier Press, 1998)

Illustration Credits

Cover:	William Powell Frith (1819–1909), *A Stagecoach Adventure, Bagshot Heath* (1848: Private Collection/Bridgeman Art Library)
Maps (except page 220):	Bernard Scale, *An Hibernian Atlas* (London, 1776), courtesy of the Board of Trinity College Dublin
Pen and ink drawings:	Stephen Dunford
Page 18:	Peter Lely, *James, 1st Duke of Ormonde*, courtesy of the National Gallery of Ireland
Page 26:	Francis Place, *Kilkenny Castle and City, Co. Kilkenny, from Wind Gap Hill*, courtesy of the National Gallery of Ireland
Page 46:	Courtesy of the British Library (ref: G 5580/2)
Page 80:	Courtesy of Shannon Heritage & Banquets (1995)
Page 86:	Courtesy of Shannon Development Tourist Information Office, Limerick
Page 104:	Ordnance survey map courtesy of the National Archives, Dublin
Page 118:	Courtesy of the National Archives, Dublin
Page 122:	By kind permission of the Syndics of Cambridge University Library
Page 139:	Courtesy of John S. Powell (http://portarlington.net)
Page 143:	Ordnance survey map courtesy of the National Archives, Dublin
Page 151:	The Wynne Private Collection © 2000

Page 155:   From J. Stirling Coyne a nd N.P. Willis, *The Scenery and Antiquities of Ireland, Vol. 2* (London, James S. Virtue)

Page 167:   Courtesy of John Donnelly

Page 181:   Photograph by Alice Beresford, courtesy of Lord Waterford

Page 194:   Private Collection

Page 200:   Courtesy of Brendan Neary and the Kilkenny Archaeological Society

Page 216:   From J. Stirling Coyne and N.P. Willis, *The Scenery and Antiquities of Ireland, Vol. 2* (London, James S. Virtue)

Page 220:   Courtesy of Meath County Library, Navan, County Meath

Page 230:   Courtesy of Father Gaffney, Rosminians (Institute of Charity) and Keane Mahony Smith Auctioneers, Estate Agents, Valuers and Land Agents, Cork and Dublin

Pages 260–1:   Courtesy of the National Archives, Dublin (ref: soc1721/110)

Page 277:   From J. Stirling Coyne and N.P. Willis, *The Scenery and Antiquities of Ireland, Vol. 2* (London, James S. Virtue)